Mirj
LETTERS I
Amsterdam, Weste

The publisher gratefully acknowledges the support of the
Dutch Foundation for Literature.

N **ederlands**
letterenfonds
dutch foundation
for literature

Mirjam Bolle

LETTERS NEVER SENT

Amsterdam, Westerbork, Bergen-Belsen

Introduction:
Johannes Houwink ten Cate and Dan Michman

Translated from the Dutch by Laura Vroomen

Yad Vashem ★ Jerusalem
The International Institute for Holocaust Research

Mirjam Bolle

Ik zal je beschrijven hoe een dag er hier uitziet

Dagboekbrieven uit Amsterdam, Westerbork en Bergen-Belsen

Translation of the Introduction: Naftali Greenwood
Academic Editor: Pinchas Bar-Efrat
Language and Production Editor: Leah Goldstein

All the documents included in this book are from Nederlands Instituut
voor Oorlogsdocumentatie (NIOD), Amsterdam, Collection 244,
reference number 1480 diary M. Bolle-Levie, unless indicated otherwise.

© 2014 All rights reserved to Yad Vashem
P.O.B. 3477, Jerusalem 9103401, Israel
publications.marketing@yadvashem.org.il
First published in Dutch by Uitgeverij Contact, 2003

ISBN 978-965-308-473-5

Typesetting: Judith Sternberg

Printed in Israel by State of Israel Government Printing, Jerusalem

Contents

Preface

I wrote these letters to my fiancé even though I knew they could not be sent, because I wanted to be able to tell him — if I were to survive — everything that happened to the Jews in the Netherlands. On my way to *Eretz Yisrael*, however, I decided not to: Let us not speak of the past, let us start our lives over. At first, of course, we spoke a little about what had happened, but only for a short time.

I concealed the letters I wrote in the Netherlands in Amsterdam, and managed to smuggle out the notebooks that I had kept in Bergen-Belsen, bringing them along with me when fortune allowed me to immigrate to *Eretz Yisrael* on 10 July 1944. In 1947, my future brother-in-law, Johan Pronk (subsequently Johanan Ron), also immigrated to *Eretz Yisrael*, and brought with him the bundle of letters that I had written in Amsterdam and Westerbork. I placed the bundle next to the notebooks from Bergen-Belsen and forgot about them. We were so busy building our lives in *Eretz Yisrael* that there was no time left to think about the past.

By contrast, my sister, Shifra Ron (Bobby), a member of Kvutzat Yavne, did speak about the past. Every year on Holocaust Remembrance Day, she told the schoolchildren on the kibbutz what had happened to us in the war, and in 2002, she described how we had conducted a *Seder* in Bergen-Belsen. When she reported this to me, I thought she had become confused: Surely the event she described had taken place on *Purim*, not on Passover. Then, however, I recalled the letters that I had written, and combed them for the answer. Indeed, one of the letters described the *Seder* in Bergen-Belsen. I sent the excerpt to my sister, who translated it and read it to her children. The youngsters showed a keen interest in the matter, and asked to have all the letters translated. That's how the first Hebrew translation came about. It was helped along by Adva Ben-Shahar, Shifra's granddaughter; my daughter Rinna also reviewed the text and added some corrections.

Even before the Hebrew translation was published, the original Dutch letters were translated into several languages. I'm glad that the English translation is now complete, thanks to the devoted efforts of both translators.

Mirjam Bolle
Jerusalem, 2014

Introduction

This book introduces the reader to a collection of diary letters that are historically unique as well as especially moving in human terms. They were written during the Holocaust by Mirjam Levie, an ordinary Jewish woman in her twenties. Mirjam worked as a secretary for the "Joodsche Raad voor Amsterdam" (the Jewish Council for Amsterdam) established by the German occupation authorities in February 1941, the powers of which were soon extended to include all the Jews in the Netherlands). She wrote the letters to her beloved fiancé, subsequently her husband — who had immigrated to *Eretz Yisrael* several years previously — during a dramatic 18 months for Dutch Jewry generally and for Mirjam in particular. During this period, the Jews of Amsterdam were deported, and the author spent time in the Westerbork transit camp for Jews (*Judendurchgangslager, Dulag*), the main stopover for Jewish deportees en route to the death camps in Poland, and in the Bergen-Belsen concentration camp, which served as an "exchange camp" (*Austauschlager*; officially, however, Bergen-Belsen was defined as a "holding camp" — *Aufenthaltslager*), where Jews who possessed foreign nationality were interned for exchange with Germans detained in enemy countries.[1]

---

1 On the Holocaust in the Netherlands and, in particular, the Joodsche Raad and the various camps, see Jozeph Michman, Hartog Beem and Dan Michman, *Encyclopedia of Jewish Communities: The Netherlands* (Hebrew), (Jerusalem: Yad Vashem, 1985), pp. 74–133. This introduction is based on an interview with Mirjam Levie by the film creator Willy Lindwer in 1994 in Jerusalem for his film on the

Although Mirjam was unable to send the letters to their destination, in late 1943 she managed to conceal the ones she had written in Amsterdam and Westerbork in a warehouse belonging to the Netherlands-Asia Trading Company (*Nederlandsch Aziatische Handelmaatschappij*), in which her father, Maurits (Moritz) Jacob Levie was a member of the board. Her brother-in-law, Johan Pronk (subsequently Johanan Ron), found the letters in 1947, and brought them with him when he immigrated to *Eretz Yisrael* under *Aliya Bet* (the illegal immigration of Jews, from the standpoint of the British Mandate authorities, during the years 1934–1948). The letters that Mirjam had written in Bergen-Belsen were removed by their author when she was included in the only exchange that set out from this location to *Eretz Yisrael* in the summer of 1944.

This book — like the memoirs of so many other Jews who went through the Holocaust — is a personal historical account of persecution, distress and anguish. It can hardly be otherwise. Unlike the memoirs, however, this is a string of correspondence that created a diary of sorts as the events were unfolding. Therefore, it lacks the *ex post* information and influence of post-liberation experiences that tend to alter, if not distort, authentic recollections. After all, all of us, Jewish or gentile, regularly adjust our memories to the ongoing course of our lives, consciously or not. The writings that follow are unique in an additional sense: They were written by an employee of the Joodsche Raad, an institution that was and remains controversial, and are the only surviving source that describes the events from the perspective of a member of its staff.

Joodsche Raad, *Het fatale dilemma* (The Fatal Dilemma). A reworked version of the film was published as a book: Willy Lindwer, *Het fatale dilemma: Joodsche Raad voor Amsterdam 1941–1943* ('s-Gravenhage: Sdu Uitgeverij Koninginnegracht, 1995). The original interview is kept in the library of the Dutch Institute for War Documentation (*Nederlands Instituut voor Oorlogsdocumentatie*, NIOD) in Amsterdam.

As a secretary with the Joodsche Raad, an institution that Jews unrelated to it viewed with envy and a "respect and suspect" attitude, Mirjam knew more about the unfolding events than the other tens of thousands of Jews in Amsterdam. Her future brother-in-law, Max Bolle, held a very high position in the Joodsche Raad until he, too, was deported. Consequently, the letters are the work of someone who knew more than others — and definitely understood more. It is especially impressive to see how Mirjam retained her composure. Although still a girl in a certain sense, she strove to maintain her equanimity and self-respect at all costs in the midst of a Jewish community that, seeing its way of life come apart under the Nazi occupation regime, lost its equilibrium in the terror of the ongoing deportations that steadily reduced its numbers — circumstances that fueled the panic all the more.

Even when deported to Bergen-Belsen via Westerbork, Mirjam continued to write — an unusual feat in itself. Thousands of Dutch Jews were deported to Bergen-Belsen, but very few kept diaries there; noteworthy among them were Abel Herzberg, Renata Laqueur and Louis Tas, whose diaries have also been published.[2]

Mirjam had good reason to keep writing: Her letters were addressed to her future husband, Leo Bolle, with whom she was deeply in love. Thus, she wrote even though she knew the letters would not be sent, because by then he was already in *Eretz Yisrael*.

As stated, the most moving feature of this collection of unsent letters is Mirjam's effort to weigh her moves judiciously, originating,

---

2   Abel J. Herzberg, *Amor Fati: Zeven opstellen over Bergen-Belsen* (Amsterdam: Moussault, 1947); Herzberg, *Tweestromenland: Dagboek uit Bergen-Belsen* (Arnhem: L. Slaterus, 1950); English edition: Herzberg, *Between Two Streams: A Diary from Bergen-Belsen*, trans. Jack Santcross (London: Tauris, 1997); Renata Laqueur, *Dagboek uit Bergen-Belsen: Maart 1944–April 1945* (Amsterdam: Querido, 1965). Louis Tas published his diary under a pseudonym: Loden Vogel, *Dagboek uit een kamp* ('s-Gravenhage: Stols, 1946).

among other things, in her love for her fiancé. She evidently realized by the very first stages of the occupation that only thus would she have a chance of saving those dear to her and reuniting with her true love. Despair sometimes gripped her at moments when she thought about him, but only then.

Once reunited, Mirjam surmised, she could use the letters "to tell him everything in minute detail, but in fact it never happened. Obviously we spoke briefly about these things after I survived," she related many years after the war, "but the events in *Eretz Yisrael*,[3] the struggle against the British, the establishment of the State [of Israel], the War of Independence and the wars that followed, our children's births and our existential struggles occupied us so much that we settled for our daily tribulations and joys. I didn't sever myself from the past deliberately; the past severed itself of its own accord."

Mirjam Bolle is a Zionist. She considered herself as such before the war, as did her husband, and so she still does to this very day.

Mirjam was born in Amsterdam to a family that lived not far from the Montelbaanstoren. Her mother, Sara Levie-Oesterman, a homemaker and mother of two daughters, was known as Celine because Sara sounded "too Jewish" in the assimilation-minded society of the time. Mirjam's parents enrolled her in the Jewish elementary school on the Roeterstraat even though it was far from their home. Her father had embraced Zionism from an early age, an anomaly at the time, especially for someone whose large family considered Zionism a "ridiculous idea." Although they respected his outlook and expressed willingness to donate a little money "for Maurits Levie's worthy goal," they maintained: "We're Dutch; what have we got to look for in Palestine?"

---

3   Mandatory Palestine, under British rule. Known to the Jews as *Eretz Yisrael*, the Land of Israel.

In 1929, Mirjam began to attend the Jewish High School on the Herengracht, a street along one of the canals in downtown Amsterdam. She received her matriculation certificate in 1934. As she displayed a talent for languages, her parents wished to send her to university, a privilege they themselves had not enjoyed. "I was rather realistic and said I want to learn languages! But I didn't want to be a teacher, which was considered the natural way to go after such studies." Therefore, she turned down the opportunity. When her parents insisted that she learn a trade anyway, she enrolled in the secretarial school at Schoevers, and finished her studies there with certification in Dutch, German and English stenography.

In 1935, at the age of 18, she fell in love with Leo Bolle,[4] who, like her, had grown up in Amsterdam in a religious Zionist family. They met at gatherings of Zichron Yaakov, the youth movement of the religious Zionist Mizrachi organization (akin to Bnei Akiva), which, while imparting its ideological values, also served as a matchmaking market.

Leo Bolle (b. 1912) attended the Dutch Jewish Seminar (*Nederlandsch Israëlietisch Seminarium*), a school for rabbis and teachers of Judaism, on the rabbinical ordination track. Although his parents yearned to see him enter the rabbinate, Leo preferred to go to *Eretz Yisrael* as a Zionist pioneer — a *chalutz*. Everyone around him considered this "a ridiculous idea," Mirjam related. "'What are you leaving the Netherlands for? Here you can find work easily and set up a family,' they kept saying. 'Why do you, of all people, want to go to Palestine?'"

Nevertheless, after a round of farewell visits to Amsterdam's Jewish dignitaries, including the Chief Rabbi, Leo set out for *Eretz Yisrael* in January 1938. His fiancée, Mirjam, stayed behind in Amsterdam for the time being, and looked for a job.

That year, she found an open position with the Committee for Jewish Refugees (*Comité voor Joodsche Vluchtelingen*), a

4   In Israel, Leo was called by his Hebrew name, Menachem.

Mirjam in Amsterdam, 1942
Author's collection

Leo in Amsterdam, 1937
Author's collection

subsidiary of the Committee for Special Jewish Affairs (*Comité voor Bijzondere Joodsche Belangen*), headed by the diamantaire and liberal politician Abraham Asscher, who also chaired the Association of Ashkenazi Communities in the Netherlands, as well as the Amsterdam Jewish community. Both committees had been established in March 1933 after the Nazi rise to power in Germany. The Committee for Special Jewish Affairs was set up to respond to events by demonstrating, disseminating information, and so on. The Refugees Committee was formed immediately afterwards, due to the arrival of Jewish refugees from Germany only several weeks after Hitler's accession. Although the leading lights of Dutch Jewry sat on the board of the Committee for Special Jewish Affairs, the *de facto* power behind both entities was a professor of classical languages at the University of Amsterdam, David Cohen. Mirjam answered an advertisement that the refugees committee had placed in the weekly journal of Dutch Jewry, *Nieuw Israëlietisch Weekblad*, and was hired because the letters she typed in German had fewer mistakes than those of the other applicants. Thus, she became the personal secretary of committee member Henri Eitje. Eitje was one of Professor Cohen's closest confidants — the two had worked together in establishing the Refugees Committee — and was one of the officials who oversaw the committee's daily work. Although Cohen was the head, as a professor of antiquity he would, for example, take trips to Greece with students and visit the committee offices only once or twice a week to make general policy. "We had lots of work to do and I worked hard there," Mirjam noted. Eitje dictated letters to his secretary on behalf of Jewish refugees from Germany, addressing them to various authorities that might be of help — the Aliens police (*Vreemdelingendienst*), the State Unemployment Authority, the Ministry of Justice, and German Jewish organizations in Germany and elsewhere. Other letters were sent to the German Jews who pleaded for aid.

One had to fight to obtain permits allowing refugees to stay in the Netherlands, and Mirjam's superordinates, whom she respected and may even have admired, indeed fought the fight. Cohen and Eitje were received by the Minister of Justice — the custom in visiting Dutch government ministers for official interviews was to wear a tall "top hat" — to whom they tried to explain that the German Jews were in mortal peril (this being the Minister's standard of measurement) and should thus be allowed to stay in the Netherlands. "Sometimes they succeeded, other times not. It was also my job to receive people and listen to their requests and stories as they poured their hearts out to me, and on this basis to arrange meetings for them with Henri Eitje if necessary. He made exceptional efforts for hundreds of people, and worked hard. He may not always have been the most welcoming of people — that wasn't his nature — but he spared no effort to improve their situation."

The horror stories that Mirjam heard included some from German Jews who had personally experienced concentration camps. At this time, before 1940, these camps had not yet become outright death factories; they were used as instruments of terror to expedite the Jews' emigration, among other goals. For this reason, Jews who had managed to obtain entrance visas to some other country (through the mediation of relatives, friends or Jewish organizations abroad) were discharged from such camps. Therefore, a permit to stay in the Netherlands was a pass to rescue.

The stories that Mirjam heard about the camps concerned "beatings and abuse, starvation and all sorts of sadistic punishments."[5] At the sound of Mirjam's stories, those of "a girl who'd just turned 20," her uncles tried to protect her — and perhaps themselves — by pooh-poohing them: "It can't be all that bad; nothing like that is happening in Holland. Really, you have nothing to fear. It's happening in Germany; there, such a thing might happen. But it could never happen here. Don't be such a prophetess of doom."

On 10 May 1940, the *Wehrmacht* invaded the Netherlands and defeated the country within a few days. Shortly thereafter, a web of legal, economic and social persecution closed in on Dutch Jewry. In February 1941, as stated, the Joodsche Raad was established, and Abraham Asscher and David Cohen were named its chairmen. They merged the apparatuses of the Committee for Special Jewish Affairs and the Committee for Jewish Refugees, which they headed, to create an organizational infrastructure for the Joodsche Raad. In March 1941, the Committee for Jewish Refugees was officially subordinated to the Raad by order of the Chief of the Nazi security police (*Sicherheitspolizei, Sipo*). From then on, among its other

5 On the Dutch government's policy toward Jewish refugees from Germany, the Committee for Special Jewish Affairs, the Committee for Jewish Refugees and David Cohen and Henri Eitje, see Dan Michman, "Jewish Refugees from Germany in the Netherlands, 1933–1940" (Hebrew), Ph.D. dissertation, the Hebrew University of Jerusalem, 1978. Though the dissertation has not been translated into English, it has an English title: "The Jewish Refugees in the Netherlands. Thesis 1978," and contains an abstract in English.

duties, the Joodsche Raad assumed the activities of the Refugees Committee as the agency officially responsible for helping the thousands of German Jewish émigrés who had fanned across the occupied Netherlands, some on their own and others in special refugee camps. Later that year, as the anti-Jewish policies became tougher and the Germans tightened their control of Dutch Jewry, the Joodsche Raad's authority was extended from Amsterdam to all Jews in the country. The Joodsche Raad now had to deal with a lengthy series of problems and issues. Jewish children were allowed to attend only those schools that the Joodsche Raad supervised; Jews were not allowed to approach Dutch or German bureaucrats except via the Joodsche Raad; and anyone who wished to move house or travel anywhere outside his or her town had to apply to the Joodsche Raad first. This made the Jews totally dependent on the Joodsche Raad.

The attitude toward the Joodsche Raad had been ambivalent at first because, apart from obeying the Germans' directives, the council regarded and presented itself — and even acted — as a representative of the Jews' interests. Now, in view of its revised duties, the Jewish community reversed its stance. In this new tendency, those who benefited from their connections with the Joodsche Raad viewed the council favorably, while the others criticized it harshly and bitterly; as time passed, some of the latter even nicknamed it *Joods verraad* (Jewish treason). The council's staff was aware of all this, of course, and it comes through in Mirjam's diary letters as well.

After July 1942, the Joodsche Raad's activity evolved into a human drama that was exceptional even within the broader tragedy of the persecution of Dutch Jewry and the deportation of more than 100,000 for "mobilization for labor in the East" (*Arbeitseinsatz*), a place from which hardly any news arrived. The Joodsche Raad staff now became a Jewish elite of sorts, a privileged claque that had a *Sperre* — temporary exemption from deportation — much to the community's annoyance, resentment and outrage. And as the deportations continued, this, obviously, led to suspicions of foul play, as a relatively small and continually shrinking group exploited its status to escape the fate of the other tens of thousands. In retrospect, historical research proves that most of the accusations against the Joodsche Raad do not stand up to the facts as discovered. Mirjam's letters augment the scientific historical picture by portraying her emotions as an employee whose status gave her privileges and, for this reason, condemned her to isolation. She describes better than others the disgust that the pedantic chairman, David Cohen, evoked in one and all, as well as the utter chaos that reigned at the Joodsche Raad offices in late May 1943, when the Germans revoked approximately half of the certifications they had issued to staff members several months earlier, temporarily exempting them from deportation — on the basis of which the Joodsche Raad had protected many Jews by hiring them. This was universally perceived as the beginning of the end, as indeed it was. On the eve of *Rosh Hashanah* 1943, the Joodsche Raad was disbanded, and anyone who failed to find a hideout was deported. Official Jewish existence in the Netherlands had come to an end.

After six-and-a-half years of separation from her fiancé, Mirjam made her way to *Eretz Yisrael*, where they were finally reunited. Six weeks later, they got married ("an amazing event"). Sometimes she spoke with him about the past, but not often, because he "strongly disapproved" of the Joodsche Raad. Afterwards, as similar stories arrived from all the occupied countries in Europe, his attitude lost its hard edge, but remained reserved.

In *Eretz Yisrael*, the couple was penniless at first. Mirjam had arrived with nothing but a rucksack full of rags. They lived on a kibbutz — Kvutzat Yavne — for some time, but moved to Jerusalem in 1947 so that Menachem-Leo could complete his studies. He obtained a teaching job, but went unpaid for months. When the War of Independence broke out in 1948, he had to interrupt his studies and joined the Haganah. (Eventually he finished his master's degree and, in 1960, presented the University of Amsterdam with his doctoral dissertation about the struggle for the emancipation of Dutch Jewry in the late 18th century.) Mirjam accepted typing jobs at home, but her earnings were obviously not enough. "We were young, and looking back today I realize how irresponsibly we behaved when we came to Jerusalem with no money, no connections, nothing." One day, the Dutch Consulate in Jerusalem contacted her because it urgently needed a secretary; the Dutch woman who was supposed to hold the job had not arrived because of the war with the Arabs. "I couldn't take the job because I had a baby about a year old. After all, I couldn't leave him untended. But they insisted: 'Look, try to find an arrangement for him anyway.' Well, I really needed the money and finally I managed to find a good arrangement for our little son, and then I began to work there."

Mirjam worked at the Dutch Consulate, subsequently the Dutch Embassy, from April 1948 to May 1981. "I loved working there, always." Her husband became principal of the highly regarded Ma'ale religious Zionist high school, where much of the Jerusalem intelligentsia enrolled its children.

Leo and Mirjam Bolle had three children: Chananya, Rinna ("my angel"), and Ilana. Chananya served in the Israel Air Force as a pilot; in the Six-Day War, his aircraft was intercepted and he was killed. Three years later, their younger daughter, Ilana ("she'd just become a private") was sent to the Golan Heights near the Syrian border, where her jeep drove over a Syrian mine, killing her and four other young passengers. Menachem died in 1992; Rinna passed away in early 2011.

The Holocaust in the Netherlands was an immense tragedy, part of the larger disaster that befell the Jewish people. However, for Mirjam, who had rebuilt her life in Israel, it is the story of resurrection and revitalization that dominates her life today. She frequently remembers her husband, Menachem, and "actually no longer thinks about" the Holocaust in the Netherlands. "But what happened to our children; that's something that never leaves me."

Johannes Houwink ten Cate, Professor of Holocaust and Genocide Studies, University of Amsterdam

Professor Dan Michman, Head of the International Institute for Holocaust Research and John Najmann Chair of Holocaust Studies, Yad Vashem, and Bar-Ilan University

LETTERS NEVER SENT

1943–1944

Lief jongetje,   27 Januari 1943.

Ofschoon ik nu op kantoor zit, en elk oogenblik gestoord kan worden, wil ik
nu toch aan de "historie" beginnen, omdat dit toch een zakelijk overzicht zal
zijn. Ik ben natuurlijk de helft vergeten, omdat er zoo ontzettend veel gebeurtenissen zijn geweest, dat het onmogelijk is, iedere byzonderheid te ont-
houden, maar Freddy heeft precies alle gegevens verzameld en ik hoop, dat ik
na de oorlog aan de hand van die gegevens, je nog meer zal kunnen vertellen,
dan wat me nu te binnen schiet. Het is wel een beetje onpersoonlijk, met de
machine te schrijven, maar ik moet er toch aan wennen, want ik wil later
toch ook mijn brieven met mijn eigen portable schrijven.

Ik moet beginnen met de Zondag voor de oorlog, toen je vader niet goed is
geworden. Hiermede is eigenlijk de ellende begonnen. Het was in de tijd, dat
ik iedere dag mijn certificaat kon verwachten en de Zondagavond zat ik in
de slaapkamer van vader en moeder te schrijven. Om een uur of negen werd er
gebeld. Het waren Freddy en Juul, die vertelden, dat je vader op straat, er-
gens in Zuid niet goed was geworden en gevallen was. Iemand die hem kende
liep juist achter hem en heeft gezorgd, dat hij naar het N.I.Z. werd vervoerd
en dat Max werd gewaarschuwd. Freddy & Juul waren tennissen en kwamen juist
thuis, toen Max hen waarschuwde. Zij hadden een auto en kwamen mij halen, om
samen naar Max te gaan, want zij wisten verder ook nog niets. Je kunt begrij-
pen hoe ik schrok. Je weet, liefste, dat het kort na de dood van je moeder
was en je vader was nog steeds ontzettend onder de indruk. We dachten aan
alles tegelijk, maar natuurlijk in de eerste plaats aan een hartaanval of een
beroerte. Bij Max hoorden we, dat nog absoluut niet bekend was, wat er gebeurd was. De toestand was zeer ernstig, maar niet levensgevaarlijk. Vader
was nog niet bij bewustzijn en de dokter zou Max onmiddellijk waarschuwen. Max
zei me, dat ik jou moest schrijven, en wel expresse. Ik vond dit niet noodig,
en zei, dat ik je toch altijd kon telegrafeeren en dat een expressebrief toch
te laat zou komen als het ergste zou gebeuren. We kwamen overeen, dat ik je
direct per gewone post zou schrijven. Toen ik in de auto op de terugweg zat,
dacht ik maar steeds: "Je zult zien, nu komt mijn certificaat en ik moet weg,
en vader sterft. En mijn kleine jongen heeft nog niet genoeg te dragen." Ik
kon toen niet vermoeden, dat dit alles bij het onzaglijke, dat in de
toekomst zou gebeuren, minder dan onbelangrijk zou zijn.
De volgende ochtend belde ik Max op. Ik had diezelfde avond jou nog geschre-
ven en de brief toch maar per expresse gestuurd, ofschoon men mij op het post-
kantoor zeide, dat het in deze oorlogstijd toch geen verschil zou maken. De
toestand was nog niet te overzien, vader was wel bij bewustzijn gekomen, maar
herinnerde zich niets. De doktoren verklaarden echter allen, dat levensgevaar
niet bestond, maar dat men toch niets kon zeggen, hoe het verder kon gaan.
De volgende dagen veranderde er weinig. Woensdag hoorden we, dat het een
zware hersenschudding was en eenige lichte verwondingen ten gevolge van de val,
maar de oorzaak stond nog steeds niet vast. Donderdag was ik bij Selma op
bezoek in het ziekenhuis. Het was prachtig weer en we liepen met de jassen los.
Voor het ziekenhuis stond een roode kruis auto. Het was een uur of zes. Selma
zei: er is zeker weer spanning, want dan staan er altijd R.K. auto's voor de
deur van het ziekenhuis. Ik dacht toen aan een radio-bericht van eenige dagen
geleden, waarin werd medegedeeld, dat jonkheer Mr. Loudon in New York tot al-
gemeen schatmeester was benoemd. Dat beteekende, dat in tijden van oorlog, wan-
neer hier iets zou gebeuren, hij gelden zou kunnen uitkeeren. Ik vond dit een
beroerd bericht. Maar toch was ik niet verontrust, toen ik die auto van het
R.K. zag staan, ofschoon ik altijd overtuigd ben geweest, dat "Olland er niet
buiten zou blijven. Maar er was al zoo vaak spanning geweest, dat ik dacht:
misschien duurt het nog wel een tijdje. Ik was toen nog zoo stom, om te denken,
dat zoo iets ergs, dat ik van jou afgesneden zou worden, mij kon over-
komen.   Diezelfde nacht brak de oorlog uit. Ikzelf hoorde niets, maar vader
heeft de heele nacht bij de radio gezeten en heeft precies alles gehoord. Hij
maakte mij 's ochtends gewoon om acht uur wakker en zei: de hel is losgebroken.
Er is oorlog. Ik bleef nog in bed liggen en dacht alleen maar: Afgeloopen.
Ik zie Leo nooit meer. Maar het eigenlijke feit, dat er oorlog was, was toch
niet tot me doorgedrongen, ik besefte nog niet, wat dit eigenlijk beteekende.
De slag was te zwaar. Ik stond op en ging jou als de bliksem een afscheids-
brief schrijven. Ik kreeg hem een paar dagen na de overgave terug en heb hem
onmiddellijk verscheurd, omdat ik hem niet om te lezen zoo sentimenteel vond.
Vader kwam thuis, met plakband, om de ramen te beplakken, voor het vermijden
van het wegspringen van scherven. We gingen met z'n allen aan het plakken, we
hadden toen nog een schat van een dienstmeisje, Dina, die hielp natuurlijk mee.
Het was een razend werk, maar 's middags was alles beplakt. Het stond afschuwe-
lijk en alles was even sinister. 's middags ging ik naar de Kalverstraat om
een leeren étui te koopen, dat op de borst gedragen kon worden, om geld en papieren in te bewaren. Het was prachtig weer, van vliegmachines was niets te-
bespeuren en je kon je absoluut niet voorstellen, dat er werkelijk oorlog was.
Maar uit de winkels hoorde je de radio, telefoon was afgesneden, je had het

Amsterdam

My dearest,

Although I'm at the office right now, where I may be interrupted at any moment, I have decided to start this "history" now. After all, it's meant to be an objective account. Needless to say, I have already forgotten a great deal, because so much has happened that it's impossible to remember every single detail. But Freddy[1] has kept a comprehensive record of events, and I hope that after the war his notes will help me tell you even more than whatever comes to mind right now. It may be a bit impersonal to write this on a typewriter, but I need to get used to it, because in future I will want to write my letters on my own portable, too.

I ought to begin with the Sunday before the war,[2] when your father became unwell. That really marked the beginning of this wretched affair. It was at the time when I was expecting my certificate[3] to arrive any day. That Sunday evening I was writing to you in my parents' bedroom, and at around nine o'clock the doorbell rang. It was Freddy and Juul,[4] who told me that your father had taken ill and had collapsed in the street, somewhere in

---

1 Leo's youngest brother, b. 1914.
2 On 10 May 1940, German troops invaded the Netherlands, Belgium and Luxembourg.
3 Visa and permit for permanent residence in Palestine.
4 Freddy's wife.

Amsterdam-*Zuid* [South]. An acquaintance of his happened to be walking behind him and saw to it that he was taken to the NIZ[5] and that Max[6] was alerted. Freddy and Juul had been out playing tennis, and had just arrived home when Max contacted them. They came to collect me, to go to Max, because they didn't have any details yet. You can understand my shock. As you know, my love, it wasn't long after your mother's death, and your father was still greatly affected by this. We were considering everything, but primarily a heart attack or stroke, of course. When we got to Max's, we heard that they had absolutely no idea what had happened. His condition was extremely serious, but not life-threatening. Father hadn't regained consciousness yet, and the doctor said he would alert Max as soon as he did. Max told me to write to you, by express mail. I thought this was unnecessary, and said I could always wire you and that, if worse came to worst, an express letter would arrive late anyway. We agreed that I would send you a letter by regular mail at once. On the way back in the car, all I could think was: Now you'll see, my certificate will arrive and just as I'm leaving Father dies. And as if my Leo hasn't enough to endure. Little did I suspect then that, compared to the awful events to come, all this would be less than insignificant.

The following morning, I called Max. I had written to you that very same evening and decided to send the letter by express mail after all, even though they informed me at the post office that it would not make any difference in wartime. We were still uncertain about Father's condition. He was conscious by now, but he couldn't remember anything. The doctors all declared that his life was no longer in danger, but that they could not say anything else. There was little change in the days that followed. On Wednesday, we learnt that he had suffered a severe concussion as well as some minor injuries as a result of his fall, but the cause of the fall remained unclear.

---

5   *Nederlands Israëlietisch Ziekenhuis*, or Dutch Jewish Hospital.
6   Leo's older brother, b. 1910.

On Thursday, I visited Selma Gazan in hospital. She is a qualified nurse now. The weather was splendid, and we walked with our coats unbuttoned. A Red Cross car stood in front of the hospital. It was around six o'clock. Selma said: "There must be tension again, because that's when Red Cross cars always park here." I was reminded of a news bulletin on the wireless a few days earlier, in which it was reported that Adv. Loudon had been appointed general treasurer in New York. It means that in wartime, if something were to happen here, he could pay out monies. At the time, the news had upset me. And yet the sight of that Red Cross car didn't alarm me, although I have always been convinced that Holland wouldn't be able to remain neutral. But there had been tension so many times before that I thought to myself: It may be a while yet. I was so naïve back then that it never even occurred to me that one day I might be cut off from you.

That very same night, war broke out. I didn't hear anything myself, but Father sat by the wireless all night and followed everything closely. In the morning, he woke me as usual at eight o'clock and said: "All hell has broken loose. We're at war." I stayed in bed a little longer and all I could think was: It's over. I'll never see Leo again. But the actual fact that we were at war hadn't yet sunk in. I failed to grasp the real meaning of war. It was too big a blow. I got up and, fast as lightning, began to write you a farewell letter. I received it back a few days after the capitulation[7] and promptly tore it up, because I found it dripping with sentiment.

Father came home with gummed tape to stick to the windows to prevent flying shards. We all began taping. At the time we still had Dina, our darling maid, and of course she helped us. It was a maddening job, but by the afternoon everything had been taped up. It looked awful, and cast a gloom over everything. Then I made my way to Kalverstraat[8] to buy a leather wallet in which to carry money

7   The Dutch army capitulated on 14 May 1940.
8   Kalverstraat was a well-known shopping street in the center of Amsterdam.

and documents under my clothes. The weather was lovely, the chestnut trees were in full bloom, there was no sign of any aircraft and it seemed quite unimaginable that we were actually at war. But you could hear the wireless from the shops, the telephone lines had been cut, the Queen had delivered her "flaming protest" address, and all you could think was: We're at war. Any minute now an aircraft may come hurtling towards us, drop a bomb and destroy the city. At the time, I had no idea how wars are really fought. The way I imagined it was a thousand aircraft dropping bombs, the city collapsing and people getting buried in the rubble or hit by a bomb. I didn't realize then that this is not what happens, but that the other method of warfare is no better for your nerves.

On Kalverstraat, all the salesgirls were busy taping up the windows. The city was deserted. I went to the office — as you know, I had handed in my resignation by then — and everybody looked at me with pity. There was nothing to do, of course. We spent the evening in a blacked-out room for the first time. We are so accustomed to it by now that we can't imagine it any other way, but back then it was ghastly. The Home Guard rang the bell to inform us of a crack of light visible from the outside, and although we couldn't see how this was possible, we switched off the lights and went to bed.

Five in the morning: air-raid warning. You have no idea what this is like, as if the whole city was wailing. We got up and went to the corridor, each with a small suitcase in his hand. You could not imagine my frame of mind at the time. I was definitely not my normal self and although far worse has happened since, I have never felt more unsettled than I did in those first few days.

On Saturday morning, I happened to be standing in front of the bedroom window. An aircraft approached, and I saw a bomb falling. It was a stray bomb, which a German aircraft had been forced to drop after taking a hit. The bomb hit Blauwburgwal, and I saw the debris scatter in all directions. The piercing wail of that bomb was indescribable. It left me utterly distraught. I couldn't eat; I was white as a sheet and shook all day. Within days I had become so thin that my belt simply slid down my hips. In the afternoon, I visited Freddy and Juul. Max and Freddy had been to see your father for the first time. Will you believe me, my love, when I say that I scarcely dared to go out into the street? There were constant air-raid warnings and I was terrified that I might have to go into an air-raid shelter — you *have* to shelter during an air raid — and that struck me as the worst thing in the world. You'd be trapped like a rat. Max and Freddy weren't dissatisfied. Father was fully conscious and although he looked a little the worse for wear because of his fall, it wasn't worth mentioning. Juul and I made plans to go see him on Sunday.

At Freddy's, the wireless was also on during Shabbat — the Chief Rabbi had ordered it — and all you'd hear was: "This is Station Wijk bij Duurstede (or any other location, of course), spotted: Twenty German aircraft, flying from South-East to West, etc., etc." You could feel the planes approaching. I went back home. The air-raid sirens sounded incessantly now. And then a fire engine parked outside our front door to protect the laboratory across the street would start whirring and the noise was enough to drive you mad. The wireless reported NSB[9] purges. Well, I'll never be able to describe what those days were like.

On Saturday afternoon I went to the main post office, because I had heard that it might still be possible to send a telegram to *Eretz* [*Yisrael*],[10] and of course I wanted to let you know that your father's condition had greatly improved. I couldn't have known then that you had never received my letter. When I reached Damstraat, I was stopped. There was gunfire on Dam Square;[11] NSB men inside Bijenkorf[12] were firing from the windows. I was allowed to go through, but at my own peril. I told you I wasn't my normal

9   The *Nationaal-Socialistische Beweging*, the fascist party in the Netherlands, led by Anton Adriaan Mussert and founded in 1931.
10 The Land of Israel, then under British rule. Also called Mandatory Palestine.
11 A square in the center of Amsterdam.
12 A well-known, major department store belonging to a Jewish family.

self. I continued, because all I could think of was how worried you might be. The scene on Dam Square beggared all description, and I'll never be able to tell you what it was like. I fled at the first shot. I couldn't get through to the post office anyway, because the entire square had been cordoned off. But I had seen enough. By the time I got home, my nerves were in tatters. My heart wouldn't stop pounding. That night, I lay in bed and heard the shelling in the distance. And all this time the enemy was advancing. From the very beginning, I recognized the futility of resistance. Even without the NSB's appalling treachery we were destined to lose, although it might have taken a few more days.

On Tuesday, Mr De Groot, our neighbour, came to see us. By then the news was so bad that everybody knew we were fighting a losing battle. The Princess was the first to leave with the children, followed by the government and the Queen. That morning I'd had a crying fit, which had set everybody else off. I had visions of soldiers getting shot to pieces, and what for... a losing battle. Actually, we were all nervous wrecks. People seemed smaller and everybody lost weight in those few days.

I forgot to tell you that on Sunday we visited your father. His face was swollen, but otherwise he looked quite normal. Except that he didn't appreciate the gravity of the situation at all, although he could hear the air-raid sirens and he also knew that we were at war. He kept saying that he wanted to go home, not knowing that every single car had been requisitioned for the Red Cross or the army.

As I was saying, that Tuesday morning Mr De Groot came to see us and told us of a chance to escape to England. There were fishing boats anchored off the IJmuiden port, and although they were heavily bombed they offered a chance all the same. The scene that followed Mr De Groot's departure will forever defy description. I was completely beside myself and begged Father and Mother to try. They wanted Bobby and me to go, but when I imagined the worry, all the anguish on our behalf and vice versa, I went quite mad. In the end they agreed to come with us, and Lea[13] would join us as well. Uncle Meijer and Uncle Moos were at our house and Grandmother wailed that we were abandoning her. The weeping, it was indescribable. The De Groot family drove off, but there was no space for us in the car. So we didn't go. News of the capitulation came at six o'clock.[14] We stood on our doorstep, talking. It's curious to see that people are very friendly and much more talkative than usual. In the street, everybody was talking to one another. A car approached and the De Groot family got out. They hadn't been able to board a ship. There had been thousands and thousands of cars in IJmuiden. Abandoned by the side of the road, anyone could have taken them. The English were bombing the harbour.

In the evening Aunt Phine came to see us, and she was picked up by Mr Luitink, who didn't want her to be out by herself. I'm telling you this, because immediately after the ceasefire Mr Luitink joined the NSB, and now no longer deigns to look at us. We would certainly not have guessed it that evening, when he made a point of escorting Aunt Phine.

I was calm then, because at least the infernal fear of bombardments had gone, as had the image of the army being shot to pieces. We went to bed, safe in the knowledge of having at least one good night's sleep.

My darling, I know my descriptions have been muddled and poor. But I can't possibly convey the state we were all in. Perhaps when I am back in your wonderful arms we can talk about it together, and how I never, ever stopped thinking of you. I'll leave it at this. It has become quite a story. The rest will follow later.

---

13 Mirjam's cousin.
14 The German conquest of Holland was swift, lasting a mere five days. On 14 May in the evening, Holland decided to capitulate; this was officially signed by the Commander-in-Chief of the Dutch army on 15 May.

Amsterdam, 31 January 1943

I'm not at all in the mood to write, since I'm dead tired. But I really ought to get started on my account, or it will come to nothing. Mind you, I have forgotten almost everything — the moment it happens, it makes a profound impression and you feel you'll never forget it, but in reality so much happens that one event eclipses the other. With hindsight, everything that happened prior to December 1941 was insignificant. That's when the real misery began.

Initially, the Dutch Jews flattered themselves with the hope that Hitler would not regard them as Jews, but as Dutch citizens. They did not even know why they believed this. I needn't tell you, my dear boy, that I never held this belief. To be sure, Seyss-Inquart[15] did promise in his first speech "to respect this country's traditions," but we knew only too well what all these German pledges amounted to. It began with Jews being banned from cafés and cinemas.[16] Not that significant in and of itself, of course, although we did say: "We may not be in the habit of going to cafés every day, but it's really rather rotten if one wants to have a cup of coffee in town and it's forbidden." Little did we know what "rotten" meant. Besides, the Dutch people were extraordinary. Most cafés had small signs: JEWS ARE NOT ALLOWED ACCESS, or: BY ORDER OF THE AUTHORITIES WE ARE NOT ALLOWED TO ADMIT JEWS. But this soon changed, when everybody received signs from the government to put up, with the words: FORBIDDEN FOR JEWS.

---

15 As Federal Chancellor, Arthur Seyss-Inquart had formed the National Socialist Austrian government that decided in favour of the annexation of Austria to the German Reich. In May 1940, Hitler appointed him *Reichskommissar* (Governor), or Reich Commissioner, for the occupied Netherlands. In October 1946, as one of the main perpetrators of the Nazi regime, he was sentenced and put to death by the International Court at Nuremberg.

16 This restriction, issued in January 1941, only applied at first to visiting the cinema; the restriction on visiting cafés, theaters and many other places was issued in September 1941. It was then that the signs forbidding entry to Jews were erected in these places.

In November 1940, all Jewish civil servants were removed from public office. A wave of indignation swept the country. Committees were formed to ensure that the Jews retained their full salaries. The fact is, they were dismissed on retaining pay, 90% to begin with, which was gradually reduced. It was on everyone's lips. Among our friends and family, Aunt Phine was the first victim, as the measure[17] led to her dismissal as head of the Montessori nursery school.

At the end of January 1941, the NSB marched through the Jewish quarter. They were expected to come armed with knives, etc., carrying out a kind of private NSB pogrom. But the Jews refused to be slaughtered and put up a fight. This resulted in the death of an NSB man called Koot. It caused a major stir, of course. Professor Cohen[18] was summoned by the German authorities — I'll tell you about the internal relations within the Jewish community some other time — and was forced to sign a declaration ordering the Jews to surrender their weapons. He did, thereby admitting that the Jews did indeed possess weapons. It applied only to the Jews in the neighbourhood around Jodenbreestraat, J.D. Meijerplein,[19] etc. A quick joke. The Jewish neighbourhood is now nicknamed

17 In October 1940, every Dutch public sector worker was requested to fill in a form in which he was to declare his status as "Aryan" or not (the form was known as "the Aryan Declaration"). Consequently, all the Jewish workers (or those of Jewish origin) were "suspended" (actually fired) in November-December 1940 from all government and municipal positions, as well as in universitites and schools and anywhere else in the public sector. At first, they continued to receive their salaries. Later they were given a form of benefit.

18 David Cohen, a professor of classical languages at the University of Amsterdam, was Secretary of the Committee for Special Jewish Affairs and Chairman of the Committee for Jewish Refugees. In February 1941, the Germans abolished these organizations and he was appointed Chairman of the Joodsche Raad (Jewish Council), together with Abraham Asscher, a well-known diamond dealer and head of the Jewish community in Amsterdam.

19 A central square in Amsterdam, named after the first Dutch Jewish lawyer, Jonas Daniel Meijer, who died there. The square had four synagogues, now the home of the *Joods Historisch Museum* (Jewish Historical Museum). During WWII, the Germans renamed the square "Houtmarkt."

"Kootwijk."[20] Some axes were handed in, but nothing to speak of. The German authorities then issued a warning saying that if no weapons were handed in, serious measures would follow.

One Shabbat in February,[21] I was on my way to Nieuwe Keizersgracht [no. 62, the home of Mirjam's future father-in-law] when, on the bridge near Weesperstraat, I spotted a German in a green uniform, a member of the *Grüne Polizei*.[22] I took little notice of him, but did move along rapidly. A little later, Max and Eva[23] arrived, who said that the "green" was stopping Jews, grabbing them and sending them on to J.D. Meijerplein. Standing by the window, we witnessed a scene I'll never forget. In the meantime, more greens had turned up and they were asking every passing man: "Are you a Jew?" And when the answer was "yes," they were grabbed and kicked about, in the most literal sense of the word, and sent to Meijerplein. Two young men and their girls approached from Nieuwe Keizersgracht, opposite the [Jewish] hospital. When they reached the corner of Weesperstraat, they were grabbed and ordered to show their *stamkaarten*.[24] The girls were sent away and the two young men had their ears cuffed so badly that their hats fell off. And everybody that had been apprehended was taken to J.D. Meijerplein.

You can imagine how devastated we were. As we stood at the window and watched what was going on on the bridge, I thought about how you used to spend hours on that bridge, talking to friends about Zionism and the duty to make Aliyah,[25] and that we could never have anticipated that this bridge might one day be the

20 "Kootwijk" is the name of a radio station. Here it is a play on words, alluding to the name of the killed NSB man, Koot, and the Dutch word "*wijk*," meaning "quarter" or "neighbourhood."
21 *Parshat Shekalim*, 22 February 1941.
22 "Green police," the German *Ordnungspolizei* (*Orpo*), or order police. Mirjam Bolle uses some German words and phrases and renders some dialogue in German. In this translation, these have been italicized.
23 Max's wife.
24 Ration cards.
25 Literally "ascent," immigration to *Eretz Yisrael*.

setting for such ghastly scenes. I believe some 250 young men were rounded up that afternoon, but I'm not certain of it. The following day it was announced that, owing to the fact that not enough weapons had been handed in, these young men would be taken to Mauthausen concentration camp.[26]

The Dutch people were appalled by this crime and expressed their dismay quite openly. That Monday, there was a general strike.[27] Neither trams nor trains were running, not a single shop was open, the city was deserted. There were public speeches. Although I was convinced it would all be futile, I had the greatest admiration for this stance. It was simply wonderful; a mark of culture as shown by no other nation. But the crowds were dispersed. German cars, manned with police, drove through the city, the barrels of their guns thrust out of the windows. Whoever failed to get out of the way was shot at. Even so, the strike lasted two days. Afterwards, the Professor was summoned by the Germans again and forced to announce over the wireless that people should resume work and that no further punitive measures would follow. And that is what happened.

Then the death notices started coming in. One person after the other received news that his relative had died in Mauthausen from the most implausible illnesses. But the people were optimistic and wouldn't believe it. The most incredible stories did the rounds about German soldiers visiting the relatives of those who had died in Mauthausen, saying they weren't dead. Today nobody believes that these young men were not, in fact, tortured to death. We may never know what really happened.[28]

---

26 The Mauthausen concentration camp was established following the annexation of Austria in 1938. The number of victims in the concentration camp complex Mauthausen-Gusen is not known. Estimates of the number of prisoners who were murdered there or killed through forced labour in the nearby quarries lie between more than 100,000 and 200,000, including some 38,000 Jews.

27 The general strike took place on Tuesday–Wednesday, 25–26 February 1941.

28 In the raid that took place in February 1941, the Germans arrested some 400 young Jewish men and sent them to Mauthausen. A short while later, death notices

BEWIJS
VAN AANMELDING,

als bedoeld in artikel 9, eerste lid, van de Verordening No. 6/1941 van den Rijks-commissaris voor het bezette Nederlandsche gebied, betreffende den aanmeldingsplicht van personen van geheel of gedeeltelijk joodschen bloede.

JOODSCHE RAAD VOOR AMSTERDAM
*

De ondergeteekende, ambtenaar voor de aanmelding, verklaart dat de aan keer-zijde aangeduide persoon, opgenomen in het Bevolkingsregister dezer gemeente, heeft voldaan aan de verplichting tot aanmelding volgens de bovengenoemde Verordening

Afgegeven op ___ 28 MAART 1941 ___

in Gemeente ___ AMSTERDAM ___

voor den Burgemeester,
De Administrateur
afd. Bev.register en Verkiezingen

Registration permit for people of Jewish or half-Jewish blood in accordance with the German Decree No. 6/1941, signed on 28 March 1941 by the Amsterdam municipal clerk. On the back was an additional blue stamp of the Joodsche Raad (Jewish Council) with a Star of David, as well as the signatures of Chairmen Cohen and Asscher. Mirjam's details appear on the back of the permit.

Author's collection

In January came the announcement of "Decree No. 6/1941 of the *Rijkscommissaris voor het bezette Nederlandsche gebied*,[29] concerning the duty to register of all persons of full or part Jewish blood." On the basis of this decree, identity cards were issued, marked with a "J." By around September 1941, all Jews possessed such an identity card. We, and with us nearly everyone else, failed to realize that by complying with this order, we played into the Germans' hands.

A second *razzia*,[30] the immediate cause of which I can't remember, followed in June. Once again, the death notices followed very soon after.

Meanwhile, more and more anti-Jewish measures were introduced, but I can't recall them all now. There was no more kosher meat, for example, because *shechitah*[31] had been outlawed. But all this is so trivial at the moment that I have forgotten all the details. I also forgot to tell you that whereas in other countries anti-Semitism began at the universities, the universities here were examples of pro-Semitism. As soon as the first anti-Jewish measures came into effect and all the Jewish professors were sacked, they went on strike. As a consequence, they were punished and the University of Leiden, for example, was closed down.[32]

---

were delivered to the families, claiming that they had died from heart disease, pneumonia and the like, as well as those who were shot while attempting escape. As Mirjam wrote, it was clear to the Jews of Holland that the young men did not die a natural death in Mauthausen, but instead were murdered, and a great fear of this concentration camp spread within their midst. Further raids took place in Amsterdam (June 1941) and eastern Holland (Arnhem, Apeldoorn, Enschede and Zwolle in September–October 1941). During these round-ups, some 500 men were arrested. They were all murdered in Mauthausen a short while later. On the death notices from Mauthausen, see later on, a letter from 27 March 1944 (p. 249).

29 Reich Commissioner for the occupied Netherlands.

30 *Razzia* — the term used in Holland for the round-ups carried out by the Germans, similar to the term *aktion* in Polish.

31 Jewish ritual slaughter.

32 In the Dutch universitites, and especially among their students, loud voices of protest were heard against the Aryan Declaration and the subsequent dismissals.

In December 1941, the first Jews were called up for the labour camps in the Netherlands.[33] There's a long story behind this, which I'll save for a letter about the history of the JC [Jewish Council, Joodsche Raad]. Unemployed men under 40 were called up. Inevitably, a run on jobs ensued. The most implausible jobs were created, so that only the people without connections were forced to leave. There were quite a few camps, in Drenthe[34] and elsewhere. The food was insufficient, the labour hard, and the families received practically no money. But the camps were Dutch and came under the administration of the *Heidemaatschappij*.[35] Treatment of the labourers seemed to be pretty fair, and the neighbouring farmers did a tremendous amount to help the Jews. Then the age limits for the labour camps were raised, and it no longer mattered whether one had a job or not. Employment at the JC provided the only chance of exemption. The examinations were initially carried out by Jewish doctors.

The run on certificates began. Everybody had some illness or other. Of course, many were declared unfit. Once nearly everybody had received a call-up — by a fluke Father didn't receive one at first — a new round of examinations by NSB doctors was introduced. After the first examination, Uncles Moos, Meijer and Nathan had been declared unfit. But after the second, Uncle Nathan was declared fit. Then Father received a call-up, too. I went to see Meyer de Vries[36] and felt just like a whore. I put on an act, sat on his lap and coaxed him into giving me a note declaring that Father worked for

---

33 At the end of 1941, the Germans ordered the erection of special labour camps for Jews. They wished to remove the Jews from city life and concentrate them together in order to make it easier to deport them at a later date. The responsibility for fulfilling the quota of Jews to be taken for forced labour fell on the Jewish Council (Joodsche Raad). In total, some 7,500 Jews were sent to forced labour. See letter from 2 February 1943 (p. 51).

34 A province in north-east Holland.

35 The Moorland Reclamation Society (literally, "the Heath Company"). Founded in 1888 as a non-profit organisation, it sought to improve people's living and working conditions by cultivating soil in arid areas.

36 An influential member of the Central Committee of the Jewish Council.

the JC. Now this was partially true — you know my father: Before there were real advantages in working for the JC, he had supplied Mr Blüth[37] with material for the camps — but he wasn't actually employed by the JC. Many would have offered thousands for such a note. We were unbelievably lucky. Father was declared unfit because of carbuncles — he happened to have one on his arm — which we could never have hoped for. You should have seen those who were declared fit — blind people, people with one leg — in a word, unbelievable. You can imagine our joy and Father never even needed to hand in his note. However, several weeks later we were quaking in our boots again, because the unfit were all called back for a new examination, except those who had handed in their note declaring they worked at the JC (which Father hadn't done, because it hadn't been necessary). Once again, we were incredibly lucky. Father wasn't called up and in the meantime the situation had changed completely — albeit for the worse.

This shows you how much strain we were under. I'm not even mentioning the fact that a Jew was not allowed to have more than ƒ1,000[38] in his possession, and was forced to deposit the rest with Lippmann-Rosenthal.[39] Nor am I raising the fact that Jews had to hand in their gold, silver and gems to Lippmann-Rosenthal. I also forgot to mention that all Dutch citizens — not just the Jews — had to hand in metals, such as copper, etc. This became such a farce, it beggars description. Everybody buried his metal in the ground or threw it in the water, rather than give it to the Germans. A little bit was handed in, just to comply with this call to hand in metals. Some people handed in metal worth a cent and a half; the "value"

37 Kurt Blüth, a Jewish refugee from Germany, and a member of the Central Committee of the Jewish Council.
38 "ƒ" is the abbreviation of florin, or guilder, the Dutch currency at the time.
39 The Lippmann-Rosenthal Bank (also known by its shortened name, Liro) was a Jewish bank that was taken over by the Germans in order to seemingly afford them legal ownership of Jewish money. In reality, it allowed the Germans to steal the Jews' money, jewellery, gold and silver, which they were forced to place in the bank.

was reimbursed, you see. And the civil servants at the office said to me, as I was paid ƒ0.375: "Fie, Miss, you handed in far too much." This is all extremely trivial, but it just happens to cross my mind right now.

Then, on 3 May 1942, came the decree regarding the Jewish Star.[40] It's inconceivable that in the 20th century, Jews are forced to walk around with a piece of yellow fabric on their clothes. At first I thought it was merely an inconvenience. A star on every single item of clothing, ruining your lovely dress or coat.

The provinces[41] were evacuated, that is to say the Jews from certain designated towns had to move to Amsterdam and the German Jews had to go to Westerbork.[42] I witnessed the first evacuation in January 1942. I was sent to Zaandam, one of the designated towns. The population showed tremendous sympathy. The people had to leave behind their furniture because they were to be housed with other Jews in Amsterdam. The Dutch hauled the valuable items out of the Jews' homes and promised to keep them safe. Burning stoves and cookers were removed from houses and replaced by useless old contraptions. The departure of the Jews was accompanied by a veritable ovation. The streets were swarming with people, and not a single member of the NSB ventured out. And this happened everywhere, not just in Zaandam. We got billeting, too: Mr and Mrs Boasson from Middelburg, very nice people. We

---

40 The Star of David or "Yellow Star," reminiscent of the medieval stigmatisation of the Jews via the "yellow mark."

41 All the areas outside of the big cities (Amsterdam, Rotterdam, the Hague). The forced relocation of Jews from the smaller towns and villages to Amsterdam first occurred in the town of Zaandam, but the process also continued in other places in the country.

42 The Westerbork "central refugee camp," in eastern Holland, was established in 1939 by the Dutch government to house the many Jewish refugees from Germany. With the German occupation in 1940, some of these refugees remained in the camp, and they were subsequently joined by other German Jews who were sent there from various outlying towns. Later on, from July 1942, the camp was used as a transit camp for Jews (*Judendurchgangslager*) until their deportation to the death camps.

had applied for this billeting, because we knew that with our big house, it would be inevitable and we preferred to choose the people ourselves. We never regretted it.

I forgot to mention the "compulsory registration of German Jews, for emigration." All German Jews had to register for so-called emigration and submit details of their possessions. After completion of the forms, some 28 I believe, asking things a person couldn't possibly remember, e.g., where and when he had bought all his possessions and how much they had cost, an inventory of their household effects was drawn up. At first, everyone was extremely anxious about this. Later, it proved to be completely unimportant.

In June 1942, the anti-Jewish laws were expanded: Jews were forbidden from using public transport; from entering shops, except between three and five; from frequenting parks and public gardens; from going to the theatre — I believe this may have been forbidden at an earlier stage; from travelling by tram or train — the train had also been forbidden before; and an eight o'clock curfew was imposed — in short, too many to mention. Furthermore, a Jew was not allowed to possess more than ƒ250, which meant that Father, for instance, only received ƒ250 of his salary, with the rest going to Lippmann-Rosenthal. And this did not apply to individuals, but to families, which meant that our family income could not exceed ƒ250. You'll understand how much swindling went on, which was just as well, because it emerged that Lippmann-Rosenthal never paid a cent of the Jews' rightful assets, save tax and some other things. People now say: I'm paid not by Lippmann, but by Black.[43] We had to hand in our bicycles, with the exception of those who received a special permit. Around that time, there was a raid on all bicycles. One Sunday evening, policemen entered the bicycle sheds and removed all the bicycles. You can imagine the impact of that in the Netherlands. All the same, many had been warned and had taken their bicycles out of the shed (so had I). It was announced

43 Black (illegal) money.

later that the bicycles had been requisitioned because the army needed them. It didn't happen again, and quite a few bicycles were left in the city.

The death blow followed at the end of June. It was a Shabbat[44] — as it happens, there was an inventory at Max and Eva's that day, because of Siegje, a little German boy they adopted and who lives with them — when the JC was convened. Max emerged from the meeting as white as a sheet and told us that Jews, men and women between the ages of 16 and 40, would be sent to labour camps in *Gross-Deutschland*, probably in Upper Silesia. I assumed that we would be put to work in factories in areas that were most heavily bombed. The Jews would be allowed to bring their families. All I could think was: Leo. We were utterly devastated that evening. Your father had just remarried, or was about to remarry, and we were all at the house on Nieuwe Keizersgracht. A few weeks later, again on Shabbat, I was summoned to the head office of the JC at Nieuwe Keizersgracht 58 to assist with the work. It had to be done on a Shabbat. The first call-up notices — at the time they only applied to foreign nationals — were dispatched. I can't tell you what that meant. The call-ups were for 15 July. One could take practically nothing. Originally, there had been reassurances that people would receive training in Westerbork[45] before being sent on to Germany. Examinations were to take place in Westerbork. The "workers" would be allowed to write. But everybody had misgivings. The postmen who delivered the registered call-ups were beaten up and placed under police guard a few days later.

Another wild run on the JC followed, as its employees were

---

44 27 June 1942.
45 On 1 July 1942, the Westerbork "central refugee camp" was turned into a transit camp under German command. Between 1942 and 1944, more than 107,000 Jews were deported from the Netherlands to concentration and extermination camps in Eastern Europe, most of them via Westerbork. Only some 5,000 survived. There were some 900 Jewish prisoners in Westerbork when it was liberated by Canadian troops on 12 April 1944.

exempted until further notice. Everybody fought for his life, and once again the people with connections avoided being called up. But the situation was tense. The communists became involved, and urged the Jews not to enter into slavery. Nobody knew: Was this forced labour or slaughter? On the Tuesday of the first transport, 15 July 1942, there were disturbances in the city. There was another raid. Unless enough people came forward for the transport to Westerbork, the hostages would be taken to Mauthausen. And although the numbers were insufficient, the Germans appeared to be satisfied and, miracle of miracles, released the hostages. I can't believe it to this day.

My darling, I'm dead-beat. My story isn't done yet; I need to mention a few more things. But I had better stop now and resume some other time. Then you'll get an account of the JC. That should bring me up to date. And I hope — more than anything in the world — that the war will be over by then. Let me end with this, the best possible conclusion. It's half-past ten now, time to go to bed and dream of you. Good night, sweetheart.

1 February 1943

Let me tell you what happened that evening of the raid, when of course we didn't know that these people would be released again. Spirits were awfully low. The Germans behaved like wild beasts and Sluzker, the Jewish intermediary between the Germans and the JC, was *ratlos*.[46] I forgot to tell you that they also took people from the JC building on Nieuwe Keizersgracht, although most of them were released again after several hours. And at your father's house the two young women, Miss Roos, the housekeeper, and Daisy, her assistant, who were both under 40, were taken away, as was Michel Kleerekoper.

46 At his wits' end.

You know Eddy Barendz.[47] The Sunday before 15 July, Max Barendz called me — we all still had telephones in those days — and asked me to come and see him. You see, Eddy had also received a call-up and would have to leave on Tuesday. Of course, his parents were at their wits' end, all the more so because a German doctor had examined him, which was rare, and had declared him fit without a proper examination. The fact of the matter is that everybody was declared fit. If only you knew how they treated Aunt Suze, it would make your hair stand on end. They asked if there was anything I could do. Actually, they had already been somewhat reassured before I arrived, because Mrs Van Tijn[48] at the *Expositur*[49] had told them that everything would be all right. I called Sluzker, whose answer was far from positive and who advised me to contact Mrs Van Tijn. Eddy was to get a job at a rest home,[50] after which his call-up would be cancelled. Mrs Van Tijn kept saying that everything would be all right, but she was unable to offer confirmation.

That Tuesday at six o'clock, his parents still didn't know whether he would have to go or not. I even cycled to the *Expo* that evening, in spite of the unrest in the city. I'll never be able to describe the scenes there. Everybody was panicking, the staff as well as the people who had to leave and who had come to ask if anything could be done for them. And it turned out that Eddy had to go. I almost didn't dare to call his parents, but I had to. To this day, I don't know where I found the courage. After about an hour, I received a telephone call from Eddy, who was utterly confused and who shouted threats down the line. I could hear his parents

---

47 Eddy Barendz had Down's syndrome. He was a handsome and strong young man, sweet, but also rather aggressive.

48 During the 1930s, Gertrud van Tijn was a member of the Committee for Jewish Refugees. After the Committee was absorbed into the Joodsche Raad, she was appointed to a senior position within the Council.

49 The division of the Jewish Council that liaised with the *Zentralstelle (Zentralstelle für Jüdische Auswanderung*, the Central Office for Jewish Emigration, i.e., a branch of the "Final Solution" apparatus in Amsterdam).

50 A pension for elderly people, housing mainly evacuees.

sobbing. It was unspeakably sad. And worst of all, Aunt Suze was still hoping he would be sent back from Westerbork so she hadn't packed him appropriate luggage. In addition to this, the people had to be at the train station at half-past one in the morning. Imagine, a boy like Eddy making his way to the station alone at night, in the dark. And imagine 17- and 18-year-old youngsters, forced to leave their homes in the middle of the night, having to go to the station with just a rucksack.

The first transport left in cattle trucks, locked and without lavatories. There were protests, and the subsequent transports took place in passenger trains. All the same, people weren't coming forward. They went into hiding, or received an exemption through a job with the JC.

Bobby, thank God, never received a call-up. At the very beginning, parents and siblings living with JC staff weren't called up either. Through me, Marc[51] had secured a job as a messenger boy at our office. This meant he was exempted, and, through him, Lea, even though both of them had received a call-up. Meanwhile, Aunt Phine had become a teacher at a Jewish school. I forgot to tell you that since September 1941, Jewish children are no longer allowed to attend state schools. One time Uncle Nathan was outside Amsterdam, where of course this measure created even more problems, and he asked a young Jewish boy who could not go to school and for whom no arrangements had yet been made: "And what do the other boys say?" The boy replied: "They'd like to be Jewish boys, too." Outside Amsterdam, the turnout was also very bad. This led to the big raid in Amsterdam in August 1942, when hundreds of Jews were dragged out of their homes or rounded up on the street.

At the time of the first transports, the people were "deposited" for two days in the former *Hollandsche Schouwburg*, later called the

---

51 Lea's brother.

Joodsche Schouwburg.[52] I worked there at the time, helping to prepare rucksacks and running errands for people on my bicycle. There was the case of a man who had gone to ask the German authorities if he could leave on a later transport, because he and his wife hadn't been able to get ready on time. The man was immediately detained and taken to the Theatre, so his wife was unaware of his whereabouts. I then went to the wife to tell her that her husband was in the Theatre and that she should pack her bags and join him with their two young children, one aged 10 and the other aged five. Their house on Tugelaweg was an indescribable mess — after all, the husband had gone because they couldn't get ready on time. A few Christian neighbour women were helping, but they only made things worse with their crying. The woman herself was completely dazed, e.g., she packed a big stack of children's books, but had no idea where to pack the most essential items. In a word, it was hopeless. Of course I tried to help as much as I could, but it's very difficult in a house where everything is scattered all over the floor and you have absolutely no idea where anything is.

I went back to the Theatre, but later I saw the woman and her two small children getting off the tram — the people with a call-up were allowed to travel by tram. It was late in the evening, and the children and the woman were trudging along. It was a scene of such utter wretchedness; I can't possibly put it into words.

On the day of the raid in August, I received a telephone call telling me to stay at home and not go into the office. In the evening, I was summoned to work in the Theatre. Petitions had to be drawn up for JC staff that had been seized, people who worked for the *Wehrmacht*,[53] people in mixed marriages, etc. We worked all night. Early in the evening, Aus der Fünten,[54] the man in charge of

---

52 Dutch Theatre, later called (by the Germans) the Jewish Theatre.
53 People who worked in factories that made products for the German army.
54 SS *Hauptsturmführer* Ferdinand Hugo Aus der Fünten was the acting head of the Central Office for Jewish Emigration. He was responsible for the registration, detention and deportation of Dutch Jews. In 1951, the death sentence he had

implementing the anti-Jewish measures, had shown up, and the JC employees were told to line up. He examined each individual case, but was unbelievably arbitrary. There was one man, for instance, who showed his JC papers. *"Wie lange bist du beim Judenrat tätig?"*[55] The man was so upset, he was unable to answer. *"In Ordnung, der Mann kann gehen."*[56] He asked another employee the same question. *"Vier Jahre,"*[57] the woman responded. *"Muss untersucht werden, wird nicht entlassen."*[58] So petitions had to be drawn up for the people who hadn't yet been released, and there were hundreds. I was pleased to learn the following day that nearly all the cases I had typed up had turned out all right.

Meanwhile, the situation deteriorated. In August, Uncle Jo, Aunt Jet and little Meta were called up, and since in Rotterdam everything had happened so quickly, I hadn't been able to find them a job. They wrote to us once from Westerbork; they were very brave. After that, we never heard from them again.

We did "celebrate" Father's birthday. That is to say, the Boassons, who slept at our house but never ate with us, joined us for dinner on that occasion. Grandmother's birthday was on 2 September. We were sitting at the table in the parlour, where we have lived for the past year, and with us were Mr and Mrs Boasson and Dina, who was visiting — we could no longer have Jewish visitors in the evening, because Jews had to be indoors after eight o'clock. Since the time I'd worked on the first call-ups at Nieuwe Keizersgracht, I'd had a permit that allowed me to be out between eight o'clock and midnight. So far, it has always been extended. It was eleven o'clock and we were just having cake when the doorbell rang, very

received in the Netherlands after the war was commuted to life imprisonment; in 1988, it was commuted to a fixed term of imprisonment. He was released in 1989 and died a few months later.
55 "How long have you worked for the Jewish Council?"
56 "Fine, the man can go."
57 "Four years."
58 "Must be investigated, will not be released."

loud. Bobby answered it and we heard: "Police." I got such a fright that for the first few moments I was unable to think, feel or move. There were two policemen with call-ups for Mr and Mrs Boasson. They were very rigid at first, but later they loosened up a bit and allowed the Boassons to pack their bags, but only gave them 10 minutes to do so. I recovered a little, and called the *Expositur* to ask what was going on, for the call-ups had never been delivered in this way [personally], which didn't give you the chance of not showing up. I was told over the telephone that this was neither a raid nor a reprisal, but that many evacuees were being taken away. It was terrible. We prepared sandwiches and helped them pack, winter clothes, etc. Luckily, they also had a suitcase packed already.

Of course I had passed the case on to the *Expositur*, with the message that Mr Boasson worked at the JC, and I expected the matter to be settled. But the following morning, Dr Sluzker told me that they had not been able to do anything. The Boassons had been too late. Aus der Fünten had stopped granting exemptions at ten o'clock. We sent luggage and provisions to Westerbork, and everything was set in motion to try and keep the Boassons there. They had a certificate saying that they belonged to the Protestant Church. A pastor and close friend from Middelburg travelled to Westerbork, even the Secretary-General of the Home Department, K.J. Frederiks, himself originally from Middelburg, intervened, but all to no avail. Two days later, they were sent on. We never heard from them again, not even from Westerbork.

But this was only the beginning. Every evening, the "black police"[59] would pick up some 500 people. On 14 September, our

---

59 Members of the "black police" received their training at the Dutch police academy in Schalkhaar, where they received "Nazi training" that included Nazi ideology and saluting. Most of them were members of the NSB, but even if they weren't, they were more than ready to carry out the orders of the Germans. The policemen wore black uniforms, and were armed with carbines — light automatic rifles. Their units were stationed mostly in Amsterdam — there the local unit was known as the *Politie Bataljon Amsterdam* (PBA) — as well as in other cities.

Zentralstelle für jüdische
Auswanderung Amsterdam

Amsterdam, den ....1..Juni.............. 194̲3̲
Adama van Scheltemaplein 1
B.Nr.................................
Fernruf: 97001

A u s w e i s

Inhaber dieses Ausweises, Mirjam Levie
geboren am   20.3.1917
wohnhaft   Amsterdam, Pl. Muidergracht 29
erhält die Berechtigung, die Strasse in Amsterdam
von 20.00 xixxxixxxxxxxxxxxxxxxxxxxxx Uhr bis zur festgesetz-
ten Folizeistunde zu betreten.
Diese Bescheinigung verliert am 31.7.1943 ihre Gültig-
keit und ist am 1.8.1943 der Zentralstelle für jüdische Auswanderung zurückzureichen.

I.A.

Hauptsturmführer

K 372

Permit issued by the *Zentralstelle* on 1 June 1943, according to which Mirjam was
allowed to stay outside in the streets of Amsterdam after 8 p.m. until the time set
by the police. This was the last such document that extended the period of time of
the original permit Mirjam received in June 1942. The permit was dated until 31
July 1943; it was to be returned to the *Zentralstelle* the following day.

Author's collection

doorbell rang at half-past eleven at night. We were already in bed,
and of course we thought: They've come to take us away. I wasn't
very anxious for myself, because I have quite a good position with
the JC, but I was truly terrified for the others. However, it was Mr
Pinkhof, our next-door neighbour. They had come to pick him up,
and he asked us to make a telephone call. By now very few people
had a telephone, but we did, also because of my "position." We made
the call, but they were also sent to Westerbork. However, through
the mediation of Bram Asscher[60] they returned — practically the
only family that did.

60 Bram (Abraham) Asscher was Co-chair of the Jewish Council.

On the evening of 15 September, i.e., the following evening, our doorbell rang at around midnight. This time it really was the police, with a list with our names on it. I had answered the door, but not before I had told Bobby to hide and smoothed her bed. We were told to get dressed and to come along. I asked if Grandmother could stay at home. This was allowed. Then I said that Mother should stay at home as well, or there would be nobody to look after Grandmother. They did not agree to this at first, but later they did, providing Father and I — remember, Bobby had hidden — were ready in five minutes. We wanted nothing better than to leave as quickly as possible, because the later you arrived at Adama van Scheltemaplein[61] — which is where you were taken — the smaller your chance of being released. And I was "overjoyed" that only the two of us had to go, because the fewer people that need releasing, the easier. And I really wouldn't have known how to get Mother ready; she was paralysed with fear.

I had to get dressed in the presence of the two policemen. Meanwhile, they were joined by somebody higher up, who searched the whole house and even shone a torch on Bobby who was hiding in the attic, but didn't see her. I forgot to tell you that the policemen asked: "How many people are in this family?" I said: "Five: Grandmother, parents and two daughters. My sister has an evening permit and is at work." Luckily I hadn't kept quiet about Bobby — this was deliberate, because her bed is in our room and during a search they would have seen two wardrobes, etc. — for one of the policemen said: "The young lady is telling the truth. I've been here before and I've seen the family in its entirety." I hadn't recognized him, but he was one of the policemen who had come to take away the Boassons. They were fairly decent, although one of them slipped a bottle of wine into his pocket, looked in all the

---

61 This square housed the offices of the *Zentralstelle*, where those Jews who had received a call-up were ordered to present themselves. At a later stage, the Jews to be deported to Westerbork were gathered at the Jewish Theatre.

cupboards and asked if we had been hoarding food. I replied: "We have no money for that." When he took the bottle of wine, I said: "That's for ritual purposes." And believe it or not, he gave it back.

As soon as I knew that only Father and I had to go, I went to call the *Expo*. The line was constantly busy. Then I called my boss and told him what had happened. So you see how fortunate we were to still have a telephone. Later, our good fortune would prove to be even greater than we realized at the time. The policeman who took us to the "Houtmarkt" — the current name of J.D. Meijerplein — was very friendly. He had come round completely, and said: "You're certain to be released, and then we'll drop by." He said it was a shame I was already going steady. He had seen my ring. He was definitely flirting with me.

When we got to the car — we were to be transported in a truck — we were handed over. And then all hell broke loose. The scenes inside that truck were indescribable. People in terrible panic were shouting, sobbing, screaming. The policemen continued to pick up more people and we heard doors being kicked in. Sick, elderly people, in nothing but pyjamas and a coat, were literally dragged out of their homes and thrown into the truck like a bunch of rags. You see, the truck had a very high footboard and the elderly people couldn't get in without assistance. So the policemen escorting the truck would pick them up and literally throw them in. All this in the pitch-dark. The drawbridge between Weesperstraat and J.D. Meijerplein was up and had to be lowered every time the truck needed to cross. We drove back and forth, until at last the truck was full.

By then it was half-past one, and I was desperate, because I'd given up hope that anything could be done on our behalf now that it was so late. But once we arrived at Adama van Scheltemaplein, I revived. It appeared that the worst was over. Our case had been passed on and dealt with, despite our absence, and we were free. As I stepped out of the truck, I said to Father: "Hold on tight, or we'll lose each other." It was like a film or a bad dream. We walked

Members of the "black police," armed with carbines, loading Jewish residents of Amsterdam onto trucks for deportation to Westerbork. A German officer oversees the operation.
Collection of the Jewish Historical Museum, Amsterdam

across a courtyard in the dark. On either side were soldiers with rifles. To the left and right, behind the soldiers, was the transport, ready to depart. As I stepped out of the vehicle, I heard Sluzker say: "Is Mirjam Levie in this group?" Then I knew that everything was all right. We weren't ushered into the room where the others were taken, but were allowed to join the line of people who had been released. We stood for half an hour. Of course we were very happy, but the sight of the others in our truck having to join the transport group was dreadful. Max was there too, as were many acquaintances, and they all came to chat with us. I'll never be able to explain how I felt. Having stood for half an hour, we filed out to Jan van Eijckstraat, to a school where we were to spend the night, because of course we weren't allowed out in the street until six in the morning. But Mr Blüth, who lives opposite the school, came to fetch us. In Mr Blüth's kitchen we cried a little and afterwards — it was half-past two — we made ourselves comfortable in the living room, together with Mr and Mrs Blüth and Sluzker, who also spent the night there. Max had already called Mother and we called her again at half-past two, which meant that she hadn't been in suspense any longer than us. I went to bed at half-past three. Father stayed up and went home at six o'clock. I slept until ten, went home and then later on to the office. Still, I felt tired and drowsy that day.

That night, at half-past twelve, the doorbell rang again. I went to the front door, because I'm always the first one out of bed. Bobby hid again. The same policemen had come to check if we had been released. At half-past midnight! What do you make of this lack of sensitivity? And these were actually the decent ones. You should know that the previous night, as we were walking to J.D. Meijerplein, I had said, when they told us that they'd come and enquire after us: "Then you'll get a glass of wine." They had come for that, I could tell right away. And if we hadn't been released, they would have looted the place. For example, I had this fine hand-cranked torch and the previous evening one of the policemen had taken it from me and given me his instead, which was actually rather decent of him.

Well, three of them turned up and flirted a little with me. They thought I had a good figure for horse-riding, would you believe it. I was in just the mood for that. I'm ashamed to say that I actually gave them a glass of wine in a bid to stay on friendly terms with them, because they told me they patrol our neighbourhood. And sure enough, a few days later the doorbell rang at ten o'clock. A call-up for Grandmother for the *Arbeitseinsatz*.[62] But while they were still downstairs, they said they weren't going to take her. It was purely a social call and they talked nicely, among other topics, about English radio. We didn't say much, naturally.

I haven't told you that on 9 September, your father's birthday, they were all taken away, and also released again. Luckily, they

62 Forced labour in Germany; the German term for deportation to the east.

were spared the ghastly car ride we'd had. Your aunts and uncle at Nieuwe Keizersgracht 56 were also picked up once, together with Aunt Leen. But Hijman and Rika were not released.

On 1 October, the roundups of people from their homes came to an end. But that didn't spell the end of the nightmare. I'll tell you about the tragedy that followed in my next letter. It's already half-past ten. Luckily it's quiet this evening. I'm having an early night, because I can't get out of bed in the mornings. Goodnight, my love. Have you hit the sack yet?

Amsterdam, 2 February 1943

Today we suffered another big blow. Yesterday, a German sub-officer was shot dead in Haarlem and the Germans retaliated by taking 100 hostages, among them four Jews. One of the four was Philip Frank.[63] Today we heard the terrible news that three of the four Jews and seven non-Jews have been executed by firing squad. The families of the Jews have been put on a transport to Westerbork. It's appalling. When someone is put on a transport to Poland it's dreadful of course, but not irrevocable. But this is irrevocable. It's truly unbearable for Frank's wife. The suffering she has been through. First her father and mother, her sister, her brother, Jo Dunner, and his family, and now her husband shot dead and she herself deported. How can one person endure so much? And the awful thing is that apparently this isn't a typically German measure. People say that when an officer is shot dead in England, hostages are taken, too. But the person affected will be unhappy for the rest of his life.

It's said that Frank wasn't shot, but hanged.

63 From 1937 until his murder, Philip Frank (1910–1943) was Chief Rabbi of the province of North Holland. From the end of 1941, he also headed the local committee of the Jewish Council in Haarlem.

Let me resume my story. At the end of September, Aunt Griet, [her husband] Uncle Meijer and Uncle Moos were taken away and sent to Westerbork. There was nothing we could do.

I should also tell you about our inventory, because that was such a farce. Towards the end of September, Father and I happened to be coming down the stairs together at half-past one. We were each on our way to our offices. The doorbell rang and three men came up, claiming to be from the *Hausraterfassungsstelle*.[64] They had come because the Boassons had been taken away. Of course, we went back up again. They sat down at the table in the living room. An older man asked questions and made notes and the others looked round the room in a really "nasty" way. They had faces "only a mother could love," and you could tell they were sizing the place up. The man asking the questions was fairly decent. We told him that the Boassons had no furniture and that we had sent them their clothes. The man asked for dates of birth, etc. and we gave him the information. When he was done, he said: "Now it's your turn." "Why?" I asked. "We have nothing to do with this. You can make an inventory here when we're taken away, but not now." He said he had been instructed that when the subtenant had been taken away, he should take an inventory of the main tenant at the same time. I replied that I thought no inventories were done at the homes of members of the Jewish Council, but he said that this used to be the case, but not anymore. "However," he said, "you can raise an objection and then we'll leave." "In that case, we raise an objection," Father and I said in unison.

---

64 The office for registering household property. This body was established along with the *Zentralstelle*, and was charged with the registration of belongings left in Jewish houses after their occupants had been forced to leave the outlying towns and move to Amsterdam, taking with them only a small amount of their property. When the deportations began in July 1942, the members of this office also, and mainly, conducted the registration of property belonging to Jews who were sent to Westerbork. Some of the members of this office later became a group known as the *Kolonne Henneicke* — Jew-hunters — who were rewarded with money for every Jew they handed over to the Germans.

In short, he wrote down that we worked for the JC and that we had raised an objection, and with that the three of them left. When they reached the stairs, they wanted to have a quick look at the Boassons' room. Their leader looked in the closet and said: "Just some *Steingut*, crockery. And what is linen again in German?" I said with a straight face: "*Wäsche*." And that, would you believe it, was the *Hausraterfassung[sstelle]*! When they finally left, their leader said: "Right, Sir, you may or may not see us again." Father said: "To be honest, I must say that I wouldn't be best pleased to see you again under these circumstances." He replied: "I understand. We don't come here as friends." The other two just stood there smirking. Then I said: "No, in that case you'd get a different reception." Then they really did leave and we haven't seen them again to this day. It really is a wonderful anecdote and it still amuses me to think how we "raised an objection."

But there were other, more wretched things. During *Sukkot*[65] the rumour went round that people at the JC would receive a *Sperre*,[66] i.e., that they would get a stamp on their identity card so they wouldn't be deported [to Westerbork or the east]. On the first day of *Sukkot* I was visiting my boss, when I heard that he had been sent for by Asscher and Cohen. That evening I had to work, and when I arrived at Eitje's[67] office the following morning — they had worked all night — I received a call-up to go to the *Zentralstelle* to

65 The Feast of Tabernacles, a seven-day Jewish harvest festival, celebrated in autumn. The festival commemorates the Jews' Exodus from Egypt and the dwellings used as they wandered through the desert.
66 From the German, meaning "exemption" (literally: "blocked"), brought into the Dutch language by the Jews. The exemptions appeared as a stamp on one's identity papers as "*Bis auf weiteres freigestellt vom Arbeitseinsatz*" ("Exempt from recruitment for labor [in Germany] until further notice"). The permits were organised according to groups of numbers, a method instituted by the Germans. This allowed for the identification of the exemption holder according to his group. Among the groups were members of the Joodsche Raad (80,000–100,000); the Puttkammer List (120,000); and so on.
67 Henri Eitje, a member of the Committee for Jewish Refugees. After the Committee was absorbed into the Joodsche Raad, he became a member of the Council.

be exempted. Eitje added that my parents and Bobby would also be exempted. Meanwhile Bobby had been transferred from the JC's public information office to the office of Mr E.E. van der Horst, the new Secretary-General of the Jewish community, to work as his secretary. I was completely overjoyed. I also received some notices for colleagues, but briefly stopped by Father's office to tell him the news. We were so happy that day. At the very least, we'd be safe for the winter months, or so we thought. Little did we know then that this safety didn't amount to very much.

Eitje was a member of the *Sperre* Commission. What that meant can't be put into words. Every JC department had to submit a list of its staff, divided into three groups: 50% A, 25% B and 25% C. Group A was certain to be exempted, B perhaps and C probably not. So the bosses had the rotten job of condemning part of their staff to death. Besides, thousands of others came to ask for a *Sperre* on the grounds of former merits, etc. People were fighting for their lives.

But the worst was yet to come. On 2 October, on the Friday before the last days of *Sukkot*, the Professor [Cohen] announced that there would be a big operation that evening. The rumour was that it would be quiet for the rest of the month of October. That Friday evening, all the labour camps were emptied and all the families [of the workers] living in or outside of Amsterdam were deported as well. Thousands were taken to Westerbork, among them those in the *kibbutz* in Elden.[68] But that day, we didn't know what was in store. This is why it was decided to dispatch all the notices for the "A" people, i.e., the people who were certain to be exempted, that very same day, so at least they would have a document. Thousands of notices were dispatched, and in the rush, of course, a great many injustices were done. That day, the notices until 22 October were dispatched. I'm not likely to forget that day. We were besieged. I

68 A centre for pioneers. They were trained by local farmers in agriculture and animal husbandry.

Zentralstelle für jüdische
Auswanderung Amsterdam

Amsterdam, den .... **28 SEP 1942** .... 194.....
Adama van Scheltemaplein 1
Fernruf: 98005
　　　　　98006
　　　　　97001

B.Nr. ....

Levie, Mirjam Sophie,
Pl. Müidergracht 29

Am **28 SEP 1942** zwischen _14⁴⁰ - 16⁴⁰_ Uhr
haben Sie bei der Zentralstelle für jüdische Auswanderung Amsterdam, Adema
van Scheltemaplein 1, zu erscheinen, damit Ihnen (bezw. Ihrem Ehegatten und
Ihren Kindern) bescheinigt werden kann, dass Sie vom Arbeitseinsatz zurückge-
stellt werden.
Sie haben Ihren Reisepass, Kennkarte (bezw. die Ihrer Angehörigen), Traubuch,
Familienbuch, Taufschein und sonstige Ihr Rückstellungsgesuch rechtfertigende
Unterlagen mitzubringen.
Diese Aufforderung gilt gleichzeitig als Reisegenehmigung für die Reise von Ihrem
Wohnort nach Amsterdam zur Zentralstelle für jüdische Auswanderung Amster-
dam und zurück für den obengenannten Reisetag.

I.A..
aus der Fünten.
╫ -Hauptsturmführer.

Den tusschen uur
moet U zich bij „der Zentralstelle für jüdische Auswanderung" Adama van Scheltemaplein 1, Amsterdam melden, om vast te kunnen stellen of U in aanmerking
kan komen (resp. Uw echtgenoote en kinderen) om van de tewerkstelling te worden vrijgesteld.
U heeft Uw paspoort, persoonsbewijs (resp. van Uw andere gezinsleden), trouw-
boekje, familieboekje, doopbewijs en verdere bescheiden mede te brengen, welke U
vrijstelling kunnen toestaan.
Deze oproeping geldt tegelijkertijd als reisvergunning voor de reis van Uw woon-
plaats naar Amsterdam tot de Zentralstelle für jüdische Auswanderung, Adama
van Scheltemaplein 1 en terug op de bovengenoemde reisdag.

i.o.
aus der Fünten
╫ -Haupsturmführer.

Notice requesting that Mirjam appear at the _Zentralstelle_ on 28 September 1942 in order to
receive a temporary exemption from being called up for labour in Germany
Author's collection

had witnessed November 1938, *Kristallnacht*,[69] and the siege of the Committee for Jewish Refugees, but this was a great deal worse. I lost my voice completely. When I got home at half-past seven in the evening, I tumbled straight into bed.

But at half-past eleven, the telephone rang. I was told to come and help. Rosien Leuvenberg[70] called me, and she was the one who came to fetch me. I was terribly drowsy when I got on my bicycle, in the pitch-dark, but later I felt better. Still, I was glad when six o'clock came and we went back home again. I had to be back in the office in the afternoon. It was a wretched situation. Everybody was begging for a *Sperre*, enough to drive you to distraction. This drama went on for weeks. I could fill books on the subject, but it really defies description. I hope, darling, I can tell you about it soon.

This *Sperre* affair is a black chapter indeed. The Germans tossed us a bone and watched with glee as the Jews fought for it. To this day, I believe that Max was sent away because he was betrayed by someone whose request for a *Sperre* he had turned down.

It was the middle of October. That afternoon, Max and I had worked together. At the time, we were working day and night. He left, and an hour later we learnt that Eva and the children had been arrested and taken to the Theatre and that Max and Sluzker were on their way there. A little later, we learnt that Max had also been arrested. Dismay all round. It was several days before we were certain that there was nothing we could do.

A few days later, Chief Rabbi Sarlouis[71] and his family were

---

69 The night of 9–10 November 1938, when pogroms took place in Germany and Austria, following the assassination of a German diplomat in Paris. A great many synagogues were set alight and the windows of Jewish shops smashed, hence the name *Kristallnacht*, or Night of Broken Glass. The term was probably coined by the residents of Berlin, who described what had happened.
70 The assistant of Max Bolle, Secretary of the Jewish Council.
71 Lodewijk Hartog Sarlouis (1884–1942) was Chief Rabbi of Amsterdam (from 1936). He lectured at the rabbinical and theological seminary, the *Nederlandsch Israelietisch Seminarium*. He was a member of the Jewish Council from its inception.

arrested, as were his son's in-laws, the Huysmans. It caused quite a stir, of course. Freddy had meetings here and meetings there, but we knew it would all be futile. And so it was. Nobody knew why Max and the Rabbi were deported. I believe the Professor genuinely didn't know it at the time, but that when he did, he never told us.

Donations for Max and Eva came pouring in. Freddy, Juul and I packed his bags. We weren't allowed to say goodbye to them. Your father said goodbye to them on the rear balcony of your Uncle Mendel's house, in Middenlaan, which was terrible, of course. We received a beautiful letter from Max and Eva from Westerbork. They were exceptionally brave. But even now, when I think about the children, I'm quite distraught. The blow was almost unbearable for your father. Max was his pride and joy, and this downfall was really rather precipitous. Needless to say, we're doing everything we can to help him get over it, but there are no words of consolation for something so appalling.

A few weeks after they were deported, we received a letter from Max, sent surreptitiously, which did give us a little hope, but in which he also said that his blankets had been taken away from him. And when you hear that the temperature in those parts is 25 degrees below zero, you can imagine what that means. We haven't heard from them since. Max wrote, which we already knew, that he had been separated from Eva and the children.

By the time the *Sperre* distribution came to an end, 17,000 people in the Netherlands had been exempted through the JC.

It was quiet throughout October, but in early November the misery started again. The first few evenings, those with exemptions were taken away as well, but after a few nights this policy was amended. Still, this wasn't much of a comfort for the victims.

At the end of November our doorbell rang once more, at half-past midnight. And sure enough, it was the police again, this time with call-ups for Father and Mother. Thanks to the fact that they had exemptions, they were allowed to stay at home, although the men kept us guessing until the very last moment as to whether or not they would be taken away.

In November, there was a major daytime operation targeting Jews working for the *Wehrmacht*.[72] A great many of them were plucked from their workshops, their families were dragged from their homes and all these people were deported. Your Uncle Isidoor had a narrow escape. And we had all thought that people working for the *Wehrmacht* enjoyed the greatest security. In mid-December we had another brief respite, due to the Christmas holidays. But at the beginning of December, during an evening that should have been quiet, our doorbell rang at half-past midnight. I thought I'd been dreaming, but I still got up and went downstairs. I asked the night nurse who was with Grandmother at the time: "Was that the doorbell?" She had been about to call us. I told her to throw the apple parings in the stove — Jews were not allowed to have fruit — and went downstairs to answer the door. There would have been no point in not answering the door, because otherwise it would have been kicked in. As I walked down the stairs, I heard German voices. I thought to myself: An arrest, we're lost. I knew that no arrests were planned for this evening, and besides, the Dutch black police [and not the Germans] always do the rounding up. But when I answered the door, I saw the silhouettes of three people, and one of them asked: "*Sind Sie Jüdin?*"[73] I realized at once that this wasn't an arrest, or they would have said my name. I replied: "*Jawohl.*"[74] "*Personsbeweis.*"[75]

I raced upstairs to the bedroom where I had my bag and was back at living room level when one of the brutes entered. I steered him into the living room, because I didn't want him to enter the

72 There was a so-called *Wehrmacht* stamp for Jews who worked in factories producing goods for the *Wehrmacht*, the German army. This stamp was considered to be a relatively good safeguard against deportation.
73 "Are you a Jew?"
74 "Yes."
75 "Identity card."

bedrooms and see the others. The fewer people these brutes see, the better. Upon seeing my identity card, he asked me what I did. I told him. He asked if there were any other people in the house. I told him the truth, because it seemed the most sensible thing to do. The nurse was in the back room, because the last time the policemen had shouted at her and called her a slave of the Jews. He had a look at Grandmother and then, believe it or not, he left. As he walked down the stairs, he said: "*Sie haben sich tapfer benommen. Schlafen Sie nun schön weiter.*"[76] I nearly broke down. When even those rogues pity us, we must be in a very bad way indeed. And you can't bear pity at such a moment. It makes you weak.

I sat up for a couple more hours. Last time they turned up with call-ups for Father and Mother, we had drunk a glass of wine to steady our nerves after they left, because your knees tremble after such a visit, I can assure you. And then we went back to bed. An hour later, the doorbell rang again. I went back down. Two other policemen, also with call-ups. I said: "Your colleagues left barely an hour ago." "God damn," one said, "did you ever see such a thing?" "Would you like to note down the *Sperre* numbers?" I asked. "No, we'll get them when the documents are handed in," they answered, and were gone. You can imagine that now I feared another visit. At three o'clock I went back to bed and said to Bobby, who was asleep: "Bob, the police were here again." "Police!" she exclaimed and sat bolt upright, rolled over and fell asleep again. The next morning, she said: "Oh well, when you came back to bed I knew they'd left and I thought to myself: It can wait till tomorrow." How phlegmatic is that? The next morning I told Mother and Father, who were frightened out of their wits. At the office, I learnt that this had been a private operation by Theatre staff, who thought the transport wasn't big enough. I heard they'd gone on the rampage and dragged scores from their homes on Muidergracht. We had

---

76 "You have conducted yourself bravely. Go back to bed now and sleep well."

been lucky again. Mrs De Groot even said they were drunk, but I never noticed.

From mid-December until early January we were left in peace, and that meant a great deal to us. At least it gave our nerves a chance to settle. But by the beginning of January, the misery started all over again. They called at Aunt Dina and Uncle Nathan's, but left after seeing their medical certificates. A few days later, however, it emerged that little had been gained by this. For two weeks now, the green and black police have been taking away the sick during the daytime. They come in trucks and are accompanied by Jewish stretcher-bearers. The latter is too awful for words. Wrecks are taken from their homes on stretchers and hauled into the truck. Sometimes they're simply hoisted out of the window. They're taken to Borneokade, a railway depot in the east of Amsterdam, and from there they are sent, with their family, to Westerbork in the evening. Then, if they are at all fit enough to be transported, they are all taken from there. So you'll understand that Aunt Dina was extremely fearful that they would come for her. And you should know that Grandmother had also been left at home on the strength of a medical certificate, so perhaps they would come and collect her as well, along with Mother. I set about trying to get her into a hospital at once. This is no guarantee either — for all you know, they'll be clearing out the hospitals, too — but at least it reduced the chance of Mother being taken. The next day, by a lucky coincidence, she was admitted to hospital. But we remain anxious about what will happen to Mother.

This round-up business takes place three times a week, in the daytime. It's heart-breaking to see old wrecks venturing out into the streets at the crack of dawn, just to be out of the house when these scoundrels come for them. In truth, very little is gained, because they are simply picked up at some other time, but a day's reprieve is still a reprieve. Originally, Aunt Dina and her family stayed with us three days a week. But last Sunday, I learnt from an official source that they are concentrating on certificates issued in

September, and that means they could turn up here any moment, because Grandmother has a September certificate. So now Uncle Nathan and Aunt Dina are no longer staying with us, and they, too, spend most of those three days roaming the streets. It's awful. I spoke to Vordemberge, Sluzker's secretary, who assured me that should Mother be taken away, she's certain to be released again. So now Mother stays home alone, because the fewer people who are at home and taken away, the better. But of course it's frightening for her, even though there's still a chance, and quite a good one, too, because Grandmother is in hospital, that she'll be allowed to stay at home. Besides, there is no point in her leaving the house, because they might come back in the evening and take the entire family. I now spend as much time as possible at home on those days, because I'm still safer than the others and I'm best at doing the talking. We hope and pray that everything will be all right.

At the moment, all hell appears to have broken loose. Until the end of last week, people were also taken away in the evening, those working for the *Wehrmacht*, no less. Everybody expected them to be allowed to stay in Holland longest, because it's in the Germans' own interest. They're not sent to Westerbork, but to Vught.[77] More on this, i.e., Vught, when I give you my account of the JC. So far this week, the evenings have been quiet. Today is Tuesday.

My darling, this has become a rather dry account. If anything is unclear, I hope to explain it to you in person. I've also left out a great deal, e.g., the saga of Aunt Ré, which is a story in itself; the deportation of Jo Dunner and his entire family; all my rushing around when a call-up arrived for Philip Keizer, our former

---

77 Vught is a small town near the town of 's-Hertogenbosch, in the province of North Brabant. The Vught concentration camp was established in January 1943. The Germans called it "The Herzogenbusch concentration camp." It came under the command of the Economic-Administrative Central Office of the SS. A total of 31,000 prisoners were held there, among them 15,000 Jews. Until the camp was liberated by Canadian troops in September 1944, at least 749 people perished there; most of them were murdered.

neighbour, a boy I grew up with; the evacuation of the German Jews from the coastal regions in September 1940 (so trivial now, but a serious blow at the time); my many unsuccessful attempts at emigrating; our hard times last winter, which was bitterly cold; the arrest of Izak de Vries and his family, with a five-week-old baby, because when he received no response to a letter to the *Wirtschaftsprüfungsstelle*,[78] the Department of Economic Affairs, he'd had the "nerve" to say: "*Wir erwarten Ihre Stellungnahme.*"[79] In short, a great deal that may come to mind later. Our regular discussions, *en famille*, on how to avoid falling into their clutches, the summons from the provincial employment office this week, ordering three people from Father's office to go and work in Germany. In a word, too much to mention. But everything is utterly inconsequential compared to this one thing: To stay here and see the end of the war.

At the moment, the news is very heartening. Let us hope our optimism will prove well founded and that the war will be over within a few months. I have a feeling that, even if we are deported, we'll survive the war, because the best part of winter is behind us again. But we all fervently wish to stay here. Father and Mother, if deported, would be wrenched apart and lose everything. And Mother especially, who has lost so much weight you wouldn't recognize her, and who might not survive the ordeal. As for myself, even if I were in Poland for only a short time, I would be part of the post-war political problem posed by these deportees, which means it might take longer for us to be reunited. Every day we spend here I'm thankful to have slept in a comfortable, clean bed. Nothing matters, except this. Let's hope that everything will soon be over and that a wonderful era for the world in general, and for you and me in particular, will finally dawn. I can't tell you, my dear, how much I think of you every day,

---

78 The German Bureau for Economic Investigation; an agency for the takeover of Jewish-controlled businesses, so-called Aryanisation.
79 "We await your decision."

how much I admire you. I've been in love with other boys, when I saw they were in love with me. But I've always known: This is just a bit of fun, something silly to while away the time. The only one I love is my darling, the best man in the world.

Next time I'll give you an account of the JC, and from then on my reports will probably get much shorter, as I'll be updating the story every couple of days or every week. May the end of the war bring all this to a speedy conclusion.

PS: Last week the Apeldoornsche Bosch, the Jewish hospital for the mentally ill, was completely cleared out. Forty goods wagons full of patients went to Germany, and 50 members of the nursing staff had to go with them. The rest of the staff had to go to Westerbork, where they may be allowed to stay. Many have gone into hiding.

Amsterdam, 3 February 1943

My dearest,

We were in a flap again this morning. As you know, we were terrified they'd come for Grandmother and also take Mother away. This morning at half-past eight, we heard Mrs De Groot calling from the back of the house. Bobby was already dressed, unlike me, because quite by chance I was working a little later than usual, at Eitje's home, as our office is moving yet again. Bob came back upstairs and told us that a green had been at De Groot and had asked about Grandmother, using her maiden name, De Vries. Mrs De Groot had said that she didn't know anybody by that name. I was awfully sorry that they hadn't come to see us, because then at least it would be over and done with, and I could have done the talking instead of Mother, who gets so terribly nervous. I said to Mother: "I'm going after them, to show them the certificate saying she's at the NIZ." I wrapped a scarf around my head, as I hadn't done my hair yet, and I was about to go downstairs in my slippers and coat, when the doorbell rang. Bobby said: "It's the dustman," but I knew right away that it was the green police. I was "glad" that at least the uncertainty was over. You may think it's mad, but at that moment I was genuinely relieved. The uncertainty is far, far worse, and now at least I was at home and not Mother by herself.

Mother stayed in the bedroom while I ushered the green policeman into the living room and signalled to Bobby to go upstairs. To cut a long story short, it was relatively straightforward, even though the chap did not read Dutch and I had to translate the medical certificate for him. He attached the translation to the call-up notice — he had the call-up from September as well as the medical certificate that the black police had taken at the time — (I actually had to give him a paper clip) and left again. Then I cycled to Eitje, from where I called Father to tell him that everything was fine before cycling back home again. Muidergracht and Kerklaan had been cordoned off by green police, who were clearing out the houses there and taking away the people, so I was still a little apprehensive. I stayed at home for a few hours until they'd gone. On paper it all sounds rather matter-of-fact, but you have no idea what those visits mean and how completely wrecked you are afterwards. When I imagine them dragging Mother into that truck, full of sick people, all moaning and groaning, and everything she'd be subjected to over on Borneokade, even if she weren't actually maltreated, I can't be thankful enough that we have been spared this ordeal. You have no idea how completely off our stroke we are. We jump at the sound of the doorbell. We flinch at any kind of loud noise in the street, e.g., the backfiring of a car. We used to pity the German Jews when they jumped at every noise, but we have long since reached that stage ourselves.

Let me get started on the history of the JC. I have plenty of time today, because our office is moving and I can't go there yet. I'll make myself comfortable at home before running a few errands for the office later.

When the occupying forces arrived here in May 1940, Professor Cohen and Asscher went to see the Germans and told

Mirjam (second from right) with her parents, Maurits (Moritz) and Sara, and her sister, Bobby, outside their home at Muidergracht 29, Amsterdam, c. 1942
Author's collection

Mirjam and Henri Eitje in the offices of the Joodsche Raad, 31 December 1942
Author's collection

them they represented Dutch Jewry. According to another version
of events, more plausible in my view, they were summoned by the
Germans and assigned the task of passing on orders to the Jews.
I don't know which version is correct: Perhaps we'll find out after
the war. I do hope it's the latter, as it would redeem the Professor
in many people's eyes. Asscher plays a fairly insignificant role in all
this. The real dictator of Jews is Professor Cohen.[80]

After May 1940, it became clear that the Jews in the Netherlands
needed a representative body, a kind of over-arching organisation
covering all associations, etc. The so-called [Jewish] Coordinating
Committee was set up, chaired by L.E. Visser from The Hague, the
former president of the Supreme Court. I witnessed these events at
close hand. This Coordinating Committee was very short-lived.[81] In
February 1941, the Germans stepped in and appointed a *Judenrat*[82]
(which the Professor respectfully translated as Jewish Council rather
than the common-sounding Jews' Council),[83] on which the highest
dignitaries had a seat, e.g., the Chief Rabbi; the Secretary (former
secretary, that is) of the Amsterdam City Council (married to a non-
Jew); Mendes da Costa, Chairman of the Portuguese community;
De Hoop (former Director of the Dutch Cinema Alliance); some of
them who in the past had never troubled themselves with Judaism.
The Professor [Cohen] and Bram [Abraham] Asscher, Chairman
of the Jewish community in Amsterdam, became co-chairs; Van
der Laan, past Chairman of the Markets Authority, was appointed

80 The application of Cohen and Asscher to the occupying German authorities in
May 1940 is not mentioned in historical sources.
81 The Jewish Coordinating Committee (*Joodsche Coördinatiecommissie*) operated
from December 1940 until November 1941, when it was shut down by order of the
Germans.
82 On 12 February 1941, in light of the disturbances in Amsterdam (see letter from
31 January 1943, p. 29), the leaders of the community — Abraham Asscher and
Rabbis Sarlouis and Francès — were summoned to Böhmcker, the representative
of Seyss-Inquart in Amsterdam, who ordered them to form The Jewish Council
of Amsterdam.
83 In Dutch discourse at the time, the term *Jodenraad* (Jews' Council) had a negative
tone.

secretary. The Jewish Council received its orders from the Germans, and was expected to pass them on to the Jewish community. At the time, I was working at the office on Lijnbaansgracht, which housed the Committee for Special Jewish Interests, which had effectively become the Committee for Jewish Refugees, and I was fairly well informed about internal affairs, because I worked for the Professor on occasion and because Eitje, whose private secretary I am still, and hope to be until after the war, and Mrs Van Tijn, for whom I've worked as well, were both members of the committee.

On 20 March 1941, I arrived at the office, but was refused entry. The Germans were inside. When I mentioned my name and position, they made an exception and allowed me in. Only the bosses, the Professor's secretary and the Germans were there. Several hours later we had to leave, and the building was sealed. The same building on Lijnbaansgracht also housed the offices of the Foundation for Jewish Labour, i.e., the Wieringen work village.[84] These rooms were sealed as well. We were temporarily housed in the building owned by the Asscher Diamond Company on Tolstraat. That very same day, the Wieringen work village was cleared and all the youth transferred to Amsterdam. The Germans requisitioned the work village. A few days later, we were allowed back into the Lijnbaansgracht offices. The Committee for Special Jewish Interests and the Committee for Jewish Refugees were now called the Jewish Council of Amsterdam: Dept. of Welfare and Social Work. The actual set-up remained unchanged. We had to sign a declaration to the effect that none of us would destroy any documents, but no investigations were ever carried out.

In April 1941, we were visited by two gentlemen from Prague, Richard Friedmann and Jacob Edelstein. They were the "Asscher and Cohen" of Prague. They came here by order of the Germans and under their command, to organize our affairs on the Prague

---

84 The village was used as a center for training where young refugees from Germany learnt a trade in preparation for emigration, mostly to the Land of Israel.

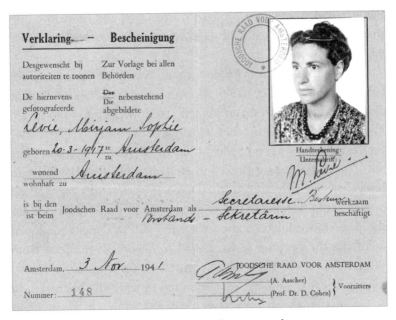

Joodsche Raad card identifying Mirjam Sophie Levie as the secretary,
3 November 1941

Author's collection

model. I chatted with these men, who were young and extremely
kind and unassuming, very frequently. I went for walks with them,
showed them round the city, and took them to the Theatre (reserved
for Jews). This was all still possible then. The concerts, for example,
were of an exceptionally high standard, and the Jewish Symphony
Orchestra was much better than the Concertgebouw Orchestra
from which Jews had been barred, and who were now playing in
the Jewish orchestra. It was a shame the Jewish orchestra was only
allowed to play music by Jewish composers.

At that time, the restrictions on Jews in Prague were already far
worse than they were here. The visit brought about the establishment
of the *Expositur*, headed by Dr Edwin Sluzker, an Austrian Jew who
had come to Holland in 1938 or 1939, after the pogroms, and who,
following his escape from one of the camps during the early days of

the war, had stayed here. I knew this man well and I owe it to him that I'm still here, because he handled our case the evening that we were taken away.

Forced registration for emigration was to be introduced for the German Jews. They had to specify all their possessions, money, clothes and furniture, down to their last drawing pin, so to speak. Everybody was expecting the German Jews to be sent to Poland once the registration was complete, just as in Germany, because all the anti-Jewish measures enforced in Holland applied to the German Jews first and only later to the Dutch Jews. But this registration proved quite harmless. The original plan probably provided for the deportation of German Jews only, but this was abandoned following the decision of June 1942 to deport all the Jews from Western Europe.[85] The term — "registration for emigration" — was a farce, because nobody was permitted to leave the Netherlands. A few extremely wealthy Jews managed to reach Spain upon payment of tens of thousands of guilders, followed some time later by another small group, but there was certainly no general *Ausreisegenehmigung*[86] and, hence, no opportunity to emigrate. We also received a visit from a certain Mr Throne from the Joint,[87] to discuss colonisation in Dominica, but this project never came to anything either.

In August, Max, who was already quite closely involved with the JC, to which all the organisations and foundations belonged, was appointed its general secretary. Van der Laan, who was often

---

85 In June 1942, Fritz Schmidt, the *Generalkommissar zur besonderen Verwendung* (Commissioner General for Special Assignments) and, in practice, also the representative of the German Nazi Party in the Netherlands, announced that all the Jews were to be expelled from Holland "and returned to the places they came from without any possessions." His words were publicized in the Dutch papers and caused great panic amongst Dutch Jewry, as many of them had believed that the Germans would expel only the German Jews.

86 Travel permit to other countries.

87 American Jewish Joint Distribution Committee: An American-Jewish organisation offering assistance to Jews around the world.

poorly, remained secretary, but in name only. Many resented Max for it, because even in those early days the JC was deemed to be "collaborating" with the Germans. It had, for example, not rejected the registration and, after those people died in Mauthausen, it hadn't said: "Go hang and do your dirty work yourself. We're closing shop. Let's see how you'll fare then." This would have been a more admirable stance, without a doubt, but I personally was of the opinion that through sabotage the JC could always mitigate circumstances and cause some delay. And it did. In December 1940, for example, the Germans had proposed to deploy Jews in German labour camps, under German command and without their families. It was not until December 1941 that this forced labour plan actually came into force, in camps in the Netherlands and under Dutch rather than NSB command. The NSB, for that matter, may be extremely unpleasant and capable of causing us a great deal of harm, should they wish to do so, but they have little say with the Germans, because the NSB is rumoured to be a mess, with a great many "traitors" within its ranks, and because Mussert[88] is a complete nonentity and an insignificant, pompous idiot.

In August we received another visit from Prague, this time Friedmann by himself. That month saw the establishment of what was to become the Central Commission for Culture, representing all denominations, including Reform,[89] Aguda,[90] etc., which sought to provide the Jews with moral support. This commission has done a fine job. When Freddy lost his job in December 1941, he became head of the office. Its chairman, until his deportation, was Jo Dunner. He was succeeded by Adv. Loonstein, who is now in prison on Amstelveenseweg. At present, Leo Seeligmann[91] is its

88 Anton Adriaan Mussert, the leader of the NSB.
89 A liberal or progressive denomination.
90 A strictly Orthodox, anti-Zionist denomination.
91 A teacher of Jewish Studies. Later, after his immigration to Israel, Izak Leo Seeligmann was appointed Professor of Bible Studies at the Hebrew University of Jerusalem.

acting chair. The commission has organised courses on all kinds of subjects. For several months last summer — in the days before the eight o'clock curfew came into force — I attended an evening class on the Jews in the Middle Ages, taught by Carolien Eitje and Mr Jacques Presser[92] at the Jewish High School. It was exceptionally good and a great morale booster. In fact, I'm still attending classes. One, on psychology, *"Individuum und jüdische Gemeinschaft,"*[93] has just ended, and one on the Marranos[94] is due to begin this week. You can choose among a range of lectures. Some JC offices have also hosted several lecture series, all of a very high standard.

Forced labour in camps [in the Netherlands] followed in December 1941. It was an immense shock, and the JC was fiercely criticized for implementing this order. For, once again, the JC was saddled with the dirty work, i.e., the administration, etc., etc. However, I was still of the opinion that they were wise not to chuck it all in, although very few agreed with me. Even within the JC itself — and I don't mean the bunch of people installed by the Germans, but those responsible for the day-to-day running and the actual work — more and more were in favour of putting an end to it all. The Professor dubbed it "the heroic standpoint." It was a question of bending or breaking, and then perhaps breaking after all if the war did not end soon enough. The fact remains that nobody has any kind of influence over the Professor. He will hear them out and then do as he pleases. It explains the immense hatred towards him at the moment. A few days ago, Freddy said: "How can this man, who has so much blood on his hands, sleep peacefully at night?" But I replied (although I have come to agree with those

92 A teacher at the Jewish High School in Amsterdam. He later wrote a book on the Holocaust of the Jews in the Netherlands entitled: *Ondergang: De vervolging en verdelging van het Nederlandse Jodendom, 1940–1945*, 2 vols. ('s-Gravenhage: Martinus Nijhoff, 1965).
93 "The Individual and the Jewish Community."
94 Spanish and Portuguese Jews who were forced to convert to Christianity in the 15th century, but who continued to observe Jewish customs in secret.

who say that the JC should stop and let things take their course, I also empathize with the Professor's standpoint): "You're wrong to blame the Professor. He believes he is doing the right thing and that's why he sleeps peacefully at night." Of course it's absurd to call him a traitor. He has the courage of his convictions. Only, he won't listen to others. If it's true that the Germans summoned him and appointed him as our representative, he's right in saying: "I am the person responsible, I shall do as I see fit." Anyway, it's a shame that we have this immense hatred within the Jewish community. These are all people whose lives have been affected, because relatives have been taken away — with the help of these traitors, as they put it.

In July[95] came the deportations via Westerbork. This used to be an assembly camp for the German Jews who had come to the Netherlands after the pogroms and who were housed first in various camps and then in one camp, i.e., Westerbork. So these people had been interned for several years, cut off from the rest of the world, in Dutch custody — the Ministry of Justice[96] — and all this time the Dutch Jews had shown them precious little concern. These people bore a deep grudge against the Dutch Jews, who had left them to fend for themselves — morally anyway; financially, they'd had to shell out a fortune. This camp now became a *Durchgangslager*[97] to Germany. The transports from Amsterdam arrive there and are sent on again after a few days.

The camp passed into German hands, under SS command, with a German commandant and guarded by Dutch military police[98] and the SS. A branch of the Jewish Council was appointed in Westerbork, with roughly the same function as the *Expositur* in Amsterdam, i.e., salvage what can be salvaged. And as one might expect, the German commandant prefers to deal with German Jews

95 15 July 1942.
96 Meaning the policemen who were subordinate to the Ministry of Justice.
97 Transit camp.
98 *Marechaussee*: A unit of the Dutch police organised in the fashion of an army.

rather than Dutch Jews, because the former have a better rapport with him. Besides, originally the camp had only held German Jews. And although various JC divisions in Amsterdam dispatched staff to Westerbork, here, too, the Germans outnumbered the Dutch. As a result, the German Jews were more or less in charge in Westerbork — those very same German Jews who were so embittered about the Dutch. This in turn meant that the German Jews received far more help than the others, because on the one hand the German-Jewish leadership had more friends and acquaintances among the German Jews — an extremely important factor — while, on the other hand, they felt greater sympathy towards their own than towards the Dutch. This, of course, fuelled the hatred against the German Jews who, in spite of everything, owe us a great deal. At present, the two groups are like oil and water.

So the problem of the JC and its friends and foes and that of the Dutch and German Jews are the two great, heart-rending problems we have to contend with, along with all the other misery inflicted on us. The consequences after the war, I fear, will be terrible, as the Dutch are sure to exact their revenge from the German Jews. The hatred towards the JC is taking on quite alarming proportions, as Max's arrest demonstrates. After all, these are matters of life and death.

In July, every single JC office needed a mounted police guard to hold back the people fighting for a job, i.e., for their lives. In October, during the rush on exemptions, there were similar scenes. It might be easier to tell you in person about the scenes that took place. The desperation in people's eyes, their grim determination to achieve their goal at the expense of everything and everyone, and dispensing with any qualms or compassion for others, are things I'll never be able to describe.

At the end of January 1943, those with *Wehrmacht* exemptions were rounded up and taken not to Westerbork, but to Vught. A camp had been built there that had originally been earmarked for the Jews, but that was later expected to house evacuees from the coastal regions. Its establishment caught everyone off guard, and only later was the Professor told that it was to be an *Arbeitslager*,[99] under *Waffen-SS* command (slightly different from the regular SS), that there would be no JC there, and that the commandant had appointed four Jews — again, German Jews — to pass on his orders to the Jewish labourers. Conditions in the camp are said to be satisfactory, with heating and fairly good food. The commandant is fairly decent. People are allowed to send parcels and even money, up to *f*15. What happens now is that the healthy are sent to Vught and the sick and their families to Westerbork and from there to Germany. The precise pattern, however, remains unclear.

I forgot to tell you that in July 1942 the JC itself had taken care of the administration and typing of the call-ups. That Shabbat when I was summoned to work, I had to do it as well, but I couldn't, and refused. I know there's no fundamental difference between typing call-ups and compiling the card index for the exempt, and yet I couldn't type the call-ups. Since September last year, the JC has been relieved of this task altogether. It really is appalling that we were forced to do this, as well as the *Sperre* distribution earlier. The Germans knew perfectly well how much discord it would sow among the Jews.

And now we're facing yet another drama. Forty people from Westerbork have been summoned to Amsterdam to help drag elderly and sick people from their homes. These are the so-called *Krankenträger*.[100] It's a wretched sight, as you can imagine. All the non-Jews are saying: "I'd rather be shot than do that." And they're right. Even so, I also understand that, when threatened with the prospect of a concentration camp, people will do anything they're asked.

I believe I've told you everything now. Our situation is so much worse than you could ever imagine. If only you knew how

99   Labour camp.
100   Stretcher-bearers.

all those people who used to live comfortable middle-class lives are faring now. Think of spoilt Uncle Meijer and [his wife] Aunt Griet, of Uncle Moos, a story in itself, which I'll tell you later. Think of Philip Frank, when we were at his wedding reception and when he taught that course in Beverwijk,[101] and who was shot yesterday, perhaps even hanged. Or think of the woman who jumped out of the window when they came to take her away and who lay dead on the ground for hours, because nobody dared pick her up. You can't imagine how much our lives have been thrown off course. We've lost the war, although something may yet come out of this misery. Let's hope that each one of us will be saved, and that we'll live to see the dawning of a beautiful era.

I'd better stop now, my love, for this has worn me out. I keep saying: Perhaps everything will be over very soon and we'll have the unbelievable luck, with all of us here, of having survived the war. For now, another hug and countless kisses. Bye, my dear one.

In my previous letter I forgot to mention that the JC staff in Westerbork has had their leave cancelled, because the commandant had heard that people had spoken ill of him. Now they won't be given leave to go to Amsterdam for four weeks.

Amsterdam, 12 February 1943

My dearest,

I think it may be best for me to write down an overview of events every week, to take a few brief notes every day to help me remember everything. Time and again I'm struck by how much is happening; new calamities every single day. Yesterday evening was dreadful again, with the transport leaving and the cars racing to and fro. It was truly awful. I felt very sorry for myself and cried a little. It's easy enough when all the others have gone to bed. I always stay

---

101 Centre for religious pioneers, in preparation for their immigration to the Land of Israel.

up very late, usually until half-past twelve, to minimize the risk of not hearing the doorbell. We're in a *Tisha B'Av* mood again today,[102] which is no wonder, really. But let me tell you the whole story in chronological order.

I believe I mentioned in one of my previous letters that the head of the volunteer legion[103] [for the German army] was shot dead. As a punishment, the people in the provinces of North and South Holland — the non-Jews anyway — are no longer allowed out after ten in the evening. On Monday, there was a huge raid on Aryan[104] men between the ages of 18 and 35. When I left the house with my bicycle in the morning to go to the office, I spotted a WA man[105] and a German policeman in front of the house. Of course I was frightened out of my wits, but they crossed the road and entered the laboratory. When I got to the office, I learnt that thousands of young men had been hauled from their beds that night and taken to Vught, some still in their pyjamas. Eyewitnesses claim they're treated like Jews there. You have no idea how wretched it is to see the WA walking around town with the green or black police. We mind that the OD (*Ordnungsdienst*)[106] takes away the Jews, but this is a tad worse in my view, because the WA men are volunteers. So our misery is compounded by this spinelessness.

---

102 *Tisha B'Av*, or the Ninth of Av, is a day of mourning and fasting to commemorate the many tragedies that have befallen the Jewish people, such as the destruction of Jerusalem and the First Temple by the Babylonians in 586 BCE and of the Second Temple by the Romans in the year 70 CE.

103 i.e., General Seyffardt, Commander-in-Chief of the Dutch army in the 1930s, who also headed the volunteer legion (*vrijwilligerslegioen*), a Dutch unit that was part of the Waffen-SS. Thousands of the legion's soldiers fought on the Russian front.

104 The author means non-Jewish Dutch men.

105 *Weer-Afdeling*, the uniformed, unarmed para-military branch of the NSB (similar to the German SA). Its members wore black shirts.

106 Jewish policemen in Westerbork. The *Ordnungsdienst* was one of the Westerbork institutions. Its members were even sent to Amsterdam to assist in the deportation of sick Jews on stretchers. In Westerbork they were also active on Tuesday mornings, escorting people who were called for transport, to the train.

On Monday evening there was another stir. The Van Geuns family next door run a rest home. They had it registered as such, because in the early days of this deportation business these rest homes were fairly safe, for staff, too. Lea owes her exemption to it. But now these rest homes are most at risk. They're emptied during the day. Of course, all the residents go out. But then on Monday, Van Geuns received notification that he and all his residents had to stay at home on Wednesday, when they would be collected. You can imagine what it must be like, having to wait patiently until they come to take you away. The Van Rijn ladies live there with their parents, who were evacuated from The Hague. They called on us around eight o'clock to ask me to come over and discuss their options. I went, but of course I couldn't tell them much. The next day they talked to various agencies, and decided to lock up and leave the house on Wednesday. That morning, Aunt Dina turned up at eight o'clock — she comes here three times a week, when the sick are taken out, first thing in the morning — and told us she had met Marie van Rijn and her sister, with a lot of luggage that she wanted to store at the orphanage. She's a teacher at the girls' orphanage, you see. What's amazing is that the Germans never even turned up on Wednesday.

On Tuesday there were terrible clashes in Haarlem, as a result of the raid on the Aryan men. Many were taken away in handcuffs. Yesterday they also took girls out of schools, including the grammar school.

As I cycled to the office, I saw scores of people in Rapenburgerstraat, on the corner of Muiderstraat. I thought they were taking the sick from Rapenburgerstraat again, but when I arrived at the office — our new address is Waterlooplein/Nieuwe Amstelstraat, just round the corner from Blauwbrug — I saw they were emptying the boys' orphanage by the Amstel. I learnt they were vacating all the orphanages, including the evacuees from Utrecht and The Hague. That day, all the orphanages were emptied and the children and staff sent to Westerbork. The thought of it is enough to turn your stomach. Mind you, a few managed to escape from Borneokade. Apparently it was pretty easy for them to escape from the train, which just stands there all day and which is where registration takes place. Some of the nursing staff got away, too. Mrs Vromen, who was among those taken, didn't want any efforts to be made for her release, and volunteered to go with the children. Amazing, don't you think? I spoke to her husband, whom I also like a great deal, and he told me that this is what they agreed. She thought they'd be taken away sooner or later anyway, and then she'd also be separated from her husband. Now at least she had a chance to stay with the children, and she wanted to seize it rather than gamble on being allowed to stay here. I think it's a tremendous attitude. So far, nobody has displayed anything quite like it.

On Tuesday evening your father and Els[107] were taken away again, because they were on a *Wehrmacht* list. You see, Els used to work at Kattenburg,[108] and had been included on a Kattenburg list. It's quite a worrying situation, because her stamp (*Sperre*) has been crossed out. Perhaps it will work out, but it will be difficult. (Meanwhile, I hear that it was all taken care of today.) It wasn't very considerate of them not to tell me about this stamp business. I heard about it from Freddy and Eitje, and also from Ro Leuvenberg. They're both rather nervous and secretive, which I think is a terrible mistake. Eitje, for example, knew nothing about this *Wehrmacht* business. I told him of course, because he thought it had something to do with Max and considered taking steps along those lines.

What is happening here is simply terror. People are shot dead all the time. Last week, Goedewaagen, one of the longest-standing NSB men, was demoted. He headed the Department of Public Information — otherwise known as Public *Mis*information — and

---

107   Leo's father's second wife, whom he married in 1942. Leo's mother passed away in 1939.
108   Hollandia-Kattenburg: A Jewish textile company, which was appropriated by the German army after 1940.

was granted an "honourable" discharge. He was replaced by a certain "Mister" Reydon, who has spent two years in prison for securities fraud. He and his wife were shot dead the other day. He didn't get to enjoy his job for very long. Although this rumour is still unconfirmed, it's so persistent it must be true. Then the Amsterdam Labour Exchange, where the call-ups for the labour assignments in Germany are drawn up, burnt down; that's to say, the second and third floors, which housed the archives, went up in flames. It must be the work of a single organisation, and I have a suspicion that the communists are behind it. We're dreading the consequences, because the Germans can't let this go unpunished.

Every now and then, there's the odd nice thing. On Wednesday, for example, I was at the National Employment Office where I spoke to the commissioner, quite a bigwig and as "kosher" as can be. The office was recently evacuated from The Hague to Amsterdam. The man told me that, of course, he has no connections in Amsterdam, and asked me about the political leanings of the Chief Inspector of the Dutch Police's Division for Foreign Citizens, H.R. Stoett. As I knew him to be trustworthy, I told him Stoett was perfectly decent. "Also with regard to Jews?" he asked. I replied: "Two hundred percent, if that's possible." It's nice to see that morale at this agency is still high. Then a travelling salesman at Father's office spoke of how he had been walking along Kalverstraat and passers-by had said: "Red Front [Communists]." In broad daylight. This is about the only pleasant news I have for you this week.

Yesterday evening the exempted diamond workers were taken away, and this operation looks set to continue today. One transport left last night, and another one is leaving tonight. Apparently the sick are not taken, so it looks likely that they will be collecting the diamond workers during the day as well. The list isn't very long — I believe some 600–700 people, including women and children. They keep changing their tactics, and although you're prepared, it's a fresh blow every time.

I'd better stop now, as I can't muster the energy to write you a sweet letter. All I do is rattle off events. The political news may be good, but it's a shame that, as we're nearing the end, we're still losing the battle. I doubt we'll pull through. Time and again I try to let things be and stop thinking about what could happen, but I can't. I hope I can write you a more cheerful letter next week, that the political news will be good and raise our hopes a little. Yesterday evening I read a book with letters from *Eretz Yisrael*. Whenever I think of the sense of freedom, I burst out crying. I have a feeling that, if we make it through this ordeal in one piece, I'll be in floods of tears for quite some time. I wish that time had already come. Lots of hugs, my love. Today I'll write you another Red Cross letter. I'm so sorry they always contain the same news. It's becoming truly monotonous. But at least you'll have another sign of life from me. It's something, even if it takes months to reach you. I understand full well how worried you must be. As it happens, I was talking about it with someone this week and we both agreed that, however worried you may be, you'll never be able to imagine what we have been through unless you were here yourself. Only a truly exceptional writer would be able to describe events in such a way as to evoke the present atmosphere. A simple summing-up of the facts can't do our frame of mind, and the atmosphere we live in, any justice at all.

My darling, I really do feel a bit better after my little chat with you. Perhaps we'll be lucky. I'm especially downhearted, because Churchill is reported to have said that something will happen within the next nine months. We'd been counting on four weeks! Of course, I know perfectly well that we shouldn't set any store by these statements. What will happen, and when, he will never reveal. Still, it's a blow, because you can't take much. A single pessimistic word and you're down in the dumps. I'm really going to stop now. Bye, my dearest.

Amsterdam, 23 February 1943. Half-past midnight

This is no life, but hell on earth. My hands are trembling so much I can barely write. This is all getting too much. This is more than anyone can bear. Another transport is leaving this evening. I had planned not to go to bed too late. Aunt Dina is staying with us at the moment. I already wrote to you that she stays at our house during the day because she has been left at home on grounds of illness and now she fears being taken away, which is what happens in all of these cases. At home on Saturday morning, she got such a bad crick in her back that she couldn't move, not even in bed. It was awful, because it meant she wouldn't be able to come and stay with us on Monday, as Jews aren't allowed in taxis. We decided to wait and see what Sunday would bring, but her condition didn't improve. She was then brought to our house by private patient transport, that's to say on a stretcher in an ambulance. It was terrible to see her stretchered in like that, but we still laughed, because fortunately there's nothing wrong with her apart from her bad back. When the ambulance pulled up at their doorstep, neighbourhood women rushed out to ask what was happening. Lea said: "My aunt has become unwell, and because she can't stay with us we have to have her picked up in this way. And would you please excuse me now, for Mother isn't at home either." This is the kind of act you have to put on, because it would be unwise to reveal too much. Well-intentioned gossip could fall on the wrong ears. Aunt Dina is staying with us now and is already doing much better. She sleeps in Grandmother's bed in the passage room. Since Friday, Mr Vromen has also been living with us. He is sleeping in the back room, our former living room.

You should know that in recent days they've been collecting and taking the sick to the Theatre in the evenings, too. They pick up the ones who are out during the day, as well as others for whom they have a call-up notice. It means that now they might call on Uncle Nathan in the evening, and discover that Aunt Dina is out. He'll tell them his wife is highly strung and has run away, but they may well force the truth out of him and make him reveal her whereabouts. And then, of course, they'll come and pick her up here. During the past few nights, the WA, in their role as auxiliary police, have been doing the collecting. They are horrible and kick in the door when you don't open up promptly, which happens because they often turn up in the middle of the night. They held a gun to my hairdresser's head last night when he didn't answer the door quickly enough.

At half-past eleven, the doorbell rang. The immense shock! And yet I knew immediately what to do. I was up, the others in bed. I said to Aunt Dina, "Stay calm, I'll do what I can," closed the dividing doors and pulled the curtains over them. All at lightning speed, but my heart was in my mouth. Then I called from the top of the stairs: "Who is it?" And heard a female voice calling out: "Decent folk." I ran down the stairs, wondering who it could be. Nobody is allowed out after eight, so I was baffled. It turned out to be a woman and a child, panting and sobbing. I said: "Quick, shut the door," and let them in. They had been picked up this evening and taken to the Theatre. They had hidden behind the truck and when it drove off, they wandered in the dark — it's pitch-dark — until they spotted a Jewish nameplate with their torch. The story came out in fits and starts. "I don't mind sleeping in the stairwell, but please don't throw us out." And the child said: "I need to go really badly." It was so wretched, so sad, to see this woman and this young child of barely eight or nine. I invited them up, let the child use the lavatory and gave the woman some water. She wouldn't stop crying. I told her there was no need to be afraid, that we wouldn't send them away.

Then we got the whole story. Her husband had been away for 10 months already, in Germany. When they had come to take them away, the woman had hurled herself off a flight of steps and had been left behind. The WA man who came this evening was very friendly, but he had orders to take them. She then asked him to fetch her something from the kitchen, slipped the call-up into her pocket and they went with him. When the truck arrived at the Theatre, she and her child didn't get in with the others, but hid behind the truck. Her escape will go unnoticed in the Theatre, because they don't have their call-ups. I destroyed them right away. I don't believe they're working their way down a list, and anyway there are so many lists, they won't notice anytime soon. They're now sleeping in our former maid Dina's room, up in the attic.

As you can imagine, we were trembling all over and it was a terrible shock for Aunt Dina. She thought, as of course we all did, that they'd pressed Uncle Nathan to reveal our address. Perhaps it has put us all in danger, but I doubt they will be looking for the woman now that the call-ups are gone. Stupid though it may be, I couldn't possibly throw her out. I'm sure, my dearest, that you approve of my actions. I know you too well.

But now I'm afraid to go to bed. With every step — every so often loud, military steps can be heard passing the house — I grow rigid with fear. You have no idea what it's like to hear those steps approach and the terrible fear: Will they stop here, will they ring our doorbell? One beautiful sunny day in June, at the beginning of the war, I was cycling along one of the canals. Despite the setbacks I had even then, when of course I had no idea how bad things would get, I was in high spirits and thought to myself: They can't break me, whatever they do to me. But this is too much, this kills your spirit. You live as if nothing is wrong, you work, which is a wonderful distraction, and yet you keep feeling: I've reached the end of my tether. I can't bear this much longer. You hover between fear and hope, which springs eternal even when you've learnt to expect the worst. Among optimists you think: It will be all right, we'll pull through. But among pessimists, you think: It's over. In recent days I've been very dejected, because I no longer believe, even though we're doing well, that we'll see it through. Unless, that is, England intervenes soon. And now that things are looking bad in Tunis, this seems unlikely. Yet despite such reasoning, you never stop hoping, against your better judgement. You know I'm brave, but my nerves are in tatters. People are carted off in droves; the old people are literally dragged away. Among the people taken to the Theatre were an 81-year-old woman and her son. The woman had to go to Westerbork, whereas the son will probably go to Vught this evening. They had to say goodbye to each other in the Theatre. Imagine that... And this is no exception. Hundreds and hundreds are deported, even 90-year-olds, but I'm telling you about this case because her daughters were with me this afternoon and I remembered their goodbyes.

The woman who fled to our house this evening told me that they took her mother last week. A railway official wanted to smuggle her out and slipped her a note with instructions. But the woman was in a complete daze and unable to take anything in, so she couldn't be helped. And so it continues, every waking hour. I have steady nerves, trust me, but these relentless blows wear you down. The tension drives you mad. But time and again hope rises within me, and I must cling to it or go to pieces. I imagine being with you. And when I do, I always think of our beautiful things. At moments of extreme danger, you forget about possessions. But as soon as the danger has passed, your thoughts return to everything you own and would so dearly like to keep. But I'll write about this some other time. It's now half-past one, and in about an hour or so I may be brave enough to go to bed. Sleep well!

Amsterdam, 26 February 1943

Let me start by telling you of the week's events. Every day I make a brief note of what has happened and then I write it all up at the end of the week. But there are general topics as well, such as the possessions I mentioned in my previous letter. Perhaps I can write about it in this letter, although I could compose lengthy epistles on any one of these topics.

On Tuesday last week, something ghastly happened in the

Theatre. The brutes who decide on matters of life and death are often blind drunk. So, too, that Tuesday night. They got into a terrible row about whether or not to release people, and it got so bad they ended up rolling around on the floor. Mr Süsskind,[109] who was there to handle cases at the Theatre[110] for the JC, intervened and pulled them apart. Now, of course it doesn't matter if these fellows want to kill each other, but as a result of this row, the 40 people who had already been released and billeted nearby had to return to the Theatre to be deported. Just imagine it. You're free and allowed to leave the Theatre with all your things, expecting to have a relatively quiet night in a private house nearby, and then suddenly you're hurled back into hell! I was in that position once myself and the feeling you have when you're free is indescribable. Imagine having to go back...

Last Sunday, a statement against the persecution of the Jews was read out in all the churches, both Catholic and Protestant, protesting against the beastly way in which the Jews are carted off, and also against the large-scale deportations of Aryans. The Catholics are forbidden from offering any kind of assistance, including administrative, unless coerced. And when they are coerced, they must sabotage the work as much as possible. Obviously, the latter wasn't said in so many words, but clearly hinted at. This isn't the first such protest and it's utterly pointless of course, but it's an exceptionally brave statement, because it could land the Bishop of Utrecht in prison. These Catholics do show some mettle. The bishops of Utrecht and Roermond are telephoned daily by the mining unions in Limburg to see if they are still in their posts and have not yet been taken away. They told the Germans that if these

109 Walter Süsskind was responsible for preparing lists in the Jewish Theatre. Together with other workers, he hid registration cards so that those appearing on them could disappear from the Theatre. In addition, Süsskind was active in smuggling children out of the Theatre with the consent of their parents, who were at the Theatre, and, together with underground organisations, moving them to places of refuge.
110 Süsskind took care of special cases in order to secure their release from the Theatre. He had (relatively) good connections with Aus der Fünten.

men were taken away, the miners would down their tools at once. Isn't that wonderful?

The Germans railed against this protest and said, among other things, that in the past the NSB (which before the war was pretty unpopular) never received as much pity as the Jews do now.[111] They are annoyed, because the Catholic Church refuses to marry or administer sacraments to members of the NSB, something that people in Catholic regions such as Brabant and Limburg find particularly upsetting, of course. I have kept a notice somewhere announcing the marriage of two members of the NSB, which mentions that because of the "obstinacy of the Catholic Church" the marriage can't be consecrated.

We've had a respite since Tuesday evening. The Theatre has to be deloused, so thankfully there are no round-ups. But even though it means a great deal, you still can't breathe freely, firstly because it will only last a few days — until Sunday evening — and secondly because plenty of other wretched things are happening. Besides, the OD has dispatched 40 of its people from The Hague to Amsterdam. Everybody fears for the NIZ and JI (Jewish Invalid).[112] The residents are all running away, or trying to, anyway. The fact of the matter is they're trapped. They're not given a relocation permit or billeting, and they're obviously all old and infirm people with nowhere to go. Everybody was expecting it to happen today, but the OD was sent into the provinces instead, to Rotterdam they say. I'm afraid we haven't heard the last of it yet.

So far the events of the week. But let me end with an example to illustrate the atmosphere we live in. A colleague at the office is

111   In February 1943, a proclamation was read out in all the Catholic churches in the Netherlands that anyone giving substantial support to the NSB would be denied the holy sacraments. This was a few months after Johannes de Jong, an ardent anti-Nazi, had been appointed Archbishop of Utrecht and was head of the Catholic Church in the Netherlands.

112   The *Joodsche Invalide*, or Jewish Invalid, was a Jewish home for the elderly and chronically ill.

the daughter of the director of the Portuguese boys' orphanage. My colleague and her parents live in the same house as the orphans, in Middenlaan. Although the orphanages have been emptied, nearly all of them have a few remaining children, and the police had now come to take these children away. The children, however, were all at school, whereupon they were told that the (green) police would be back in the evening. Needless to say, the boys, as soon as they found out, all scarpered. That evening her parents were at home, petrified, but the police never showed up. They didn't know what to do, with this constant threat looming over them. They applied for billeting or a relocation licence but were met with refusal, because the JC, which may grant billeting, may only do so when people are genuinely unable to return to their home, because it has been sealed. This was not the case here, so these people were effectively forced to wait until they were rounded up. Besides, their chances of being released again were minute; firstly because all the boys had fled, for which they might be punished,[113] and secondly because they had been exempted on grounds of the orphanage, and with the closure of the orphanage their *Sperre* had become worthless.

On Friday evening, my colleague came to see me and told me that the police had come back. Nobody had been at home, but the neighbours had told them. She gave me their details and asked me to keep an eye on things. She had to go home, because you *have* to be at home. You put other people's lives at risk if you spend the night with them without permission. So they planned to make sure they were home by eight, fully expecting to be taken away that evening. Imagine having to go home in the knowledge that you'll be taken away. The next morning I was up at the crack of dawn, to see if anything had happened. Luckily, the police had not returned.

---

113 The Jews marked as *Strafgeval* (a punishment case) for not obeying the law — through "transgressions" such as hiding, not donning the Yellow Star, holding false identity papers, travelling by train or tram, etc. — were sent immediately to Westerbork, and from there, in most cases, on the first train to a death camp.

In fact, nothing has happened so far, so it seems fair to assume that the case is closed.

An amusing incident now. Last week, Mrs De Groot, our neighbour, bought fish on the black market. You see, Jews can't get fish legally, because Jewish fishmongers don't get an allotment, so they can't sell any, and we're not allowed to buy from Aryans. This applies to fruit, vegetables and fish. But there is so much black-market trading, by Jews as well as by Aryans, that everybody has fish. It's frightfully dear, to be sure, but money is no object at the moment. This is another topic I intend to cover at length some day. So she went into a shop and bought fish. When she left, she found a policeman outside. Of course it frightened the wits out of her, because she was convinced she had been caught. The policeman noticed her shock and said bluntly: "You must have bought fish. I say, would you mind giving me a piece of paper, if you have any, otherwise I have to carry the fish unwrapped in my bag." In other words, he had bought fish illegally himself, since it wasn't an official fishmonger. He even winked at her!

This letter has become longer than I thought it would be and I have no more time to regale you with observations on various subjects. Perhaps I'll have the time and inclination on Sunday, for I do need to be in the right mood or you end up with a dreary tale. Perhaps it's wrong to try and cover them all in a single letter. It might be better to slip them in here and there, but because I worry about forgetting things, I mention them all in the same letter. I expect to come back to them in my next couple of letters.

Darling, your father received another Red Cross[114] letter yesterday. How wonderful to hear you're doing so well.

114   It was possible to send a letter once every three months via the International Committee of the Red Cross. The letter had to be written on an official form and could not exceed 25 words.

Amsterdam, 18 March 1943

My dearest,

I'm writing at the office. Actually, I still have a lot to do, but I can organize it in such a way that I can afford to play truant for an hour. I can't say whether this letter will be any good. It all depends on whether or not I get interrupted a lot. The other week I reread my last few letters, and noticed that I forgot to give you the outcomes of some of the stories. Let me do this first.

First of all, Miss Roos was also released the following day. It was close for a while, but in the end everything turned out all right. She told me that she had been with Eva Eitje. This is a ghastly affair. Apparently Eva is rather nervous, and when she was in the Theatre she went and stood with her arms crossed in front of some high-ranking Hun and called him every name under the sun. The fat was well and truly in the fire then. Miss Roos told me, among other things, that JC staff had to stand to one side, and then they were considered for exemptions on a case-by-case basis. Eva joined the group; after all, she's a nurse and therefore in JC service. But when the chap spotted her, he went wild and shouted: "*Sie haben hier nichts zu tun. Raus! Mit dem erstfolgendem Transport kommen Sie weg.*"[115] Sluzker advised her to go to Vught, but she refused and was therefore bound for Westerbork. According to Sluzker, it would have been an easy matter to resolve, but her outburst in the Theatre spoilt everything, it goes without saying. It's terrible for her father, who has nobody now. And on top of it all, she was smuggled out of the train at Borneokade. She's in hiding now. One has no way of knowing whether or not this is good, for hiding has become an extremely risky business. I expect to write to you about that at length some day.

Our arrangements for Grandmother fell through. Professor Roegholt, the professor who came to see us, is the successor of Professor Noordenbosch. The latter was removed from his post as

---

115 "You have no business here. Out! You are leaving on the next transport."

director of the WG[116] because of his anti-German sentiments. The Wilhelminagasthuis, incidentally, is now called Westergasthuis. People greatly resented Roegholt for accepting the appointment, but he's not an NSB sympathizer and seeks to prove it in all kinds of ways, e.g., by doing a lot for the Jews. It really was extraordinary that he came to see us at once, between two operations. He was extremely friendly, and even spoke to the director of the Municipal Health Service, but nothing can be done. And we haven't received her identity card back yet, so we can expect something any day. I do remain hopeful that she may be admitted at some point, but I'm very fearful that something will happen in the meantime. And what is worst, is that Mother will be at home all by herself. We can't get any help either, because all the nurses are working at the NIZ and are not allowed to leave. Selma was with us, but her parents were taken away on Friday and sent on, and now she's so down in the dumps she doesn't want to be away at night. Besides, because her little sister doesn't have an exemption she wants to be at home in the evenings, to be there in case something happens.

Something dreadful happened. There was terrific shelling here on Friday evening. Everybody is always glad to hear the English. Not me, I'm always anxious, but there's scarcely a soul who isn't happy. But then Elie Pakkedrager's little boy was hit by a piece of shrapnel and killed instantly. Isn't that awful? You're glad to hear the shelling, but these people will never be glad again.

Let me tell you a few quick jokes. An NSB man has a hutch with rabbits he's fattening up so he can eat them. One morning, when they're almost big enough, he finds the hutch completely empty, save for a note saying: "Evacuated according to plan." I don't know if the English papers report any of this, but every time the Germans lose a position, our papers write: "Evacuated according to plan." And now a true story. The trams here are always jam-packed. There are far too few and on the running boards, and everywhere,

116 A well-known hospital.

people stand and hang on to the straps. One such overloaded tram left Muntplein. Standing on the running board were a couple of true Amsterdammers. A German officer came running by and one of the chaps grabbed him by the scruff of his neck and yanked him onto the tram with the words: "Hop on, Fritz, 'cause if you take a tumble we'll have to be inside an hour earlier again." Isn't that funny? The mood here is so incredibly anti-German, you have no idea.

Somebody is married to a *Reichsdeutsche*,[117] but the couple has lived in the Netherlands for 20 years and the woman herself is as anti-German as they come. But her Dutch is poor. A while ago, she was waiting at the Central Station to meet some guests. She was sent from one platform to another until finally, dead-nervous, she found herself on the other side, on the IJ waterfront. And when she's nervous, her Dutch is even worse than usual. In the end she went home, where her visitors had been waiting for half an hour. The woman told me this herself. She also told me that in the shops the hostility is almost palpable. Of course, nobody could possibly know that she's also anti-German, and everybody regards her as the enemy.

It's curious that I can never really evoke the atmosphere we live in. We're okay during the day, but the evenings are quite miserable. On the face of it we're quietly going about our business, but at times — some evenings are worse than others — you sit there with heart palpitations, expecting to hear the doorbell any moment. And you can rationalize as much as you like, that you may well escape again, and if not, then for God's sake you will share other people's fate, but it makes no difference. Last night I woke with heart palpitations, because I dreamt I heard the doorbell. This had never happened to me before. Others tell me they dream this all the time. The hopelessness slowly grinds you down. A short while ago we were much more hopeful, but it's clear now that the English aren't

---

117   German national.

doing anything, which means we're well and truly lost. These past few days I've been very down. But every bit of slightly more positive news raises your hopes, and that's the trouble. You're torn, unable to be objective. Sometimes I try to be firm with myself and face up to all the possibilities. And then, when I reach the conclusion that there's no more hope for us, I think to myself: But surely it's possible that with my excellent position at the JC I could hold out for another six months or longer. After all, there are still some Jews working at the *Reichsvereinigung*[118] in Germany. But when I think of Father, Mother and Bobby, I lose heart. But at the same time I think: What if Hitler is really dead, or the Germans themselves grow sick of it all, or the English finally take some action, etc. And then every evening this round-up business with the trucks racing to and fro, and the news the following morning: So-and-so has been taken away and such-and-such. It drives you mad. I do all I can to keep my nerve, because once you go to pieces, you're lost. But it's terribly difficult.

And always, and this is the worst, I'm doubtful whether I'll ever see you again. It leaves me frantic. My longing for you is killing me. I always managed to reassure myself, but the situation is so hopeless now that I've lost all faith in a happy ending. When I think that all our courage and fortitude may have been in vain, I can't bear it any longer and yet I know I must. When shall I be with you again, my love, and when can we share our cares and our joys? My darling, I realize that all my efforts to convey the mood are futile. I can't do it and I doubt anyone can.

I'd better stop again, as I'm becoming tiresome, and try as I might, I can't tell you what I really want to tell you. Let me end, as always, with an awful lot of hugs and kisses. Bye, my dear young man.

---

118 *Reichsvereinigung der Juden in Deutschland*, the Association of Jews in Germany.

Amsterdam, 21 March 1943

My very dearest,

I have just, for the umpteenth time, reread all of your Red Cross and other letters in a bid to get in the mood. At home I still have the letter you wrote to me on my first birthday after your departure. I wanted to reread it yesterday, but I didn't get round to it. I'll enjoy it later.

I went to Zichron[119] this morning and listened to the *Megillah*.[120] Then I went to the office — it's Sunday morning — and now I'm sitting here, all by myself, quietly writing to you. I have a fair bit of time and can talk to you as much as I like. Unfortunately, I have quite a lot of horrible news to tell. On Thursday morning I was at the office, when somebody from our staff came to see me and told me that Uncle Nathan, Aunt Dina and the children had been taken away on Wednesday night. He told me that when they had not answered the door, the police had gone next door to ask for an axe and when the neighbour replied that he did not have one, he had to go and help kick in the door. Uncle Nathan is said to have been beaten, and the children, who had hidden, were found. I got a terrible fright, for I was convinced they would be treated as punishment cases, and then that would be the end of it. First I went home to fetch the copy of the letter I had given them in the event that something should happen to them, and then I cycled to the *Expositur*. I knew that Uncle Nathan would not answer the door to the police, because we had discussed the matter, and I had told him many a time that it makes no difference, that if you don't answer the door, they'll simply kick it in. But he'd say: "They have no right to enter my home if I don't want them to. I'm under no obligation

---

119 Zichron Yaakov: a well-known religious-Zionist youth organisation that organised synagogue services on the Sabbath and religious holidays. During these services, Hebrew was pronounced in the accent of *Eretz Yisrael* (i.e., not the Ashkenazic pronounciation).

120 The Scroll of Esther. The story of the delivery of the Jews in Persia under King Ahasuerus by Esther, a Jewish girl.

to let them in." True, of course, but he doesn't seem to know that we've lost our rights. Anyway, no point dwelling on it; this is the way things were. When I arrived at the *Expo*, I saw that Asscher and Cohen were with Sluzker, so I knew I had no chance at all of seeing him. Instead I asked to speak to his secretary, whom I know quite well. As I sat there waiting, I suddenly saw Marc. I couldn't believe my eyes! And a moment later, Lea, too. They told me the whole story.

At half-past ten in the evening the doorbell had rung. They hadn't answered. At first, Uncle Nathan had wanted to answer it after he had concealed Aunt Dina and the children had fled onto the roof, but they took so long to get ready that in the meantime the police had smashed down the door. Aunt Dina was indeed hiding in a closet and the children on the roof. The police burst in with guns and gave Uncle Nathan a bloody nose. They realized at once that there had to be more people in the house, for there were dirty cups on the table and Marc's bed, which is in the passage room, as you enter the house, had been slept in. He had just gone to bed. They found Aunt Dina and, after a brief search, Marc as well. Lea was on the roof, all huddled up. They walked past her a few times, but found her in the end. Just imagine what she must have gone through, every time those thugs walked past her. I can't remember whether I told you that when *we* were picked up, Bobby was hiding in the attic. They shone a torch on her, but luckily they never found her. But then I hadn't concealed the fact that there was a second daughter; I just said she had evening duty, which wasn't true either. Still, back in September it was all much less risky. In the worst case you were found and taken away. If you didn't hide, you had to go along as well, so if you did, at least you still had a chance. But now the situation is different, because the policemen will report the fact that you hid and then you become a punishment case. And that's the end of it, even if you have a *Sperre*.

These brutes ransacked the place. It was quite a catch for them, because Uncle Nathan still has his gold and silver jewellery business and they found lots of gold and silver. As you know, Jews are not allowed to have any gold or silver in their possession, but they had a permit. These fellows confiscated it all straight away, as well as all of Uncle Nathan's papers, including the letter to Sluzker I had given him. Luckily it contained nothing incriminating, but it shows how you can walk into a trap without even realizing it, because of course my name and address were in that letter. The "police" raided the entire sideboard, ordered them to unpack the rucksacks and took what they fancied, put all the silver in bags, and turned the whole place upside-down. In a word, it must have been chaos. But Marc is a shrewd one! He simply put a lot of what they had taken and laid out on the table back into his rucksack. But still, fountain pen, etc., are all gone, as is everything important. They stayed for hours, and of every shiny object they asked if it was silver. Meanwhile, Lea packed the rucksacks again and at three o'clock the truck arrived and took them to Adama van Scheltemaplein. Lea told me they were held separately, not in the same room as the others. They met a young man from the *Expo*, an acquaintance, and early in the morning Lea's and Marc's names were called out and they were free. But because they hadn't received their identity cards back, I didn't know whether they had been listed as punishment cases. In that case, their *Sperre* would be crossed out and an "S"[121] stamped onto the identity card. At any rate, they were lucky to be free.

I discussed the case with Sluzker's secretary, who held out little hope, but promised to do what she could. Then I briefly spoke to somebody else about Lea's and Marc's identity cards, about whether they might get them back, but this person thought it best not to become involved in the case and to apply for new identity cards. When I went back downstairs, I happened to bump into Sluzker, whose birthday it was that day. I congratulated him and spoke to him about the case, pointing out that Uncle Nathan did have

---

121   For "*Strafe*," or punishment.

a permit to own silver, but that his papers had been confiscated. He promised to do what he could and this raised my hopes a little, because I had now done everything in my power. In the afternoon I learnt that they had been transferred to the Theatre, and this raised my hopes even further, because they were evidently not being treated as special cases. Otherwise they would have been left at the *Zentralstelle*. In Eitje's name, I wrote a letter to Mr Susskind, who pulls some strings in the Theatre. It was all I could do at that point. Of course it was another big blow for Mother, who has absolutely no resilience. She's a dreadful sight to behold and completely apathetic. We're expecting the worst.

The following morning I wrote another letter in Eitje's name, this one to Sluzker, in a bid to keep the case warm. In the afternoon, I learnt that a transport had made its way from the Theatre to Borneokade, from where the transport to Westerbork would depart at eight. Uncle Nathan and Aunt Dina weren't on it. I spoke to Leo de Wolff, who told me they still stood a good chance. But shortly before the transport left, they were sent to Borneokade and on to Westerbork. I can't keep them there, it will be impossible. They do know Ab Wijnschenk at the JC in Westerbork, and perhaps he can do something for them, but I fear the worst. It's a shame Uncle Nathan is 56. At present, everybody up to the age of 55 is sent to Vught, where at least you have a little more certainty of staying in Holland for a while. Luckily, Father is only 52. We're trying to keep Uncle Nathan in Westerbork on account of his diamond skills, but I don't have much faith that they'll accept that.

So now Lea and Marc are billeted with us. We have yet to discuss the practicalities of this, because of course Mother can't look after this huge household all by herself, but I'm sure we'll find a solution. We have made no further progress in Father's case, but I'm going to write Mr Blüth a note tomorrow. Eitje has urged me to do so.

On Friday morning, Aunt Phine came to see me at the

office to tell me that she had received an *Anweisung*[122] to move
to *Oost*.[123] People from the "Rivierenbuurt" area — the Jews, that
is — are forced to leave their homes and move to *Oost* to make
way for evacuees or other people who have to move. Curiously,
everybody always expected the Jews from wealthy *Zuid* to have to
leave their homes. In a few cases, when the *Wehrmacht* fancied a
house, this did happen, but not on a major scale. Meanwhile, every
week some 20 families from Rivierenbuurt are forced to move to
Oost. They're allotted a house, and the majority of these houses
are terrible. For the most part, the people that lived there were
deported, so thieves and burglars have made their haul, smashed
windows that can't be replaced, etc. But the curious thing is that
very few people now mind having to leave their home and move
into such a hovel — besides, there are some decent houses, too. It
pales into insignificance compared to everything else, although
it's certainly no trifling matter to leave your house within a matter
of days — you're given three to four days. You're allowed to take
your furniture, which is tremendously generous, of course. But if
they catch you in your old house after the appointed date, they will
deport you to Westerbork.

As it happens, people are seldom forced to move from Aunt
Phine's neighbourhood (Stadionbuurt). But when she went to the
Expositur to apply for a deferment, she was told that her house had
already been rented out and that she owes her move to some NSB
people who wanted her out of the house. I have already written
to you that the Luitinks, who live downstairs, joined the NSB
and even the WA. When the people upstairs — Jews — were taken
away, Luitink helped NSB members to move into their home. So
Aunt Phine no longer fit into that house and they drove her out.

122 Relocation order.
123 The eastern part of central Amsterdam, called *Oost*, where many Jews,
    mostly of low income, lived. The Germans called the area *Joodsche Wijk*
    (Jewish Neighbourhood). Due to the concentration of so many Jews in the
    neighbourhood, it became a kind of open ghetto.

She has to be out by Wednesday. She doesn't know where to. She could apply for billeting in another neighbourhood, but if she does, she will lose all her furniture and she will also run the risk of having to move again when the people she's staying with receive an *Anweisung* themselves. But living in *Oost* is dreadful, because of the nightly "visits" (always by the black police, WA, green police, etc.). What happens is they carry out house-to-house searches, looking for people without a *Sperre*. Aunt Phine had wanted to take her sister, Aunt Ré, with her, who could then be her so-called "carer" and receive a certificate to this effect. But Aunt Ré hasn't been exempted yet, and would therefore run an even greater risk there than anywhere else. You see, our worries come thick and fast.

So now we have a big crowd of people in the house, while anticipating yet another visit from the police, in connection with the fact that Grandmother's identity card has still not been returned to us. Perhaps we'll be lucky. It all depends on the fellows who turn up. If they are "decent," we may be allowed to stay at home; if not, the whole lot of us will be taken. And although we're all exempted, you never know whether or not you'll be released again. We'll just have to wait and see.

I forgot to tell you again that we had another visit from the police, but this one had a very happy ending. At half-past twelve in the evening (or night rather), the doorbell rang. I was still up; the others were already asleep. I ran downstairs and opened the front door. There were a Hun and three Dutchmen. The German spoke, the Dutchmen were silent; I suspect they didn't even understand German. He enquired after the number of people in the house and I answered truthfully, which I always think is best. They wanted to come upstairs, but I said we were all exempted and it would therefore be a waste of their time, or something to that effect. I just chattered on and all of a sudden the green started crying, honestly, crying out loud. And he said: "*Sie sind ein tapferes Mädchen und ich bin ein Schuft.*"[124] And off they went! I double-locked the door and walked up the stairs, my knees trembling, I can assure you. Then straight to bed. (With hindsight, I think he may have been drunk.)

Let me tell you a bit about the black-market trade now. It's a truly fascinating subject. You should know that black-market trade in food is punishable by death, for both vendor and buyer. When this law came into effect, we agreed we would no longer buy on the black market, because it was too great a risk. But the fact of the matter is that black-market trade is incredibly common and relatively few people are caught and shot, so everybody lives off black-market purchases. Money can buy you literally anything. Let me quote you a few prices, just for the fun of it. This past winter an egg cost as much as ƒ0.85, at the moment ƒ0.60. Butter costs ƒ18 per pound and is quite scarce. Jam is ƒ1.85 for a jar. Tea ƒ100 per pound. Coffee I'm not entirely sure about, roughly the same I think. A half-pound of dark chocolate, very difficult to get hold of, costs ƒ12.50. A loaf of bread, on the black market, costs ƒ2. I don't know the prices of meat, because kosher meat is unavailable. We sell our ration coupons. What usually happens is that you buy a coupon on the black market. The food itself is then fairly cheap, i.e., roughly the normal price. The coupons make everything so dear. Tea, for example, is in very short supply, as is coffee, but sugar, jam, bread, etc., are still available with coupons. Salad oil costs ƒ40 per bottle (I'm not sure of this) and is also very difficult to get hold of. You have no idea just how widespread this "trade" is. At the market, for example, mounted police must keep an eye out for any black-market dealings. But they actually do it themselves. Cigarettes cost ƒ5 per packet of 20, a cigar costs ƒ1.70 or more. This trade is so widespread because people no longer turn over every penny. You can buy little else besides food. Especially the Jews, who are no longer allowed to go out, travel, etc. Besides, you feel you have to eat as well as you possibly can in order

124 "You are a brave girl and I am a bastard."

to preserve your health. You can't live off the coupons, or only very badly.

There's a good joke on the subject. A man wants to commit suicide by hanging himself. But the new make of rope was of such bad quality that it broke. Then he wanted to gas himself, but the gas had been disconnected (which is what happened last winter, between two and five).[125] In the end, he decided to live off his coupons and he succeeded at once. Besides, the Jews, more than anyone, feel that money is no longer an object. If you're deported, it's gone, too. But you end up spending ridiculous amounts of money, whereas officially you're not allowed to earn more than ƒ250 per month. Another silly thing is that a household of two, for example, is entitled to ƒ250 per month, the same as a family of, say, 10 people. I wrote to you before that we're not allowed in greengrocers. The Jewish greengrocers receive very little in the way of fruit and vegetables, but the Aryans are a great help and supply the Jews with vegetables, etc. The support and sympathy we receive from the Christian people is really rather extraordinary. It means that, provided we have enough money, we want for nothing. It's strange, but you can't imagine now that you used to think something was too dear. To give you an example: In the old days, I would often buy a chocolate bar for breakfast. They cost five cents back then. (If you can get hold of a bar now, which is quite rare, it will cost you ƒ1.25 on the black market, whereas in the old days, when you used to buy six, you would even get one free.) At the time I thought it was very extravagant to buy such a bar every morning. I can't imagine it now.

This is all for now, my darling. I hope this has given you a little bit of an idea of the black-market trade. People say things such as "You look like you're living the black-market life" when somebody looks quite well. Our nerves consume a great deal of energy, so we all

125 The gas in Amsterdam was supplied to houses from a central reserve, via a pipeline.

eat much more than ever before. Besides, the food is less nourishing — e.g., bread and cheese, skimmed milk, which is undrinkable, just a bit of powdered milk, etc., etc. — and you feel: I *must* eat well to be healthy when the war ends and to be strong in case, God forbid, of sudden deportation. I'll stop now for I'm the only one left at the office, which is a bit spooky. Perhaps I'll write you a short letter this evening about my birthday.

Amsterdam, 28 March 1943

Let me start with some good news today. The population registry burnt down last night. As you know, Dutch men are being sent to work in Germany. The call-ups are, of course, issued with the help of the population registry's card index.[126] The population registry is guarded. For approximately a year now, it has been located in Plantage Kerklaan, in a building in Artis,[127] which has been completely renovated. Last night it burnt down to the ground. And although we live close by, none of us noticed a thing. Very queer. Word has it that around eleven — it was pitch-dark last night — a German car pulled up, carrying men in police uniform. It's said that they forced their way into the building, gave the guards an injection, taped their mouths shut and then left them in the garden at Artis. After that, people say, they took the documents out of the cabinets, doused them with paraffin, set the building alight, using time bombs among other things, and then cleared off. It must have been quite an inferno. It was on everybody's lips today. Whether this colourful account is true — it sounds like Chicago — I don't know. At any rate, it's sabotage, and I'm curious to see what the reprisals will be. I only hope they won't shoot any hostages.

---

126   Non-Jewish men who were taken for forced labour in Germany due to a severe shortage of labour there.
127   The Amsterdam Zoo.

We're still paying the price for last time, and are only allowed out until nine o'clock — the Christians, that is, and the Jews with an evening permit, your future wife among them — but it doesn't matter very much. The whole of Middenlaan and Kerklaan has been cordoned off. And today, Sunday, it was a veritable place of pilgrimage. Muidergracht was swarming with people. I haven't seen it this busy in years. It was literally teeming. The atmosphere was wonderful, and there was even a cart selling flowers, like a funfair. This morning I overheard somebody saying: "We're going to the flower show." Very jolly. But I doubt it will have any effect, because nobody knows whether the intended documents were actually destroyed. I believe they were, but there are copies in other buildings, which is a shame, of course. Perhaps they'll set fire to these as well, although the Huns are bound to be extra vigilant now.

Another nice anecdote. Doctors are obliged to become members of the so-called *artsenkamer*,[128] the equivalent of the chamber of culture that actors are obliged to join, etc. These are all run by the NSB. Now the doctors are refusing to do this, which means they lose their title. They have covered their nameplates with plaster or gummed tape. For example, next door to us lives a doctor whose nameplate reads: DR J. WESHOF, PHYSICIAN. "DR" and "PHYSICIAN" have now been covered with a plaster. Some have put gummed tape across their nameplates. Almost all doctors have done this, so that, in theory at least, there are hardly any "doctors" left, only quacks. Naturally, they're not permitted to write prescriptions, sign death certificates, etc., etc. And the worst thing is, most of them don't sleep at home for fear of being arrested, so if somebody needs a doctor in the middle of the night, e.g., for a delivery, they're in a real pickle. We're very curious to see how it unfolds, for surely they can't get by without doctors. I do admire the attitude, though.

128 Chamber of doctors.

A few more examples will show you just how anti-German the Dutch people still are, and increasingly so, mainly as a result of the forced labour in Germany. There are advertising posters that show a woman lying dead amidst rubble and a small child asking: "Mother, is that the second front?" Pasted over it are stencilled slips bearing the words: "No, silly, that's Rotterdam." You should know that during the fighting in May 1940, Rotterdam was heavily bombed, and later the Germans showed footage in Germany of a city said to be bombed by the English. That was Rotterdam. Another billboard shows a Dutchman in German uniform on the eastern front and another with a haggard face, a cigarette in his mouth, a red, white and blue[129] handkerchief in his breast pocket and the head of a matchstick sticking out of his buttonhole: Hold your head up high, i.e., don't give up. The caption reads: "Who is the true Dutchman?" Across it is pasted a stencilled slip with the words: "Neither of the two. It's the striker, the saboteur." But these are about the only nice things I have for you. The rest is just more misery.

I told you that Lea and Marc are wanted by the police. It appears that the police are not prepared to accept that the gold and silver found in the house was there legally, because Uncle Nathan had not been forced to liquidate his business, so now they have been charged with black-market trade. I went to see Sluzker, who told me that we should not keep them in our house, because it would be too dangerous for us. But it really is wretched that we, the only family they have left, can't even offer them our house. It's extremely difficult to find them a place where they can hide. Besides, Lea looks very Jewish. She has spoken to a number of people about going into hiding. I'll tell you about that later; I think it may be too dangerous to put in writing, because I might end up getting others in trouble. Other things I have written to you are also extremely dangerous, but they would only get *me* into trouble, and not jeopardize other people's lives. Imagine the feeling: As soon as you hear that your

129 The colours of the Dutch flag.

parents have been deported, you must go to the hairdresser's to have your hair dyed and pick a pair of spectacles to change your appearance, and it's still not enough. Lea was to spend the night elsewhere, not with us. Marc, too, but he found a place right away. But because Lea didn't know the way, I agreed to take her.

We pretended not to know each other and, from a certain point, when we no longer knew the way, I would ask for directions, fumble with my bike and, as soon as Lea came into the street, cycle to the next corner. We even had a bit of a laugh. At some point I beckoned for Lea to keep going, after which I would give her further directions. It took longer than we had anticipated, so she had already reached the end of the street, had turned right and then retraced her steps. It meant that she passed me just as I turned into the street. I stood still at the corner and asked somebody for directions. The next morning, Lea told me that she had nearly died laughing, because she thought I had wanted to ask *her* for directions. But you have no idea how sinister it was, in the semi-darkness in a completely unfamiliar neighbourhood, knowing there may well be NSB people on that street who will betray her. It was terribly forlorn and wretched and I felt so sorry for her, so all alone in the world. She now has a permanent place of hiding and is no longer with us. She took nothing, since she never intended to go into hiding straight away, but apparently she had no choice. This week we're going to send her clothes to an agreed location, since we don't know exactly where she is. Just imagine, Leo, being snatched from your familiar surroundings and loved ones, deposited with complete strangers, no more kosher food, no contact with us or with Marc, so she has no way of knowing whether we are gone or still here.

Meanwhile Aunt Ré has also been taken away, and there was nothing we could do for her. Aunt Phine has been allotted a decent house. That, at least, is one thing I managed to arrange. She could have a decent house if she agreed to billeting. Miranda, whom I know well, telephoned the office of the JC to say she was to have billeting and then she did, indeed, get the house. The alternative would have been a hovel, because she lives by herself.

Father's case shows little sign of progress. I'm afraid it won't make much difference now. Perhaps I may still get him through as a special case, but I'd rather not, because I detest all this cronyism. But when I think that the alternative is deportation, I only have one thought: I must do everything I can, proper or not, to keep Mother and Father here as long as possible. This week, the German authorities are said to have decided not to close the company where Father works, although other factors are said to be casting doubt on this again. In any case, they have given him *plein-pouvoir*[130] to join the JC if he wants to. He will go and talk to Blüth this week to see if he can get a position. There may be an opening at the preparatory commission for Vught. I happen to know that this commission, which is made up of three German Jews, among them Mr Blüth who is nearly always away, would like to have a Dutch Jew. It may be an option. Once again, let's wait and see.

We were downright lucky again this week. On Thursday, the police carried out house-to-house searches in the daytime, looking for people without exemptions. Mother was on the doorstep when the police turned up at our house and asked her if all members of the family are exempted. She was so taken aback she said yes, even though it's not true, since Grandmother isn't exempted. The man was a rather decent sort, for he didn't investigate further and went on his way. A charwoman who works a few doors down, but doesn't live there, had to give her address. She will be taken away. A lot of people were told to gather at a particular address from were they were taken in the afternoon. So you see how lucky we were. In more than one respect. The *Shammes*,[131] Deen, didn't say there were people without exemptions in his household. His house was searched, those without exemptions were found and he himself

130 Unrestricted permission.
131 Beadle.

deported as a punishment case. The same could have happened to us. I've now pressed upon Mother that it's better to tell the truth. But the problem is that she gets so flustered that she ends up saying all the wrong things.

Grandmother is probably going back to hospital this week. I'll be relieved when she does. It's absolutely impossible for Mother to nurse her and besides, she could be taken from here at any moment. I do fear the worst though, because the *Zentralstelle* has removed the identity cards, hers included, from the distribution centre, so that doesn't bode well. But, as ever, our motto is: Let's wait and see.

One more thing. The children who are taken to the Theatre are allowed to spend the night in a private house on Parklaan, which has been especially designated for this, and during the day they're allowed to go out for walks, escorted by nurses. It's a dismal sight, all those poor children bound for deportation walking around in small clusters. Seeing it makes you sick. All these sad things destroy you. Think of Marc, for example, who hasn't found a [permanent] hiding place yet and is now roaming the streets. Our house is too dangerous, both for us and for him, which is why he sleeps in a pitch-black barn somewhere and doesn't know what to do with himself during the day. I used to think, when I heard a poor man say he was prosperous once, that this was surely impossible. Now you see people who were once respectably middle- or upper-class living like vagrants, completely uprooted. At least Lea and Marc have money, but how many have lost that, too? Once-wealthy people are now penniless. It goes to show how ephemeral everything is, and that people you thought would be powerful forever are now unbelievably poor and powerless.

I'm going to call it a day, Leo. I always intend to give you detailed reflections, but such an awful lot happens I can only describe it all in a nutshell and there isn't even any time left for some tender words. I'm going to bed now, because the clocks go forward tonight. Otherwise I miss an hour's sleep and I can't afford that. The constant strain we're under is extremely tiring. I can't do a thing in the evenings.

[Undated — first page is missing]

My inspiration has gone out the window because of a conversation taking place here, but I'll save it for later. First I have the weekly newsreel for you, and quite eventful it is, too. I already told you about the population registry. The incident did indeed pass as told. The press published a "Notice," signed by Lages,[132] offering a ƒ10,000 reward. Ten thousand guilders isn't even all that much. This week the mayor of Baexem, a hamlet in Limburg, was murdered, and the reward offered was no less than ƒ25,000. Of course they'll never find the perpetrators, and I expect we're in for more punishment. The curious thing is that on Monday the curfew was extended from nine to ten o'clock. On Sunday, we witnessed a veritable pilgrimage. Hundreds and hundreds went to look at the population registry. Middenlaan had been cordoned off at the corner of Parklaan, as was Kerklaan up to Muidergracht, so everybody flocked onto Muidergracht. There was a flower stall, too — a wonderful atmosphere.

Sunday morning at a quarter-past two — our clock already said a quarter-past three, for that night was the beginning of summertime — the doorbell rang. (I can't concentrate; there's terrific gunfire outside and we're talking incessantly.) I didn't hear the bell, but Grandmother's nurse woke me up. It's what we agreed, you see, since I'm the *chef de réception de la police*.[133] I was down in a jiffy. The police, of course. Let me keep it brief. I'd better hurry up, it's already half-past ten and I don't want to go to bed too late. It was

132   SS *Sturmbannführer* Wilhelm Lages, head of the *Zentralstelle* (and head of the SD, the German security police, in Amsterdam), supervisor of Aus der Fünten.
133   Responsible for receiving the police.

a house-to-house search for people without a *Sperre*. I told them that Grandmother isn't exempted, but is completely bed-ridden. They were Dutch police in plain clothes. Not bad-mannered, but not well-mannered either. Father went to fetch the whole family's identity cards: Aunt Phine, who was staying with us because she hasn't quite settled into her new home yet and therefore can't cook; the nurse; Mr Vromen; the four of us — all in all, quite a crowd. But at least we're all exempted. Not only is Grandmother not exempted, we don't even have her identity card. It's still at the *Zentralstelle*. I had intended to say, should the policemen ask for it, that Grandmother doesn't have one. While Father was still upstairs fetching the identity cards, I showed mine to one of them and told the nurse to show them hers. He waited a few minutes for Father and then said: "So except for the one, everybody else is exempted?" "Yes," I answered. "All right," he said, and left. So he never noticed that Grandmother has no identity card. Sheer luck, don't you think? We had a drop of wine again and then hit the sack. I do think it's worrying that I didn't hear the doorbell, because on Monday Grandmother will be readmitted to the NIZ and we will no longer have a nurse in the house. Let's hope for the best.

On Tuesday, a rumour went round that the Theatre was to be disinfected, in other words, that we were to have several days' respite. Such was indeed the plan, Sluzker had told Eitje, but unfortunately it was called off. People are now being taken day and night, with three transports a week to Westerbork, carrying 500–700 people each, and one a week to Vught, approx. 300, but the latter varies constantly.

Wednesday evening, at a quarter-past eight, the doorbell rang. It's always a shock to hear the doorbell after eight, because even those with an evening permit seldom visit nowadays. I myself prefer not to go out, because you're at risk wherever you go and besides, when you come home, you may well find the place ransacked. I heard shouts of "Home Guard!" I was just having a nap in our bedroom, Mother was lying on the sofa in the parlour, Father was sitting in the big chair, Bob was in the kitchen, Mr Vromen was out. I thought to myself: No light could possibly be seen from outside, for none of the lights are on. Mother later told me that a man with a torch had suddenly appeared in front of her and had said: "Are you alone in the house?" Mother replied: "No, I'm with my husband and two daughters." "Identity cards!" I heard and ran downstairs. In the hallway stood a green with a helmet. "*Was wünschen Sie?*"[134] I asked. They were looking for Grandmother. Two policemen, one black and one green, with a call-up notice. I told them she was in hospital and turned on the light in the back room, because it's easily blacked out. The green was charm personified. He pushed aside some papers on the table and said: "*Ich muss da einiges in Unordnung bringen, aber ich werde es wieder zurecht legen.*"[135] We showed him the old NIZ certificate that we had showed last time. I told him we had handed it in before. "*Die wird wohl verloren gegangen sein,*"[136] he said kindly. "*Verwahren Sie diese nur gut.*"[137] The black policeman was vile. He searched the whole house, and at one point he said: "There was somebody in the bed, a small child, you concealed it." "That was me," I said, which was the truth. He accepted the explanation. Aren't you offended, Leo, that they called your future wife a child? Anyway, they left again. A lucky escape, don't you think? And I am so "glad" that he wrote down "since 16 January," because now it looks as if she never left the NIZ and got to stay after the hospital clear-out.

This is it, my love, it's getting late. Lots and lots of kisses. I wish I could fly to your side, because I know only too well how anxious you are. To be continued.

134 "What do you want?"
135 "I am afraid I will have to displace a few things, but I will put everything back in order again."
136 "It must have been lost."
137 "Please store this one safely."

Amsterdam, 14 April 1943

I think this is going to be a very long letter, because we suffered another blow yesterday — the last but one, I suspect — and I have a feeling that soon I will no longer be able to write to you. So I'd better seize this opportunity now and give you a detailed account.

Do you remember that winter evening, a Saturday evening, when we went shopping together on Kalverstraat? We went to Hoying, where we bought those lovely fruit knives. I'm sure you remember how happy we were then and how wonderful it was to buy things for our home together. I remember how much I enjoyed it, what everything looked like. The weather was mild, all the shop windows were beautifully lit and each shop window was a work of art in itself. When we came out of the shop, the street was one big, surging mass, and everything was bright and gay. And turning onto Dam Square, which was so spacious and so beautiful, and seeing the illuminated windows of Bijenkorf and the cafés crammed with people, it all felt so cosy. And Munt Square, with its cars and trams going to and fro and flashing neon signs, and Reguliersbreestraat packed with people! You know how much I enjoyed it all.

I have drawn you this picture to tell you what the city looks like now. Kalverstraat is a sea of shutters. Even in the daytime only some of them are removed; most of them are nailed shut. Shop windows all display the same wares. Wooden brooches, for example, are sold by lingerie shops, furniture shops, department stores — in a word, by everybody — because there's nothing else to sell. Goldsmiths have shut up shop, so the windows are boarded up and the doors are locked, also boarded up. Bensdorp is closed. Focke and Meltzer, that beautiful china and ceramics shop, is also closed, while the shops that remain open have almost nothing in their windows. And of course it's dead quiet in the evening, with all the shops closed and the windows boarded up, even on Saturday evening. Munt Square is so quiet now that there's no more police. Cars have become quite a rare sight in Amsterdam for that matter, only those belonging to the *Wehrmacht* and the odd other one. There are fewer bicycles, too, and all this has made traffic so much more orderly that we no longer need even a single traffic warden. Munt Square, and I'm not exaggerating, resembles a busy junction in a small provincial town. All over the city the streets are damaged, because the Germans' heavy vehicles race across them and destroy the asphalt, which isn't repaired. And everywhere similar scenes of poverty, unpainted doors, cracked windows that can't be repaired, and shutters, shutters and yet more shutters. That is what the city looks like now.

And now the Jewish quarter, e.g., Breestraat.[138] It's dead quiet, because a large part of the population has been taken away. Many of the houses have been ransacked. They're emptied by a company called Puls[139] and we refer to it as "pulsed by the Dutch pilfering corporation." Until they're emptied, the doors are sealed with gummed tape, the windows boarded up and the black-out curtains are usually down because people are taken away in the evening and therefore don't have a chance to draw the curtains. A scene of utter poverty and despair, which you can't picture unless you have seen it with your own eyes. And on, say, Tugelaweg, windows have been smashed and shutters broken by "ordinary" burglars, who beat the Huns at their own game. Rumour has it that there's an organisation of professional burglars who ransack the homes, and if the inhabitants return after the war they will receive their possessions back, provided they pay a storage fee. *Si non è vero...*[140] The city looks like a battlefield. The whole city does, wherever

---

138   Amsterdam has two streets called "Breestraat," beginning off as Joden Breestraat and continuing as St. Antonies Breestraat.

139   The Puls company was a removal company that emptied out property from the houses of Jews who had been sent to Westerbork or Vught. The company worked for the Germans, and the looted property was later transferred to bombed-out towns in Germany. Abraham Puls himself was a Dutch Nazi who was personally responsible for the arrest of many Jews. After the war he was sentenced to death, but the sentence was later commuted to life imprisonment.

140   *Si non è vero è bene trovare* is Italian for "even if it isn't true, it's a good idea."

houses have been emptied. During the day, you see the big removal vans all over the city. These vans dump their contents into Rhine barges moored along the Amstel. Somebody told me he had found a volume of Levy's dictionary on the embankment at Weesperzijde. It must have fallen out of the van, missing the barge.

I wanted to tell you this, because the city looks poor, derelict, dirty. Words can't describe it. It looks a little bit better now, because spring has come exceptionally early this year and everything is such a beautiful soft green that, despite all the misery, you can't but enjoy the lovely weather. I hadn't yet begun to write to you last year or the year before, otherwise you would have had laments about the bitter cold and the misery when we ran out of coal and were unable to get hold of any because of the distribution problems. But thanks to this year's wonderfully mild winter, it's such a distant memory now that I couldn't possibly give you a vivid description. So you'll have to do without. Isn't that a pity? Oh yes, you do miss out on an awful lot!

Another subject I wanted to write about, but kept putting off, is German propaganda, so effective in Germany and yet a complete failure over here, because the Germans seem to be familiar only with their own mindset and not with that of the Dutch. In various letters, I have mentioned the comments on the billboards. The army bulletins, too, are always so insane you wonder how the Germans can expect us — the Dutch, that is — to believe them. For example, when the Huns are forced to retreat, a standard line from the *Wehrmacht* bulletin reads: "We have withdrawn to previously prepared positions." Or: "Without enemy force." Or: "Without enemy obstruction." We also love: "Evacuated according to plan." You really wonder how they can be so naïve as to think we would swallow all this. The other day, a decree was issued to stop people from leaving the cinema during the newsreel or coming in after the newsreel. That says it all. People either come in after the newsreel, or if the newsreel is played after the feature, they leave early because they don't want to see the German lies.

The rabbinate has issued a comprehensive circular on the occasion of *Pesach*,[141] with all possible kinds of advice, such as different daily menus (also for children and babies), consisting mainly of potatoes, potatoes and yet more potatoes (and vegetables, if we have any). This is our first year without *matzot*[142] (and I hope it will be the last). We're short of so many things, we don't even know how to celebrate the *Seder*.[143] Never mind, we'll manage one way or another. At least we're still better off than the people in the provinces. You see, yesterday evening we learnt that, as of 23 April, the provinces of North Holland, South Holland and Utrecht must be clear of Jews, who are to go to Vught. So you can imagine the kind of *Seder* these people will have, knowing they'll be gone the next day.[144]

We, too, have gradually come to accept that we won't see it through. Amsterdam still has a relatively high number of Jews — estimated, I believe, at 20,000–40,000, whereas the three provinces probably have some 2,000 — and we don't know if Vught will be able to absorb them all and what will happen in Amsterdam, but if they proceed at this rate it will be a matter of weeks until we've been

141 *Pesach*, or Passover: the Jewish festival celebrating the Exodus from Egypt, as narrated in the Book of Exodus. During the eight-day festival, only unleavened food is allowed.
142 Unleavened bread.
143 A special family ritual during which the *Haggadah*, the book detailing the Exodus from Egypt, is read out. In Israel, the *Seder* takes place on the eve of *Pesach*; outside Israel, there is also a second *Seder*, on the eve of the second day of *Pesach*.
144 On 30 March 1943, the press publicized an announcement from Hanns Albin Rauter, Commissioner-General for Security (*Generalkommissar für das Sicherheitswesen*) and Highest SS and Police Leader (*Höhere SS- und Polizeiführer*, HSSPF) for the occupied Netherlands, according to which, from 10 April 1943 Jews would be forbidden from living in eight of the 11 provinces of the Netherlands, and they would have to move to the Vught concentration camp. This did not include Jews in mixed marriages. Holders of temporary exemptions would have to turn to the *Zentralstelle* to check whether the exemption was still valid. On 13 April 1943, a new declaration of a similar nature was publicized, relating to the additional provinces, not including the city of Amsterdam, mentioned above.

cleared out. And I'm very fearful they will start at the beginning of May, perhaps even the end of April.

We've just learnt that on 23 April, a train full of [Jewish] *Frontkämpfer*[145] from World War I is to leave Amsterdam for Theresienstadt. It's supposedly a special favour, as conditions there are said to be good. The other transports are currently taking place in goods trains, with a bucket near the entrance or a hole in the floorboards serving as a lavatory. The sick and elderly are laid on mattresses and suspended, one above the other, from the ceiling. The family sits on the floor underneath. Imagine it! I dread to think what it means.

Father, Mother and your father actually have a chance of staying in Westerbork should they, Heaven forbid, end up there. A list is being drawn up of former NZB (*Nederlandsche Zionisten Bond*)[146] honorary officials, which will be presented to the German government for a possible exchange. Apparently this list, which is kept to a minimum, is certain to be accepted. Father has been included on this list, as has your father, because of Max's good work. These are the only documents with any value at present. What their value will be in half an hour, I don't know; the situation changes constantly. What is good today is bad tomorrow. The *Wehrmacht* was always considered safest, yet its workers were taken away first, whereas in the provinces the Jews exempted on account of the *Wehrmacht* are allowed to stay. It's utterly confusing and lacks any kind of consistency. But, for the moment, we welcome this option, because we're still hoping to see it through, even if our hopes are quashed over and over again. And even if we don't see it through in our own home — which I personally don't mind too much, because I don't have that much to lose, but it would be wretched for Mother and Father to lose all their furniture, etc., at the last minute — it will

145 "Front Soldiers": soldiers of the German army during WWI.
146 Union of Dutch Zionists.

make all the difference whether we're still in Holland or already in Poland.

I also want to tell you about the problem of going into hiding. At the outbreak of war and the subsequent armistice, several people disappeared. They were social-democrats and the like who had openly campaigned against Hitler. These people hid with farmers, and because their numbers were, of course, quite small compared to the population at large, it was simple enough. There were problems obtaining food, to be sure, as these people received no ration coupons. But their families would take care of the coupons, either by saving them up or buying them, or else the farmers they were staying with had enough food to spare some. So it continued for a very long time. Some people even went to work as farm labourers. This went well, except for the odd betrayal. In July 1942, many Jews went into hiding, i.e., they hid with Aryans. There are organisations that organize this, produce fake identity cards — identity cards without a "J" and in a different name — etc. They also take care of coupons and food, with somebody either collecting coupons on the old identity cards or buying ration cards. The former goes wrong from time to time, because in many cases the identity cards have been blocked. That is to say, somehow or other the Germans find out, because they turned up with a call-up perhaps, that certain individuals have gone into hiding and tell the distribution centre not to issue any coupons on the identity card of the person concerned and to arrest the person presenting the card. The people in hiding are then often discovered, because the Aryan in question will be subjected to all kinds of torture until he reveals the Jews' whereabouts. (For example, they will flash extremely powerful electric arc lamps in his face.)

Then there are the people who have Christian friends who are prepared to hide Jews. Of course you need extremely strong nerves for this, because you don't hear from your family and you're confined, enough to drive you mad. Besides, there's the risk of accidents. To give you an example: Someone had gone into hiding in Haarlem. One Sunday afternoon the family in question left the house, while the hidden Jew stayed behind. The neighbours, who knew the family had gone to a wedding, thought the house was empty. At some point, they heard the lavatory being flushed and because of the recent spate of burglaries — burglars sometimes think that houses have been emptied when they're still occupied — they alerted the police, who found the hiding Jew. And often Jews are caught because of carelessness, because they can no longer bear the isolation and visit or write to one another. Betrayal lurks everywhere, and virtually every street has a member of the NSB, bent on informing on Jews. Then there are Christians who

```
            Office Palestinien de Suisse


                                Geneve, le 11 August 1943
                                8, Rue petitot
Téléphone :  5 12 10
Cte de chèques post. : 1. 4889



        Herrn
        Mozes Levie Oesterman
        A m s t e r d a m .


        Betrifft :

        Sehr geehrter Herr Levie,

        Wir teilen Ihnen hierdurch mit, dass Sie auf der
        Liste für Veteranen-Zertifikate die
                Nr. V/II/43/77
        erhalten haben .
        Gleichzeitig geben wir Ihnen bekannt, dass diese Liste
        von der Schutzmacht bereits den zuständigen deutschen
        Behörden überreicht wurde.
                            Mit vorgüglicher Hochachtung

                            Office Palestinien Geneve

                        w.g. Dr.Posner
```

Notice from Chaim Posner from the *Eretz Yisrael* Office in Geneva to Moses Levie-Oesterman, i.e., Maurits (Moritz) Jacob Levie, in Amsterdam, confirming that his name was included on the list of immigration certificates for veterans. This list was then passed to the German authorities. 11 August 1943

Author's collection

harbour Jews for financial gain. When the ƒ1,000 note was recalled and the Jews had trouble paying, some of them simply kicked the Jews out. Often the Christians themselves are sent to Germany, so the Jews end up on the street, or the house is searched for some reason or other and the Jews discovered. Sometimes they simply go to Westerbork and onwards, in which case nothing has been lost because they would have been deported anyway; sometimes they go to Amersfoort, to a CC (concentration camp), which has now been moved to Vught and which I mentioned before. Sometimes they go to the prison on Amstelveenseweg and then to Westerbork as a punishment case. I must go now, for my boss has sent for me. Perhaps I'll continue later.

It's evening and I'm at home and want to write some more. Do you know what they call a house where a Jew has gone into hiding? "*Duikjoodbasis.*"[147] Isn't that funny?

This afternoon, I happened to hear about the case of a family with seven children, number eight on the way, who were hiding a Jewish child. Not very conspicuous, you'd think. But they were betrayed and the couple arrested. The wife was sent home because she was heavily pregnant, and was told that if she named five families hiding Jews, her husband would be released. If not, he'd be sent to a CC. The wife didn't betray anyone and the husband is now in Vught. Imagine the wife's dilemma, with a family that size! The Aryans aren't always arrested. Again, there's no consistency at all.

I completely forgot to tell you that we received another visit yesterday evening. They were looking for people without exemptions. Luckily, we're all exempted. Still, it gave us quite a fright. And we were a bit shaky already, because somebody had a panic attack right on our doorstep and had to be taken away by the Municipal Health Service. It sounded terrible and unnerved us as well.

147 "*Duikboot*" is the Dutch word for "submarine" or "U-boat" and rhymes with "*jood,*" the Dutch word for "Jew." The term for "going into hiding" is "*onder-duiken*" (going under, diving or submerging), hence the term "*duikjoodbasis,*" or "base for submerging Jews."

Amsterdam, 22 April 1943

I'll continue my account now, although a great deal has happened in the meantime and I'm really too agitated not to tell you the whole story straight away. On Monday evening I had a bath, and at half-past nine we began the *Seder*. Father began by reading texts from the *Rosh Hashanah*[148] prayers: "So shall the righteous see it and rejoice... wickedness shall vanish in smoke, for Thou wilt remove the rule of arrogance from the world," whereupon Mother burst out crying. She recovered soon enough, and we had a very pleasant *Seder* evening. We never expected to have everything, but we even had a delicious *Pesach* cake and roasted almonds during the *Seder*. We went to bed at midnight.

On Tuesday morning I went to Zichron. The service was excellent. Mossel spoke. He wept a great deal and I found it a bit soppy, but it's terribly difficult to speak well these days. After *shul*[149] I went home with Freddy and Bram de Jong. That morning, Bram de Jong had received an *Anweisung* to move to *Oost*, and not even to *Oost* proper, but to Asterdorp, across the IJ, where you're really rather cut off from everything. Freddy then accompanied him to Van Dam, his former colleague at the Bank voor Onroerende Zaken,[150] who now handles housing matters for the JC, to try and undo the whole thing. I dropped by Juul briefly to say that Freddy would be late. Then home, where we had a lovely meal of *matzot* with sugar and potatoes, with a kind of ersatz gravy for afters. Then I had a blissful time in the sun, reading and smoking. I have eight cigarettes left, not counting a packet in my rucksack, and now only smoke on Sundays and holidays. At a quarter-past three I changed — I had worn a velvet dress in the morning and put on a silk one in the afternoon, because I thought: I probably can't wear

---

148 Jewish New Year.
149 Synagogue.
150 Real Estate Bank.

it during *Shavuot*,[151] who knows where I'll be, so I might as well put it on now. Then I went to visit Eitje, where I happened to hear that in Belgium it's such bedlam that everybody walks around with fake *cartes d'identité*,[152] so the anti-Jewish measures are nowhere near as sharp as they are here.

Against this backdrop I'd like to pass on the story Lex W. told me the other evening, about Jaap Spitz. He was the administrator of the DV (*Deventer Vereniging*),[153] a position Freddy used to hold. He didn't feel very safe, and went into hiding in Deventer. Even that wasn't safe enough for his liking, so he went to Antwerp, from where he was taken to Paris. There he was left in the lurch, and so he returned in the hope of making his way again from Antwerp. Back in Antwerp he was caught and held in a building with the same function as our Theatre. He was put on a train to Poland. Near Mechelen, the train slowed right down. A man sitting opposite him said: "Jump! I can't myself, because my wife is in the other wagon, but you're by yourself." "I have no money," Jaap said. The man gave him money and the story goes that Jews were jumping left, right and centre. The best moment was when Jaap saw the lights of the train fade in the distance. He was smuggled across the border and then, exhausted, he went to have a cup of coffee in a small café. A military policeman walked in. "Documents!" "I don't have any," Jaap said. What else could he say? "Then you must come with me." On their way to the station, the policeman asked him: "Are you a Jew by any chance?" "Yes," he replied. "Clear off then, I never saw you." He reached Sint-Oedenrode, where he knew a few Jews were living still, but because he was afraid to approach people in the street, he went to see the mayor, passed himself off as somebody working for the Germans, asked for and obtained the Jews' addresses. He went to see these Jews, received money and food and travelled back to

---

151 The Festival of Weeks, when Jews celebrate receiving the *Torah*.
152 Identity cards.
153 Deventer Association: A Zionist organisation representing the interests of pioneers to *Eretz Yisrael*.

Amsterdam, 22 April 1943.

Ik zal m'n verhaal voortzetten, hoewel er al weer een heeleboel gebeurd is in die
tusschentijd en ik eigenlijk te opgewonden ben, om je het heele verhaal niet meteen te vertellen. Maandagavond ben ik eerst in het bad gegaan en om half tien zijn
we begonnen te seideren. Vader heeft eerst de *פרק* *זה* uit de *הגדה* voorgelezen van *לו*
זאת voorgelezen en moeder begon natuurlijk te huilen. Enfin, het was nogal gauw
over. Verder hebben we heel genoeglijk geseiderd, we hadden alles, zooals ik je al
schreef en tusschen de seider hebben we een heerlijke plevekoek gegeten en gebran-
de amandelen. Om twaalf uur gingen we naar bed. Dinsdagochtend was ik naar
Zichron. De dienst was heel goed. Mossel heeft gesproken. Hij heeft ook gehuild en
ik vond het een beetje kwijlerig, maar het is ook ontzettend moeilijk, om nu goed
te spreken. Het einde was goed, n.l. een verhaal van Agnon over een *זקן* *מאד*
die in een plaats in het Galuth komt, waar het mooiste *שול* *פאריז* is. En die mensch
waren zoo met zichzelf tevreden, dat ze de *שול* zóó opvatten als de plaats,
waar de meeste geleerden woonden. En de *זקן* *מאד* neeft zoo vaak gedacht aan
de *בית* *הכנסת* dat het *מקום* *מן* zich tenslotte verheven heeft en zich verplaatst heeft
naar.. *ארץ* *ישראל*. Na Sjoel ging ik met Freddy en Bram de Jong naar huis. Bram de
Jong had n.l. die ochtend een Anweisung gekregen, dat hij naar Oost moest verhui-
zen en nog wel niet eens naar Oost, maar naar Asterdorp, aan de Overkant van het Y
waar je natuurlijk wel erg afgesloten zit. Freddy is toen met hem naar van Dam
gegaan, van de bank voor Onroerende zaken, om te probeeren, de zaak te niet te
doen. Ik ging even bij Juul, om te zeggen, dat Freddy later zou komen. Toen naar
huis, waar we heerlijk hebben gegeven, Matzes met suiker en aardappelen met een
soort namaakju toe. Toen heb ik zalig in de zon zitten te lezen met een cigaret,
- ik heb er nog acht, behalve één doosje, dat in m'n rugzak zit en rook nu alleen
nog maar op zon- en feestdagen -, heb me om kwart over drie een beetje verkleed
- ik had 's ochtends s een fluweelen jurk aan en heb 's middags een zijden aange-
daan, omdat ik dacht: met *טלית* kan ik hem waarschijnlijk niet dragen, dan doe ik
hem nu maar aan. Toen ben ik bij Eitje op visite geweest. Daar hoorde ik toevallig, dat in Belgie zoo een bende is, dat iedereen er met valsche cartes d'identité rondloopt en dat daardoor de Jodenmaatregelen lang zoo scherp niet zijn. In dit
verband wil ik je even het verhaal vertellen, dat Lex W. me die avond tevoren gedaan had van Jaap Spitz. Die was administrateur van de D.V. in Deventer, wat
Freddy vroeger is geweest. Hij voelde zich niet erg veilig en is in Deventer on-
dergedoken. Ook dat was hem nog niet safe genoeg en hij is naar Antwerpen gegaan,
en werd vandaar naar Parijs gebracht. Daar heeft men hem in de steek gelaten en
hij is toen naar Antwerpen teruggegaan, in de hoop, vandaar wel weer verder te
komen. In Antwerpen is hij gepakt en werd in een gebouw ondergebracht, wat hier
de schouwburg is. Hij werd in de trein gezet, naar Polen. Bij Mechelen ging de
trein heel langzaam rijden. Iemand, die tegenover hem zat zei: spring eruit. Ik
kan het niet doen, want mijn vrouw zit in de andere wagon, maar U bent alleen. Ik
heb geen geld, antwoordde hij. De man gaf hem geld en volgens het verhaal, zouden
links en rechts de Joden uit de trein gesprongen zijn. Het was het mooiste oogenblik voor hem, toen hij de lichten uit zag flauwen. Hij is toen over
de grens gesmokkeld en is uitgegut in een café'tje een kop koffie gaan drinken.
Er kwam marechaussee binnen. Papieren ! Die heb ik niet, zei hij natuurlijk. Dan
gaat U maar mee. Op weg naar de kazerne vroeg de marechaussee hem: bent U soms
een Jood ? Ja, antwoordde hij. Kijk dan, maar uit, ik heb U niet gezien. Hij kwam
in St.Oedenrode, waarvan hij wist, dat er nog eenige Joden woonden, maar hij durf-
de de menschen niet te vragen, is toen naar den burgemeester gegaan, heeft zich
voor iemand, die voor de Duitschers werkt uitgegeven en heeft de adressen der Joden opgevraagd en gekregen. Is naar ze toegegaan, heeft geld en eten gekregen en
is naar Deventer teruggereisd. Hij kwam net in de Sperrtijd aan en is toen ge-
sperrd. Toevallig ontmoette ik hem verleden week. Hoe gaat het met je ? Goed, hoor
Ik wist toen nog niet, wat hij achter de rug had. Hoe vind je dit verhaal !!!
Enfin, ik zat dus bij Eitje en hoorde die meneer spreken en toen drong het eigenlijk plotseling tot me door, hoe verschrikkelijk het is, dat we nog maar een paar
weken hebben. En ik dacht er ook over om onder te duiken. Vervuld van die gedachten ging ik naar de *grote* vader, bleef tot kwart voor zes en toen naar huis. We
aten weer lekker, stamppot en heele echte gremschlen, zalig in echte boter ge-
bakken, met rozijntjes en amandelen, enfin, goddelijk. We hebben n.l. nog één of
twee blikken boter en die gebruiken we nu. Daarna heb ik amandelen gebrand en
toen was het weer tijd voor de tweede seider. Die vind ik nooit zoo leur als de
eerste en ik was ook erg moe. En de gedacht e aan het onderduiken liet me niet los
Ik peinsde en peinsde en overwoog maar steeds het vóór en het tegen. Als je naar
Vught gaat weet je wel waar je begint, maar niet waar je eindigt. Als je gepakt
wordt, is het meteen afgeloopen en ga je misschien dood in een strafkamp. En dan
het zwerven...Gisteren weer naar Sjoel, naar huis, gegeten, roode kool en stamppot en heerlijke aardappelkoekjes na. 's middags zou Bobby eerst naar je vader
gaan en mij dan komen halen en we zouden dan samen naar tante Phine gaan in haar
nieuwe huis. Vader en moeder gingen er ook heen, maar vroeg. Om half drie werd er
gebeld. We wilden juist naar boven gam om ons op te knappen. Laten we maar niet
open doen, zei Bobby, want als we nu visite krijgen kunnen we niet weg. Dat deden
we. Een paar minuten later werd er zoo ontzettend gebeld, dat we onmiddellijk ver-
moedden, dat het politie zou zijn. Maar omdat we visten dat het rustig was, konden

Deventer. He arrived during the time of the exemption distribution and got a *Sperre*. I met him last week. "How are you?" "Just fine." At the time I didn't know what he had been through. What do you make of this story!

As I was saying, I was at Eitje's, listening to this gentleman's story, and then suddenly I realized just how dreadful it is that we have only a few weeks left. And I considered going into hiding. Possessed by this idea I went to see your father, stayed until a quarter-to six and then went home. We had another nice meal, mash[154] and proper *gremchelich*,[155] fried in real butter with raisins and almonds. Delicious! You see, we're using up our last one or two cans of butter. Afterwards I roasted almonds, and then it was time for the second *Seder*. I never like it as much as the first and I was also very tired. And the thought of going into hiding kept haunting me. I mulled it over and over, constantly weighing up all the pros and cons. If you go to Vught you know where you start, but not where you end up. If you're caught, you're finished, and you may well die in a prison camp. And as for the drifting...

To *shul* again yesterday, then home, food, red cabbage and mash and delicious potato latkes for afters. In the afternoon, Bobby was going to see your father before picking me up to visit Aunt Phine in her new house. Father and Mother were going there, too, but earlier. At half-past two, the doorbell rang. We were about to go upstairs to freshen up. We'd better not answer, Bobby said, for if we get visitors now, we won't be able to leave. So we didn't. But a few minutes later, the doorbell rang so outrageously loudly, we immediately suspected it might be the police. But because we knew it was supposed to be quiet, we couldn't quite believe it. When I went to answer the door, I said to Bobby: "Remember, we were playing ping-pong in the attic and didn't hear the doorbell." And

---

154 In the Dutch edition: *stamppot*. This is mash made from potatoes and vegetables cooked together.

155 A special *Pesach* treat. Patties made of soaked *matzot*, eggs, raisins and almonds, fried in a pan.

indeed, it was the police. They came up, two officers in plain clothes, and said: "Identity cards." Bobby showed hers, but mine was in my bag, upstairs in the bedroom. "Oh, Bob," I said, "would you mind going up and fetching my bag?" Bobby wanted to go, but one of the policemen said: "You're not going anywhere. We know all about this fetching-from-upstairs. It happens all the time." I said: "But my identity card is upstairs, so I can't show it to you." "Too bad," he said.

Then they began to ask us a lot of questions: How many people were in the house, names and maiden names. They said that somebody who had gone into hiding had been caught, and that a parcel with coupons and money for this man was thought to have been delivered here yesterday (i.e., the day before yesterday). "How long have you lived here?" one of them asked. "Some 12 years, I believe," I replied. "Right," he said, "then how would you know what happened yesterday, having moved here so recently." And so it continued. They also asked me everything about the neighbours and I gave them the information, because we've been living together too long not to know these things about each other. They pretended to leave, but then suddenly one of them took off his coat again and said to Bobby: "You're coming with me for a look around the house." He searched everything, rummaged through my bag, which really was upstairs, and also through another bag. Bobby had to take out my rain hat, which was folded up in one of my bags, and unfold it. He mistook a Reveillon gift voucher, which has been in my bag for years, for a coded message, tapped on the walls, etc., etc.

Meanwhile, the other fellow took me *à faire*,[156] told me that his intelligence was always accurate, that I was lying and that it would cost me dearly, etc., etc. He told me that a few hours ago the man had confessed that the parcel had been left with us, and that he had mentioned my name. All of a sudden, a thought crossed my mind and stupidly, without thinking, I said: "That can't be

156   To task.

true, because you don't even know my name." That shut him up. Then he wanted to see our coupons. This had me quaking in my boots, because we always buy extra coupons and they were in the ration book. I said that I didn't know where my mother keeps the coupons. "You people never know anything." I said that I worked at an office and never concerned myself with household matters, but I was definitely quaking in my boots. Luckily, he did not search the cupboard where we keep the coupons. The other policeman came back down with Bobby, picked up one of Mother's bags, which was hanging from a chair, opened it without a word and searched it. I could have killed him! He did it with such impertinence and arrogance, as if he owned the place. Words fail me. I had to clench my fists to stop myself from boxing his ears.

Again they pretended to leave, but one of them suddenly said: "You (addressing me), come with me to the other room." There he looked in Mr Vromen's linen cupboard, which had one of Mother's hats. Odd, a lady's hat in a gentleman's cupboard. I explained to him that Mother had asked Mr Vromen and that he didn't mind. He pointed at a parcel, containing books to take into hiding, and asked: "What's this?" "Books," I said. "Show me." I opened the parcel and he looked at the books, never suspecting that they were destined to go into hiding. They searched the kitchen. We had eggs, fish and the opened can of butter, but luckily they didn't notice.

Then they went to De Groot. They did wish us a good afternoon, but I didn't bother to switch on the light in the stairwell, nor did I reply. De Groot later told me that they had gone there first when we hadn't answered the door and had then returned, saying: "Didn't we make ourselves perfectly clear? We asked you about the number of people in the house and now the neighbours tell us something completely different." All lies, for our information had been entirely truthful. From there, they made their way to Pinkhof, our next-door neighbour, whose wife was sick and home alone, and they said: "Your friend and neighbour De Groot has just told us that you're hiding the sister of Mr Hamburger (the man who had been caught)." A lie, of course. In the end it turned out that this sister is in hospital and is a cousin of Mrs Pinkhof. I suspect, therefore, that this affair won't come back to haunt us.

Bobby then went to Aunt Phine to inform Father and Mother, because I didn't know then whether the police would be back. Besides, with Bobby at my side, I had spotted a few things that Father and Mother ought to be aware of, in case those fellows were to return. Later I went to see Gretha[157] and Ies, ate with them, and chatted for a couple of hours. They live in Amsterdam now, together with Daniel Klein. He's having a truly rotten time of it: First his father and mother were taken away, his father died in Westerbork, and his mother was sent on. Then last year his brother passed away unexpectedly, and now his widowed sister-in-law, who was living in The Hague, was taken to Vught with her children. I went home at ten, chatted a bit, and to bed. This morning I had mashed potato for breakfast, went to the office, and dealt with the mail. Not a lot to do today. Eitje arrived at half-past nine; I worked with him, told him the story, told Marianne van Stedum[158] the story, and now I'm writing to you, because I'm not very busy. It's twelve o'clock, and I'm going back to work, for I haven't done much yet. Of course my nerves were in tatters yesterday, but I'm better today. I'll write about the problem of going into hiding later.

Yesterday morning there was an air-raid warning, but no shelling; there was shelling in the afternoon, but no warning. There are heaps of military targets here now, U-boats, etc., so we're expecting bombardments. A speech from Seyss-Inquart was in yesterday's evening paper. I'll read it this evening.

---

157 A good friend of Mirjam's.
158 The social worker of the Committee for Jewish Refugees.

Amsterdam, 23 April 1943

I wrote to you yesterday afternoon, at midday, and now I'll continue my report. We're not very busy this week, because luckily it's quiet and we don't have to call or write or walk or cycle places on behalf of people who've been arrested. I was in Eitje's office, chatting a bit about the *Frontkämpfer* who left for Theresienstadt yesterday. They were bragging about it, as if they're better than the other Jews, just because the Germans, in a fit of I-don't-know-what, happen to be treating them a little differently. One of these people had said that it was now well and truly *Pesach* for him, he was leaving *Mizrayim*[159] and returning to his *Heimat*.[160] How is it possible that after all these years these people haven't learnt a thing?

One of the department heads told us a nice story, the kind you no longer expect to hear. A German Christian woman was married to a Jew. They had become stateless, and the wife had been *ausgebürgert*[161] as well. The husband lives in Holland, the wife in Berlin. The wife filed a petition for divorce, protesting that as a *deutschblutige Frau*[162] she can't be *zugemutet*[163] to live with a Jew. The judge ruled that the wife was stateless, as was the husband, but that as the husband lives in Holland, Dutch law prevails. And there is nothing in Dutch law that allows for a petition of this kind, so the divorce can't be granted. What do you make of that? The judge acted as if justice still exists.

Home at half-past twelve, had some food — turnips and mash and another potato latke. Put away some clothes, watered the plants, back to the office. No wait, I first went to Nieuwe Keizersgracht to discuss a few identity card matters, then back to our office and from there straight to Joachimsthal[164] to return a few books that

159 Egypt.
160 Birthplace.
161 Denaturalized.
162 Woman of German blood.
163 Expected.
164 A Jewish book shop.

Eitje had taken out on spec. He had given me a voucher for my birthday, and I bought a book on efficient housekeeping and took away two novels on spec. I look forward to reading them over *Yom Tov*.[165] Naughty, don't you think? Then back to the office again, where I worked with Eitje, dealt with the mail and received a few people who wanted to speak to Eitje. I made appointments, and at a quarter-to five left on my bicycle to Parklaan for a big JC gathering, organised by the Central Commission for Culture.

There were three parallel meetings for different departments. An awful lot of people attended, and it was actually quite heartening to see so many people together. The Professor was there, Dasberg, Brandon, Van der Laan, your father, Frederik, Albert, etc., etc. The gathering itself was a bit of a disappointment; I'd had extremely high expectations. Jo Gomperts was a master of ceremonies of sorts. He did a good enough job, but the whole affair didn't really grab me. A quartet played several Yiddish songs, a kind of medley. Lichtenstein sang and Erich Schönlank recited an extract from the prophet Habakkuk. This I liked best. The man recites beautifully. The event was certainly good, but for some reason I was expecting more. It was funny to hear the diverse opinions. One thought it was splendid, another absolutely awful, a third had yet another opinion. Your father liked it. I'm curious to hear what Freddy thinks. He organised it, but I don't think he put the programme together. Seeligmann probably did.

Home at half-past six, had food, vegetable soup, brown beans, potatoes and another *gremchelich* each. Then I made the beds, did some more tidying upstairs and spent the rest of the evening darning stockings. The stocking problem is terrible. Stockings are almost impossible to get hold of, so mine are all completely threadbare. Mind you, when Aunt Griet was taken away I was given her stockings, which means I have plenty of pairs, but of course they're all rather thin. It means non-stop darning.

165 Jewish holiday, in this case *Pesach*, or Passover.

Telephone: ALgonquin 4-3600   Cable Address: ZIONISTS

הסוכנות היהודית לארץ ישראל

JEWISH AGENCY FOR PALESTINE
PALESTINE OFFICE FOR U.S.A.
111 FIFTH AVENUE
NEW YORK CITY

OFFICERS:

DAVID WERTHEIM
   Chairman

MAX HAGLER
HERMAN QUITTMAN
   Vice-Chairmen

DR. S. BERNSTEIN
   Director

משרד ארץ ישראלי
לארצות הברית של אמריקה
פאלעסטינא־אמט

September 4, 1940

TO WHOM IT MAY CONCERN:

This is to testify that we have been officially notified
by the Jewish Agency for Palestine in Jerusalem that an
immigration certificate has been issued for

Miss Mirjam LEVIE,
Amsterdam,
Pl. Muidergracht,29,
H o l l a n d

to enable her to proceed to Palestine for permanent residence.

As soon as Miss Levie will arrive in a neutral country
steps will be taken in order that the British Passport Control
Office be instructed to grant her the necessary facilities
enabling her to depart for Palestine in due course.

Cordially yours,

Dr. S. Bernstein, Director,
Palestine Office for U.S.A.
JEWISH AGENCY FOR PALESTINE

SB:tf

Notice to all interested parties from the representative of the Jewish Agency
in the US that an immigration certificate had been issued for Mirjam Levie. 4
September 1940

Author's collection

This morning I had turnip and mash for breakfast, popped into no. 62 before nine to drop off a few soup plates, as all of us, i.e., Freddy, Juul and I, are eating there tonight and Els doesn't have enough soup plates for *Pesach*. Then to the office, where I dealt with the mail, made telephone calls and now I'm writing to you. Eitje is away, so I'm making the most of it, although there's still plenty of mail. I'm going to stop now; I just chatted to a girl about our adventure the day before yesterday.

I have more or less made up my mind not to go into hiding. First of all, there's a possibility of a permanent ghetto in Amsterdam, in which case we may still have a small chance. If I were sent to Vught, I might also be able to stay there a while; after all, I'm quite an accomplished seamstress. And even in Westerbork I still have a chance, thanks to the Palestine papers.[166] But if I go into hiding and get caught, I'd be finished. Unless I could get a very, very, very good hiding place. But I doubt it. Besides, I would lose all contact with you. Let's hope the war... Bye, my love.

It's difficult to remember precisely how I spent the day, and of course tomorrow I can't write. But on Sunday I'll give you the whole story again. I promise!

25 April 1943

I haven't written since Friday afternoon. When Shabbat finished yesterday, very late, I wasn't in the mood to begin. Now it's Sunday evening, a quarter-past seven, and we've just had dinner. I'll try

---

166 The Germans had all kinds of plans to exchange German citizens who were under British rule, so they "guarded" those Jews with British citizenship (or that of a neutral country), as well as those with certificates of emigration to Mandatory Palestine (including those who had submitted a request for such a certificate). Some of these Jews were sent from Westerbork to Bergen-Belsen, but in July 1944 a swop actually took place, in which 222 Jews were transferred to the Land of Israel (among them, Mirjam).

to call to mind what happened over the past few days. Luckily, nothing special.

I can't remember whether I told you last time that Lea telephoned on Friday morning. As you know, she has gone into hiding. She asked for Marc and I had a bit of a fright, because I thought something had happened. At first it was very difficult to get hold of Marc, but when I came home at half-past twelve he was there. I then sent him to one of Lea's cousins, whose address she had given me over the telephone. In the afternoon, Marc came to see me and said that Lea had asked for a coat. I had already sent her her coat, so I was very surprised to hear that she hadn't received it. Besides, about a week ago she had asked for ƒ500, which surprised us greatly, too, for we knew she had taken enough money. Now Marc told me that she said she never asked for, or received, any of it. In other words, it was a swindle by the man with whom she's hiding or by whoever is acting as an intermediary. I decided to talk to somebody at once, which I did, and he told me he was grateful for the information. This intermediary does a great deal for Jews, but is completely unreliable when it comes to money.

Nothing special happened at the office. Mrs Van der Heyden, Tiny's mother, came by to see me, but I was out. I was at Nieuwe Keizersgracht 58 again to discuss a few matters. Some members of staff there asked me for advice. The *Expositur* is taking on 60 people, because they work shifts and the hours are too long. The department in question employs mainly German Jews and is now hiring almost exclusively Dutch people, because everybody is up in arms about the dominance of the German Jews. But the people who are taken on argue as follows: As soon as the *Expositur* has to cut back on staff, we'll be the first to go, so we may be more secure at our current department. It's very difficult to give advice on such matters, because you don't know what the future holds and how they plan to clear out Amsterdam. The latest rumours suggest a ghetto.

When I came home on Friday afternoon, Ezra de Lieme, the son of Nehemia de L.,[167] was there. He travelled illegally from The Hague to Amsterdam, and has been billeted with Tiny van der Heyden for five days. He came to ask if he could live with us. He would then change his identity card and signature himself. I don't believe this is risky as such. The policemen who turn up don't check whether or not you're in the population registry. Only you'd have to buy a ration book every month, because you're not registered with the distribution service. But he can't stay with us, firstly because Mother can't look after yet another person, and secondly, if there were another incident like the one with those detectives last week and they don't find whoever they're looking for — which luckily in our case they didn't — and they investigate the matter and discover such a young man in the house, we'll all be in trouble, not just him. When I came home that evening, Father told me that he had promised to let Ezra know. We did discuss the matter, but came to the conclusion that we couldn't do it, much as we regretted not being able to help and having to let him down. On Friday evening I got home at around nine, where we talked a bit more about Ezra's case and then had an early night.

To *shul* yesterday, where I heard a beautiful, if rather theatrical, recital of *Shir Hashirim*, the Song of Songs. Afterwards to Hectorstraat[168] with Tiny van der Heyden, Daniel Klein and Ezra. We had a lovely time, and I didn't walk back home until almost four o'clock. Your father and Els had been to visit us, and when I came home, at five, Sam Salomons and his wife were still there. I had some food — I honestly can't remember what; it must have been mash — and then I had a good read. Mr Vromen came home and asked to speak to me. We talked for about an hour, about whether or not the children who escaped the orphanage clear-out should go

---

167 Nehemia de Lieme: former Chair of the Union of Dutch Zionists. Kibbutz Sdeh Nehemia, founded by Dutch pioneers in Israel, was named after him.
168 To the home of the Van der Heydens.

into hiding. He has received a good many offers to take children into hiding, but it's a difficult decision; there's so much at stake, e.g., the safety of the families taking in the children, the children's characters, whether or not they're suited to it, whether they have younger brothers and sisters who would be left on their own, etc., etc. We also talked about me and about his position, and I didn't go to bed until midnight.

I rose at half-past eight this morning, arrived at Eitje's at a quarter-past nine and discussed a few issues with him, chiefly staff salaries. Then I went to the office to fetch paper and carbon, for Lex Wolfsberg was coming over to work with me in the afternoon. From there I dropped in on Els, originally to collect the plates we lent her, but she wanted to keep them a few more days. While I was there, she asked if I could roast some sugared almonds. She also had some hazelnuts. I did, and I'm pleased to say they turned out quite well. I also made a cup of hot chocolate, quite delicious, though I say so myself. Els has always worked in an office and is obviously not a consummate housewife, although she's managing quite well. But your father is used to perfection, and this creates conflict sometimes. He may deny it, but your father is really rather demanding. Still, they're happy enough together.

Home at a quarter-to twelve, played the piano for a bit, had some food — French beans and mash. This morning I had mashed potato for breakfast — and then I made a pudding with water, potato flour and the caramel left over from the hazelnut roasting. Lex arrived at half-past two and we got a fair amount of work done. I can't remember whether I told you that a report is being drawn up about Transjordan, so there will be some proposals on the table after the war for those Jews in Poland who have nowhere to go. Of course, it's almost impossible to find sources. A great many people are working on the project, but it has to remain a secret because it could be mistaken for political activity, which is strictly prohibited, so one person isn't aware of another's involvement. Like a whodunit, all very furtive. Afterwards, we talked a bit. He really is a splendid fellow, just "fickle." He has trouble sticking things out, I believe. He left at half-past four.

Selma was at our house, and we had a bit of a chat. Then we had some food — onion and vegetable soup, mash left over from lunch, beetroot and potato salad and three-quarters of a fried egg each. And now I'm writing to you. So you see, we spent these last few days more or less as normal. As for what happens next, we try not to think about it too much. And now I'd better stop. It's nearly eight o'clock and I'm going inside for a cup of tea. More after *Yom Tov*. Happy *Yom Tov*, darling, in so far as that is possible.

27 April 1943

I completely forgot to tell you that in *shul* on Shabbat I learnt that Bram de Jong doesn't have to go to Asterdorp after all, but is allowed to live in *Oost*. He has been allotted a beautiful house, a real stroke of luck for him.

Now I'll proceed in chronological order. On Sunday evening I read a little, then had an early night and a lovely kip. Cold potatoes for breakfast, to *shul*, jam-packed, perched on three-quarters of a chair. Sieg Leuvenberg was the *chazzan*,[169] Jaap Meijer spoke, well, but rather chaotic and heated. There is one thing I liked a great deal though, and that is that he mentioned the brochure on the occasion of the 50th anniversary of the emancipation of the Jews,[170] which featured an article by a certain Dr Liepman, rector of the rabbinical seminary in Amsterdam. This man was baptised[171] two years after writing the article. The fact that he was baptised doesn't matter in and of itself; as rector of this seminary, he was the most competent

169 Cantor.
170 The text referred to by historian Jaap Meijer is probably a brochure from 1846 on the 50th anniversary of the emancipation of the Jews in the Netherlands in 1796.
171 Converted to Christianity.

person to do it (said Jaap M. ironically.) What does matter is that the children who were then, at the start of the emancipation, in the cradle, are now people aged 90, 100, going into *galut*[172] with their rucksacks on their backs. I thought he put it extremely well.

Home through a gale, and there I made a delicious pudding with coffee, potato flour and skimmed milk, roasted hazelnuts and also some nougat and a potato casserole. Lovely meal, peas and refried potatoes, something we hadn't eaten for months because we had too little butter. But for *Pesach* we had opened one of our last cans, hence this little treat. Afterwards, I sat in the sun with one of my last cigarettes, but only very briefly. Then I changed and went to Isidoor and Anna, back again, all with this gale still blowing. I passed a group of *Jeugdstorm*,[173] and overheard somebody entering his house saying: "I'd better turn my back on them." Then briefly to your aunt Rachel and uncle Marc in Franselaan, home, dinner, soup, tinned carrots and peas (you see, we're finishing absolutely everything we have), potatoes and pudding. Then I read, with a cup of tea, roasted almonds and delicious, coffee-flavoured nougat. I'll make you some soon! I promise! To bed.

Terrible gunfire last night. I believe I never told you that we've been having very frequent air-raid warnings of late. And once in a while there's shelling during the day, but without warning. Last night, the fighting was extremely fierce. One aircraft was shot down and crashed behind the Carlton Hotel, which is in use by the Germans. An entire block of houses was destroyed, and the Carlton Hotel is said to have been gutted. Lots of people got up, but we stayed in bed, because we don't do anything anyway. We don't go down to a shelter, since we don't have one. Besides, with a whole house on top, I wouldn't feel any safer in a shelter.

I slept very late this morning, rose at half-past ten, had mashed potato for breakfast, which didn't agree with me, so I ate hardly

172 Exile, Diaspora.
173 The youth organization of the NSB.

any cabbage and mash at half-past twelve. Read a while, then went to your father and from there to Freddy, where Jo Mossel gave a Hebrew *sicha*.[174] I understood it quite well. Juul told us that the police had called on her parents that afternoon to tell them that her blind uncle, who's staying with them, will be taken away tomorrow. And there's nothing they can do, because if he doesn't stay at home, they will be taken instead. Appalling! Then home, dinner, soup, carrots and peas, potatoes. I read a bit, and now I'm writing to you. I intend to write to you every day until Friday. Then I'll hide the letters somewhere, for I'm finding it a bit too risky to keep them all with me. I'll also make notes and give you a monthly telegraph report, i.e., a report in telegram style. How much longer?! Right now I'm drained, numb, and worn out for lack of sleep last night.

Sunday, 4 July 1943, half-past four, Barracks 65, Westerbork[175]

Although I can't muster the peace of mind to write and it's also rather difficult to write on the second tier of a bunk bed, with your head down so as not to knock it against the third tier, I want to find some comfort with you and tell you "briefly" how we ended up here in Westerbork. The blow has come at last, and in some respects it's worse, in others less so, but certainly very, very different from what we ever imagined. In actual fact, we could never really form a picture of any of this. Such an awful lot happened during the month of May that I can't for the life of me mention it all. I saved some newspaper cuttings and notes, but it remains to be seen whether I'll ever lay hands on them again. I do remember a few things. For example, all the men in active service during the fighting in May 1940 have been made prisoners-of-war. The paper keeps publishing

174 Conversation lesson.
175 This letter was written later, in Westerbork, but it is inserted here as it relates chronologically to this period of time — May 1943.

call-ups for certain regiments. And all men aged 20–35 are being recruited for the *Arbeitseinsatz*. The students who didn't sign the declaration of loyalty have been deported to Germany. Even all the Christians have to hand in their radio sets. Unbelievable!!! What it comes down to is that, practically speaking, nobody will be left.

During May we received another nocturnal visit, and the blighters took down Father's name and his *Sperre* number. The following morning, when I made enquiries, I was told that we were bound to receive an *Anweisung* to move to *Oost*. Besides, that week we had just sent Mother to the doctor's because she was so awfully thin, and he had found a small lump in her breast and referred her to Dr Kropveld. I went with her, and he said she needed surgery. A dreadful thing in these precarious times of deportations and possible invasion, etc. Just what we needed. Then there was the added problem of housekeeping, but quite by chance I bumped into Selma Gazan and she was prepared to come and help us. Except that this turned out to be impossible, because the JC needed qualified nurses very badly and wouldn't allow her to do domestic work. By the grace of G-d, the JC's medical commission granted that if, after her release from hospital, Mother was still too weak to do her own housekeeping, Selma could come and stay with us. But it would all take a rather different course.

I headed east on my bicycle to find a house. Houses are allocated, but if you say: "I would like such-and-such a house," and the woman in charge of allocating the houses (Mussert's niece!) is in a good mood, you usually get it. I found nothing. Many of the houses were unoccupied, but they hadn't yet been "pulsed." Besides, the *Anweisung* hadn't arrived yet, and Sluzker advised me against applying for one myself. I was in a hurry because of Mother's hospital admission and the fact that some kind of new *Sperre* process was hanging over our heads, which meant I'd be insanely busy again.

On Friday, 21 May 1943, the bombshell dropped. The JC was

The first letter written by Mirjam in Westerbork, 4 July 1943
Author's collection

convened,[176] and late in the afternoon it was announced that "part of the JC will be called up for the *Arbeitseinsatz* and everybody must be prepared." (I forgot to tell you the trifling fact that those without exemptions had had to report at Polderweg, but that only a very small percentage had showed up.) So now the JC's turn had come. I received word to go to Nieuwe Keizersgracht, where Eitje was. Everybody there looked glum, but what the actual percentages were, nobody knew. I was told to come back at eight in the evening. It was Friday evening and Mother was to go to the NIZ that Sunday. But it couldn't be helped.

That evening, the four of us (the secretaries of the members of the *Sperre* Commission, made up of Meyer de Vries, Jack Brandon, Professor Cohen and Henri Eitje) convened all the department heads required to submit staff lists that would then be presented to the commission for evaluation. In addition to the above-mentioned four, Henri Edersheim from The Hague was also a member of this *Sperre* Commission. We went home at eleven o'clock and that was the last night I got any sleep. I'm not in the mood now to give you all the details. It's a shame I didn't write it down sooner, for I can't possibly convey the tension and anxiety of those days now. Seven thousand people would have to be called up by Tuesday 25 May, and the Huns had warned of "terrible things" if not enough people came forward. The Professor took this to mean firing squads, but whether this was said in so many words, I don't know. It meant 60 percent (I believe) of the JC, so all people you know well. Not to

176 De Jong wrote that during this meeting, Aus der Fünten told the JC representatives that on 25 May, 7,000 of their workers would have to report for "work in Germany." The JC was ordered to take care of the order. They were given 20 minutes to deliberate, but were warned that if they did not submit the 7,000 names as requested, worse things would happen to the Jews. In light of this threat, the leaders of the JC agreed to cooperate. Louis de Jong, *Het Koninkrijk der Nederlanden in de Tweede Wereldoorlog* ('s-Gravenhage: Staatsdrukkerrij-en Uitgeverijbedrijf, 1969–1991), vol. 7, pt. 1, pp. 286–289. See also the protocols from the Central Meeting of the JC, nos. 94 and 95 (21 May 1943; 28 May 1943), and here, pp. 143–144, 155–157.

mention... the parents! The four of us, the secretaries, could talk of nothing else.

Having seen the departmental lists, I realized they would never fill the quota. You see, every department had included on its blacklist those people who were certain to be indispensable for another department. The seminary, for example, had dropped Leo Seeligmann, knowing that the Jewish High School would keep him. All the departments were doing this, with the following result (Meanwhile, I've done the laundry, eaten some mash and now I'll resume. A beautiful view: Some of the laundry is fluttering between two beds):

1. Mistakes were made, because the seminary, for example, would say: The Jewish High School will put Leo Seeligmann on its list of indispensable people, so we can remove him. Meanwhile, the Jewish High School would say: The seminary will include him, so we can put him on the blacklist.

2. The list was far too short, owing to the fact that too few were actually struck off the list of exemptions, because naturally people such as Seeligmann were not blacklisted[177] and therefore not included in the required 7,000.

I hope this makes sense and, more than that, I hope to explain it to you in person. It's not easy to gather your thoughts in a barracks with 1,000 people, and so much happened afterwards that this has already faded from memory.

Saturday, 22 May

Worked with Eitje during the day, the night on the card index.

---

177 After Seeligmann appeared on both the seminary and High School blacklists, the mistake was discovered and he was placed on the exemption list of one of the institutions.

Sunday morning, 23 May

I went home at eleven, where I said goodbye to Mother who was going into hospital. As soon as she and Father had gone and I was by myself in the house, I cried my eyes out because I knew the game was up, and because I was so upset that the JC had once again lent itself to this barbarity instead of saying: Enough is enough, go hang. It reminds me of the following sick, but very telling, "joke": Asscher and Cohen are sent for by the Huns and are told that the Jews will be gassed, whereupon the Professor's first question is: "Will you supply the gas or should we?" Such was our predicament.

I slept until two, then went back to the office. There I had to strike all the bigwigs' friends and family off the (interim) call-up list. How about that? In a word, I was given a list of their cronies and had to check whether they would be called up and, if so, I had to strike them off the list. I almost wept with fury and indignation, but there was nothing I could do. Home at half-past six, back at eight.

Sunday night, 23–24 May

I'll never forget that night. I was working on the call-up list, collating it with cards from the card index. A group of accountants had been called in to do the counting, Ab Vreedenburg and Karel Hartog among them. I forgot to tell you that Freddy had refused to draw up the lists, as had Elie Dasberg. But they knew they wouldn't be dropped. And as for the parents: Elie's brother, Simon Dasberg (who has since become Amsterdam's acting chief rabbi), would take care of his mother, while your father, as funeral director, was safe, so they could afford to refuse. This team of accountants (I was helping Jo Pinkhof) did nothing but count and count, but the figures just didn't add up. They remained well below 7,000, which was quite understandable (see above) and had in fact been anticipated by us, but not by their lordships themselves. This resulted in a "raid," i.e., the entire card index was reviewed (so no longer just the departmental lists) and call-ups written for the cards that were pulled out. Utterly indiscriminate. Our team, which received the call-up lists — every now and then we were summoned to the Professor's office, the scene of the massacre, to fetch the lists — was beside itself with rage. Of course we kept coming across the names of good friends, colleagues, sometimes even relatives, brothers and sisters and even parents and children! The mood became more and more charged, until one of the men (a former theatre director and impresario) burst into tears and shouted that he refused to go on. At that point, we all chucked it in and one of us went to tell the Professor that we couldn't possibly do this insane and barbarous work.

Then the entire commission convened in our office and the Professor spoke to us as follows: "If we fail to do this, terrible things will happen." When he was told that there wouldn't be enough people in any case, he replied: "Then that's the will of the people. But I can't shoulder the responsibility for refusing the order." It all sounds very matter-of-fact, but everybody was crying and barely capable of voicing their objections. The Professor, too, was almost in tears.

Then I said, on the verge of tears: "But Professor, surely the people would have wanted you to refuse this order. And if the terrible things you keep speaking of will happen anyway (you see, the Professor had told us that the Huns had said that if insufficient numbers of people came forward the 'repercussions would be unimaginable.' He had also said that he was convinced the turnout would be poor), then why do this nauseating work instead of lying in the sun and gathering our strength for Poland?" Everybody agreed with me and nodded their approval. The Professor replied: "Miss Levie, that's not for you to judge." I was incapable of replying that it's all very easy to fob somebody off like that.

The Professor looked round at all the sobbing men — I was the only woman — and said: "Please don't make things difficult for us, the call-ups *have* to be dispatched." (Remember, they had been given the order on Friday and the people were expected to report on Tuesday!) Anyway, we went back to work.

At six in the morning (i.e., Monday 24 May), Lies (who'd had a terrible crying fit, out of fear for her parents. If it hadn't been for Father and Mother, I would have chucked it all in a long time ago and told them: Go hang, I quit), Ab Vreedenburg, Dorus Hijmans, Karel Hartog and I were summoned to the commission and asked whether we were physically and emotionally fit enough to continue the raid through the card index, which had remained unfinished. We refused en bloc, whereupon their lordships looked at one another and said: "In that case, we shall carry on ourselves." Then we left. I got home at two, slept until four, and then went back to the office.

Meanwhile, many people had learnt that they were to be called up, e.g., from typists. The typists had suffered panic attacks that night, e.g., when they had to type out call-ups for their own parents. The first such call-up could usually be cancelled, but not the second. It was all so arbitrary, down to mood and chance. It was my task to receive these people and collect their details. At approximately six o'clock, we received news that staff at the NIZ, as well as any relatives living with them, would be interned at the JI building for five days. Panic and conjecture were rife. An hour later, the Professor issued a statement: The announcement is incorrect. Only hospital staff *with* call-ups will be interned, without family. In the meantime, however, entire families had walked over to the JI. But our minds had been put at rest, because we had thought that these people were to receive special treatment, whereas the revised version implied that the hospital staff would be safeguarded against measures aimed at the rest of the population.

Home at approximately half-past six. Then to Freddy, because I wanted to talk to somebody. Everybody looked like they had done during the first few days of the war: nervous, pale and gaunt. I chatted to Freddy for a couple of hours, then (i.e., Monday night) returned home, slept (after two nights) and at nine o'clock on Tuesday 25 May went to Waterlooplein to find out who had received call-ups and whether there had been any mistakes. By then I had already heard that dozens of friends and relatives had received call-ups, including Grewels, other aunts and uncles, etc. At ten o'clock, to Keizersgracht. There I was summoned to the commission (the other secretaries hadn't arrived yet) and the game began all over again. Cancelling call-ups at the rate at which they had been issued. And it shows that we had been right in saying that it was an impossible task, because in a great many cases the commission said: Oh no, that's absolutely out of the question! And then the game of chance began all over again. Call-ups were cancelled until five in the afternoon, while the people were expected to report at Polderweg that very same day. One thousand call-ups were returned undeliverable, so things weren't looking good for the 7,000 quota.

JEWISH COUNCIL OF AMSTERDAM

Amsterdam, 2 June 1943

Minutes of the 94th meeting of the Central Commission held on Friday 21 May 1943 at three o'clock in the afternoon at Nieuwe Keizersgracht 58, Amsterdam.

Attending: Professor Cohen, Chairman, Mrs Van Tijn and Messrs Asscher, Barmes, Van den Bergh, Blazer, Blüth, Cahen, A. Cohen, Diamand, Edersheim, Eitje, Dasberg, Hendrix, Kauffmann, Krouwer, Van der Laan, Van Lier, Moser, Van Oss, Sluzker, Spier, Spijer, Van der Velde, De Vries and Brandon, Secretary.

The Chairman opened the meeting and announced that this morning the German authorities ordered the Jewish Council to assist in the call-up of 7,000 Jews for transport to Westerbork on Tuesday 25 May.

In order to allow those attending to define their positions, the meeting was adjourned for five minutes.

After reopening the meeting, views were exchanged on the principles of the order. It was announced that the Jewish Council has reached the decision to implement the order. The meeting resolved to take immediate action. A commission, comprising Messrs Edersheim, Eitje, De Vries and Brandon, will be charged with the implementation.

The heads of department will be asked to lend their assistance as a matter of urgency.

The meeting resolved to read out the following announcement in the Jewish Council offices: "In accordance with the order of the Commissioner-General for *Sicherheitswesen*, some of the Jewish Council will shortly be called up for forced labour. Who will be selected is as yet uncertain. People are advised, however, to prepare for imminent departure."

Westerbork, Monday, 8 o'clock in the evening, 5 July 1943

Tonight is transport night, so we have to be in by nine. Otherwise at ten! Silly, isn't it? In Amsterdam, you were picked up if you ventured out one minute after eight. Let me continue my account now, although I doubt I'll get very far. Lex Wolfsberg will be visiting shortly to collect a few items, food and soap, that he has run out of, because he may have to go on the transport tonight.

Now that so much time has passed, I'm less capable than ever of conveying the immense turmoil of those days. That Tuesday night, I slept very badly. Nerves and utter exhaustion, I suspect. At around six in the morning I suddenly heard a loudspeaker in the street, and I knew at once: This is it, we're done for! But what it would be, I didn't know, of course. I stayed in bed, actually without thinking. Then I heard Father and Vromen talking in the hallway. Father said he had caught something about "*deutsche und holländische Polizei.*"[178] Vromen rushed downstairs and came back up again a moment later to say that the Jews had to stay at home, because they would be picked up. The Aryans weren't allowed out either. Only then did I stir. I got out of bed and got dressed, without washing, without combing my hair. Vromen, extremely agitated, came to say goodbye, because he had a hiding place and wanted to try and get there. I thought we would be taken to the Theatre and wasn't very anxious for myself. Honestly, my thoughts were all about Father and the fate of the NIZ. I said to Father: "I want you and Bobby to go to the NIZ; then at least you'll be together." "But we're not allowed out!" Father said. "What does it matter, you'll be picked up either way." It was a quarter-to seven. And off I went! I'll never forget the sight of Father sitting at the table, preparing sandwiches. Such an image becomes ingrained in your memory.

Off to the NIZ. Of course it was dead quiet in the street, although there were a few Aryans about. They all said: "You're not allowed out," but I feigned ignorance and kept going, fast, but not too fast either. When I arrived at the NIZ, I saw Vromen across the Nieuwe Keizersgracht talking to somebody, surrounded by a bunch of green police. In trouble already, I thought to myself. At the NIZ I asked for a certificate saying that Mother was in hospital, thinking it might be useful. As I stood there waiting, the NIZ staff interned at the Jewish Invalid were brought in by a green. Oh dear, oh dear, I thought, he will see me in my coat and ask me where I've come from.

Westerbork, Tuesday morning, 9.15 in the morning

The morning after the transport. I'm writing amid an infernal din, tucked away in a corner on the bottom tier of a bed. I'll try to tell you the rest of the story in a coherent way.

178 German and Dutch police.

I walked into the waiting room, as did all the people in the corridor, was given the certificate saying that Mother had been admitted for surgery, and stuck my head round the corner. When the green walked past, I slipped out behind his back. But just as I was about to leave the building, I heard a voice: "*Wo gehen Sie hin?*"[179] I replied, as if it was perfectly normal: "*Ich muss eine Strecke weiter, ich muss zur Arbeit.*"[180]

"*Danngehenwirzusammen,*"[181] he replied. And off we went. It was swarming with green police, but I wasn't stopped, since I was being escorted by one. I asked him whether he knew what was happening that day, but he didn't say; he probably didn't know either. I decided to go to the JC and he even rang the doorbell for me. They were all thunderstruck when they saw me and begged me to stay and not to go home. I allowed myself to be persuaded, for we no longer had a telephone at home and I thought I could be of more use to Bobby and Father at the JC.

Meanwhile, I learnt that the entire city centre had been cordoned off, bridges pulled up and the people taken to Houtmarkt (J.D. Meijerplein), to the "New Synagogue" (!), for registration. The personal details of the detained Jews were written down, and the Jews destined for deportation were then taken to the Theatre. The Huns behaved disgracefully. Mrs Van Tijn, who lives in Nieuwe Amstelstraat, had already been collected and immediately released again. But she was the only one! At that point Lages, the man in charge, hadn't arrived yet, and Aus der Fünten had released her. Nobody else was released that day. When Lages arrived, Sluzker was dismissed. Chief Rabbi Dasberg, Mrs Eitje (my boss's wife),

179 "Where are you going?"
180 "I need to be on my way, I need to go to work."
181 "Then we shall go together."

Freddy and Juul, Rabbi Vredenburg, Rabbi De Lange, they were all sent on to Westerbork. Only Ru Cohen, the Professor's brother, was released. He had the 120.000 stamp.[182]

In the afternoon, the Huns came to see us at the JC. We all pretended to be busy and suffered fits of nervous laughter. When Asscher and Cohen told them that we were working on German orders, we didn't have to leave. A moment later, your father called (there's an internal telephone connecting nos. 62 and 58. Because the line at no. 58 is always busy, the Huns often telephone no. 62 and then your father passes the message on via the internal system) to say they were about to be taken away. We said goodbye, to Els as well. They were quite distraught, naturally. I sat by the telephone and kept calling them, and every time I did they were still there. And then the Huns disappeared from the street! They had been overlooked!!

At around five o'clock, we all set about cleaning the building. It had become a pigsty after five days and nights of work. But it lifted our spirits considerably. Then we had some food, small rations of course, for nobody was allowed to enter or leave the building. And then we went to sleep, right there in our chairs, with our heads spinning. I knew that Father and Bobby had gone. Ab Vreedenburg was beside himself with worry about his wife and child, because everybody expected *Zuid* and *Oost* to be next. Later, three of us lay down on a sofa. I had written a Red Cross letter to you that day, without a form, since I didn't have one, asking the Red Cross to copy the letter onto a form. The letter was never sent, because I'd forgotten your address. It just goes to show how nervous I was.

182 Those who managed to acquire the 120.000 stamp, bearing the words "exempt until further notice," had proof of being "invaluable for the economy." These stamps were also sold by the SS for considerable sums of money. Through intermediation of Herr Puttkammer, a German clerk in the Rotterdamsche Bank, it was possible to get a temporary exemption stamp with the numbers 120.000 in exchange for industrial diamonds (or for other valuables such as large sums of foreign currency). These valuables and monies were then transferred to the Germans.

In the morning, I washed and perked up a bit, telephoned the NIZ (I knew that everything was still all right over there) and asked when I could come and visit. The answer was: half-past eight. Upon my arrival, I was told that Mother had just been taken upstairs for the operation. I went home because I was worried about our luggage, Mother's and mine, which was still in the house. There were guards everywhere; the *Expositur* had advised me against going home, but I thought it was worth a try. I had been given a certificate saying I had worked at Nieuwe Keizersgracht on Tuesday night (not true, of course) and that I was therefore "legally" in the cleared-out city centre. It was wretched coming back home. I could tell they had left calmly. My luggage had been put to one side, with a note, and so had Mother's. I lugged everything to the Leuvenbergs, in Parklaan, including food, peeled potatoes, a big pan of rice, vegetables, etc., and on my way back I bumped into Tiny van der Heyden, who had come to see if there was anybody left. It was amazing! He helped me carry everything, and invited me to spend the nights at their house, because he lives in a neighbourhood with few Jews. I gathered together the food and packed it in some spare rucksacks. Then to Mother. When I asked the doctor whether I could tell her about Father, he replied: "No." I had expected as much. Mother was still asleep. To the office, where I found Eitje. Sad to see how few were left. The others were busy putting together parcels for those who had gone away. I wrote a letter to Father and Freddy.

Back to Mother. The operation had been successful, but you have no idea how difficult it was to put on a happy face and tell her that Father and Bobby were fine and to see how glad she was. Back to Nieuwe Keizersgracht, where I gathered some toiletries which, as a precaution, I had already taken to the office on Waterlooplein, and to Tiny around nine. Had dinner with them, they were very warm and friendly, and then went to bed. Up early, to Muidergracht, where the JC was collecting food in rucksacks — strictly speaking, you're not allowed to remove anything from the houses, and rucksacks look the least conspicuous — to take to Waterlooplein.

Let me run through the rest for you. Told Mother the truth after a couple of days. She didn't take it too badly; perhaps it didn't sink in properly. To Sluzker. Advice: Move house at once. To Leeman, who is *Verwalter*[183] of the Dutch-Asian Trading Company now that the Jews — Father among them — have been thrown out, and discussed the matter. The next few days: Move, move, move!! A nightmare!! All on my own!! I had agreed with Leeman that some of our furniture would be stored in the depot of the Dutch-Asian on Hoogte Kadijk. Then to Hein van Dam, someone I'd met during the call-up business, who had an apartment. I applied for the *Anweisung* and decided what should and shouldn't go into storage. I can't tell you how much work it was. Plus — to the office, to Mother, hiring the removers, fixing myself something to eat, for I was too busy and too grubby to eat with others. And all the while I felt as if I'd bitten off more than I could chew. But I managed it.

The *Anweisung* (I had been worried the application would be declined) was for 9 June, *Shavuot*, and because I only discovered this on Friday, I was forced to postpone the move until Tuesday. I even quarrelled with the woman from the Housing Association. This is how it works: You receive your *Anweisung* to move from the *Zentralstelle*. You can also apply for one, in which case you're given an "order." This you take to the JC, where you receive a permit to move which, together with the *Anweisung*, also serves as a permit for transporting furniture. Finally, you have to go to the Municipal Housing Association (Mussert's niece), where you are allocated a house. But if you happen to know of a house yourself you can apply for it, and if she's in a good mood you'll get it. So off I went, with a note from Van Dam saying he wants to let this apartment to me. At first she was very friendly and asked me, when

183 All Jewish company managers were dismissed by the Germans and were replaced by a *"Verwalter"* or manager. These were mostly NSB or German cronies, without any knowledge of, or experience in, the business. In this case, however, the Jewish management succeeded in having Mr Leeman, their former non-Jewish employee, nominated as *Verwalter*.

she saw my occupation, whether I have a nice boss and whether my mother would be home soon. But when I produced my note, she flatly refused to give me the apartment, claiming the Germans hadn't released it yet. I knew they had, for Van Dam had had it "pulsed" for that express purpose. But she refused, and gave me an apartment on Afrikanerplein. If it's any good, I thought to myself, I might as well take it; after all, I'm not wedded to Van Dam's apartment. Besides, I hadn't seen that one either. So off I went to Afrikanerplein. A hovel! The rooms were poky. Then to Van Dam's apartment, Pretoriusstraat, close to Linneausstraat. A gem of a place. No bathroom, but otherwise grand.

Off I went to Van Dam, who telephoned to say that the apartment had indeed been released. Dashed back to the Housing Association, because Van Dam had said: "She's furious. Hurry or she'll give it to someone else, just to spite you." So I went and she was fuming! "I'm sick and tired of your race's scheming." And: "It's so unfair towards the other landlord. His apartment has been empty for much longer." As if I was some philanthropic institution for this landlord. Anyway, she gave it to me in the end, because she thought my case was "tragic." Moved house, and toiled, toiled, toiled.

7 July 1943, 17.45

It was a mad rush, but by Shabbat, 19 June, I was all done: Curtains washed, cupboards stocked, floors waxed. Everything was shipshape, even if I say so myself. I had slaved away, because I wanted it to look good for Mother. That day I had an "open house." I invited your father and Els, Eitje, Jo Pronk (Bobby's boyfriend, who had been a great help. He is very handy and did all kinds of odd jobs for me) and Aunt Phine, ordered delicious fondant, baked proper biscuits with butter that I bought on the black market (cheap at 10 guilders for half a pound) and also bought a cake, a real butter cake, on the black market.

I forgot to tell you that on that Thursday we had been forced to hand in our bicycles. A new list had been submitted, and a number would be engraved on our bicycles.[184] I would have it back by Monday. That week, the Professor had been told that as of Monday (i.e., 21 June), some measures favourable for the Jews were to come into effect, which prompted me to say to Eitje: We are bound to receive some bad tidings now. When the Huns say "favourable," it really means "unfavourable."

My "open house" was a great success. Everybody stayed a long time and inspected the house from top to bottom. I even had some proper lemonade; everything was just perfect. Eitje also brought me half a real butter cake. Extremely kind. At six o'clock, I ate with the Dunners, in Den Texstraat, and got back home at ten. Little did I know that, for the time being, this was to be my last night in Amsterdam. For how long? That remains to be seen. As it happens, I slept badly that night (not unlike King Ahasuerus),[185] but when I turned in I did think to myself: how wonderfully soft and warm.

The following morning, at the crack of dawn, I heard the roar of a loudspeaker outside. I couldn't believe my ears. On a Sunday, and after all the reassurances we'd had! Perhaps it's something else, I thought, but then I told myself: You know what this means, it's over. Then suddenly I thought: Mother! All alone in hospital. So I got out of bed, this time I did get washed and dressed, put on stockings (despite the heat), smart shoes and a beautiful silk dress as well as an elegant tailored coat and a nice handbag, because I wanted to impress the Huns. I wanted to get through. From the balcony I understood what was happening. The Jews were being rounded up, of course! So off I went, without breakfast. I was in two minds about what to do. You see, the Professor once told us

184 The list was of those eligible to own bicycles, with their numbers matching those engraved on the bicycle itself.
185 The king mentioned in the Book of Esther. He is said to have had a bad night's sleep, which had serious consequences for the Jews.

that in an emergency, he would have us picked up. I was now living in Pretoriusstraat and the two other secretaries in Ingogostraat, so the three of us lived quite close to one another. But then I thought: Perhaps there's no time to lose. So off I went.

Everything had been cordoned off again, and as I made my way, I learnt that it was the same story in *Zuid*. At Nieuwe Weesperpoortbrug I tried my luck with the green police, who had cordoned off the place. No luck whatsoever! Not even with my "most charming smile." I retraced my steps to try at the Amstel Brewery. Along the way, a Jew asked me: "Shall we try together?" The soldier who had spoken to us told us to go to the Colonial Institute for an *Ausweis*.[186] I have no intention of putting my head in the lion's mouth, I thought to myself (that is where the green police were based), but my companion said: "You've got nothing to lose; you'll be rounded up anyway. At this early hour, they may still issue one." I let myself be persuaded, and headed for the Colonial Institute. But on my way there, I was stopped by a green who asked me where I was going, and when I told him I wanted to go back home to fetch my luggage, he grabbed me by the arm and took me to... the Colonial Institute. I was hopeful at first. We received a polite welcome, and were asked to hand in our exemption papers and identity cards. My exemption paper happens to be rather good, with a low number (the same as with cars), an old date and the personal signatures of Professor Cohen and Asscher, instead of the later stamp. We had to stand facing the wall (there were four people already). But as more and more time passed, and more and more people came in, and we still didn't receive any further information, I thought to myself: It's over, I backed the wrong horse, better not dwell on it, it can't be helped. It was mainly hospital staff coming in. Later I learnt that they had telephoned Dr Kroonenberg, the

186 The Colonial Institute was the headquarters of the German (green) police in Amsterdam. *Ausweis* here refers to a permit to stay in Amsterdam, an exemption from deportation to Westerbork.

director of the NIZ, and had been advised to go to the Colonial Institute, where they would be given an *Ausweis*.

Despite the fix we were in, I couldn't help but laugh at the sight of us, standing there, staring at the wall. One woman needed the lavatory and stood there moaning: "I really need to go!" And then one of those fellows would bark: "*Wenn Sie nicht schweigen gebrauche ich mein Schutzwaffe*,"[187] or something to that effect. If somebody else had told me this, I would have thought: How awful. But now I didn't think it was awful at all, only insane, that these men would fly into a rage whenever you as much as turned your head.

Around eleven o'clock — we had been standing for approximately three-and-a-half hours — we went outside. I forgot to tell you that meanwhile hundreds of green police, who had been called in from outside, were filing into the building. One of them had jumped off the train too early, and was carried in dead on a stretcher. Too bad it was just the one. I briefly harboured hopes that we would be taken to the Theatre, but no. We were taken to Polderweg in trucks. This is the area, not far from Muiderpoort Station, where those with call-ups had had to report. For a moment I thought we would be boarding the train straight away, but we were taken to a sandy area enclosed by a wooden fence. The weather was splendid and we had plenty of space (there were only about 100 people at that point), so we decided to lie down in the sand, awaiting further news. One man, Rennig, lorded it over the others and he split us into hospital staff and JC staff. There were only about six of the latter, among them the assistant to De Miranda, head of the Municipal Office for Jewish Billeting, who had a special stamp, signed by Wörlein, one of the bigwigs. He walked up to Rennig, showed him the stamp and said: "*Unterzeichnet von Herrn Obersturmführer*

187 "If you do not shut up, I shall use my gun."

Wörlein.[188] *"Und ich bin Rennig,"*[189] the man said, and dismissed him. He later learnt that Rennig and Wörlein were sworn rivals and enemies, and that these stamps, initially signed by Wörlein, were later issued exclusively by Rennig.

It would take too long to tell you everything in detail. It was all fairly easy-going. Rennig served as our lavatory attendant, and we took turns going to the lavatory in a hut housing the Dutch military police. I seized the opportunity to telephone Eitje. The military police were really very decent. Heilbut, one of the heads of the *Expositur*, showed up, but wasn't allowed to enter the enclosure. Later on, Mrs Sluzker arrived, followed by Sluzker with Aus der Fünten. Everybody's hopes were up. But to no avail. Sluzker had no say. I even went up to Aus der Fünten (I had nothing to lose) and showed him my papers, but he said: *"Spielt keine Rolle,"*[190] and to Herz he said: *"Es wird nur noch auskwartiert."*[191] When the NIZ staff was taken to one side, I thought they might be released. Later on it emerged that only a few were let go. Apparently, a couple managed to go into hiding, that's to say, I saw Manuel Ossendrijver that Sunday, but the other week he turned up in the punishment barracks here.

We were herded to the station. This is it, I thought to myself; what I've been dreading so much is actually happening now. Cut loose and driven out. Luckily I hadn't had my luggage sent home yet (it was at the JC), so it could be forwarded. But Mother's suitcase was lost, because it was still at the Leuvenbergs, who had since been taken away and whose home would be "pulsed."

Still, I thought, they're bound to pass over the apartment in Pretoriusstraat; all the other people in the building are non-Jews, and very decent ones at that, and there was no name or *mezuzah*[192]

---

188   "Signed by *Obersturmführer* Wörlein."
189   "And I am Rennig."
190   "Those are irrelevant."
191   "From here on, it is all evacuation."
192   Small, decorative tube affixed to the door frame containing a piece of parchment with the prayer from Deuteronomy VI, verses 4–9, "Hear, O Israel" and XI, verses 18–20.

on the door yet. I had intended to put "Do not ring for letters" instead of my name on a plate the same size as the nameplates of the upstairs neighbours. After all, a removed nameplate means as much as "Jew." I also thought that they might not have found me so easily, for I had quite an excellent hiding-place. But I forced myself not to dwell on these things. This is how it is, now stop thinking about it!

At the station, the wagons were waiting. Goods wagons, cattle trucks rather. "*8 chevaux*," 8 horses, it said in French on the wall of my wagon. I hope to bring the story up to date tomorrow and then write more regularly again. It's nine o'clock and I'm going to hit the sack.

JEWISH COUNCIL OF AMSTERDAM

Minutes of the 95th meeting of the Central Commission held on Friday 28 May 1943 at 10.30 at Nieuwe Keizersgracht 58.

Attending: Professor Cohen, Chairman, Mrs Van Tijn, and Messrs Asscher, Aal, Blazer, Blüth, Cahen, A. Cohen, Diamand, Edersheim, Eitje, Hendrix, Kauffmann, Jacobs, Jacobson, Krouwer, Van der Laan, Moser, Van Oss, Sluzker, De Vries and Brandon, Secretary.

The Chairman opened the meeting and reported on the events of the past week. This week has been one of the most dreadful in the history of the Jews in Amsterdam. The flower of our nation has fallen victim to these events, which shall never be forgotten. Amsterdam has been described as a mother in Israel and the history of Jewry has taken root here as it has in few other places. A history stretching back 300 years has been destroyed in a single day. We watched the people on Houtmarkt and among them recognized many of our dearest friends; people whose forebears and who themselves have done a great deal for the Netherlands. They bore their ordeal with a dignity befitting the nobility of Judaism.

This leaves us to consider how to proceed with our work. But before we do so, we would like to express our gratitude for everything that those who are leaving have done, and to wish them the strength to bear this terrible fate. Let us hope for better times and await the liberation of, and reunion with, those we cannot do without.

Subsequently, the speaker reported on his meeting with Messrs Lages, Aus der Fünten and Blumenthal,[193] which took place last Thursday, 27 May. During this meeting we stated that our organisation had been decimated, and requested that some of our employees be released from Westerbork. Our request, however, was turned down. We must attempt to rebuild our organisation with the Jews who are still with us. The sole exceptions were made for Chief Rabbi Dasberg and Mrs Eitje. We have also been granted permission to submit a list of the deported wives and children of employees who were not taken to Westerbork. It is beyond dispute that the German authorities appreciate the continuation of the Jewish Council's work.

Subsequently, views were exchanged on the inventory of our remaining staff and the reorganisation of the departments.

It was decided to send out a circular instructing the heads of departments to draw up an inventory of their staff as a matter of urgency.

With regard to the question whether statements can be issued about those members of the Jewish Council who have received a call-up for forced labour in Germany, it was reported that no information can be given, but that in view of the transport, the question has probably become irrelevant.

The possible transfer of employees from departments with a surplus of workers to departments with a shortage will also be considered.

The next item on the agenda was the rearrangement of the card index. We intend to distribute a circular on the matter next week. Regarding this matter, the speaker is of the opinion that the heads of

193   Hans Blumenthal, the commander of the security police and security services in Amsterdam.

department must start thinking about the future reduction of their department.

Following some deliberation, the Chair said he would return to the issue soon and probably impose binding regulations.

Subsequently, the speaker called on the heads of department to pay no heed to the many rumours circulating in the Jewish community. The speaker is of the opinion that these may be attributed to a lack of discipline. Finally, in reply to a question, the Chair declared that members of the Jewish Council should not issue statements to the effect that an applicant does not appear on the transport lists.

The employees who worked in one of the offices on the day of the operation were asked to give the names of their deported wives. This request was complied with.

There being no further business, the Chair closed the meeting.

JOODSCHE RAAD VOOR AMSTERDAM.   Amsterdam, 2.6.1943.

Notulen van de 95ste vergadering van de Centrale Commissie, gehouden op Vrijdag, 28.5.1943 te 10.30 uur in het gebouw Nw.Keizersgracht 58.

Aanwezig Prof.Cohen, Voorzitter, Mevrouw Van Tijn en de heeren Asscher, Aal, Blazer, Blüth, Cahen, A.Cohen, Diamand, Edersheim, Eitje, Hendrix, Kauffmann, Jacobs, Jacobson, Krouwer, Van der Laan, Moser, Van Oss, Sluzker, De Vries en Brandon, Secretaris.

De Voorzitter opent de vergadering en doet verslag van de gebeurtenissen van de afgeloopen week. Deze week is één der vreeselijkste geweest in de geschiedenis der Amsterdamsche Joden. De bloem van onze menschen is daaraan ten slachtoffer gevallen en de gebeurtenissen zullen nimmer vergeten worden. Amsterdam is wel eens genoemd een moeder in Israel en de geschiedenis van het Jodendom is hier verankerd als op weinig andere plaatsen. In één dag is een geschiedenis van 300 jaar vernietigd. Wij hebben de menschen op de Houtmarkt gadegeslagen en daaronder veel van onze goede vrienden herkend; menschen die zelf en menschen, wier voorouders veel voor Israel hebben gedaan. Zij hebben het gedragen met een trots, waarin men de adel van het Jodendom kan herkennen.
Thans valt slechts te beraadslagen hoe het werk moet worden voortgezet.
Voor wij hiertoe overgaan, dienen wij een woord van dank uit te spreken voor alles, wat zij, die heengaan, hebben gedaan en hun de kracht toe te wenschen op het vreeselijke lot te dragen. Wij kunnen slechts gelooven in betere tijden en verwachten redding en hereeniging met hen, die wij niet kunnen missen.

Vervolgens geeft spreker een verslag van zijn onderhoud met de heeren Lages, Aus der Fünten en Blumenthal, welk onderhoud Donderdag j.l. heeft plaats gevonden. Bij dit onderhoud werd medegedeeld, dat onze organisatie stuk was gemaakt en wij verbonden daaraan het verzoek een aantal onzer medewerkers terug te mogen krijgen uit Westerbork. Dit werd echter afgewezen. Wij moeten trachten met de aanwezige Joden het apparaat weder op te bouwen. Slechts werd een uitzondering gemaakt voor Opperrabbi,' Dasberg en Mevrouw Eitje. Voorts mogen wij een lijst indienen van vrouwen en kinderen, die meegenomen zijn van hemp die op het bureau aan het werk waren en welke laatsten niet naar Westerbork zijn overgebracht. Vaststaat, dat de Duitsche autoriteiten de voortzetting van den arbeid van den Joodschen Raad op prijs stellen.
Over de wijze, waarop een inventarisatie zal plaats vinden van het aanwezige personeel en over de wijze, waarop de afdeelingen zullen worden gereorganiseerd, wordt vervolgens van gedachten gewisseld. Besloten wordt, een circulaire uit te sturen, waarbij den afdeelingchefs zal worden opgedragen met spoed een inventarisatie van de employé s te maken.
Omtrent de vraag, in hoeverre mededeelingen kunnen worden gedaan over degenen, die door den Joodschen Raad opgeroepen zijn voor tewerkstelling in Duitschland, wordt medegedeeld, dat hieromtrent niets kan worden gezegd, doch dat vermoedelijk de kwestie van de actie de aangelegenheid van het transport teniet heeft gedaan. Het eventueel overhevelen van employé s van afdeelingen, dien een surplus hebben aan werkkrachten naar afdeelingen, die daaraan tekort hebben, zal mede onder oogen worden gezien.
Over den opbouw van de kartotheek wordt vervolgens gesproken. Hieromtrent zal in de loop van de volgende week een circulaire worden uitgezonden. In dit verband meent spreker, dat reeds nu de afdeelingchefs zich moeten beraden op de toekomstige inkrimping van hun afdeeling. Na eenig debat zegt de Voorzitter hierop binnenkort terug te zullen komen, waarbij vermoedelijk de regeling van deze aangelegenheid zal worden opgelegd.
Vervolgens doet spreker een beroep op de afdeelingchefs te bevorderen, dat men zich niet stoort aan geruchten, die in de Joodsche gemeenschap rijkelijk circuleeren. Als grond daarvoor meent spreker, dat hieraan ten grondslag ligt een gebrek aan discipline.

Ten slotte wordt op een desbetreffende vraag geantwoord, dat het niet in de bedoeling ligt verklaringen af te geven, dat men niet op de transportlijst voorkomt. Gevraagd wordt nog op te geven die vrouwen, die op transport gesteld zijn van de employé s, die op één der bureaux op den dag van de actie hebben gewerkt, aan welk verzoek wordt voldaan.

Niets meer aan de orde zijnde sluit de Voorzitter de vergadering.

Protocol from the Central Committee meeting of the Joodsche Raad, 2 June 1943

Author's collection

Westerbork

My darling,

I'm all alone in the school at the moment. "Alone" is a relative notion, for there are at least 100 children outside, with all the noise that playing children make. But with all my bosses gone out, I can write to you for a bit. That said, someone could walk in any moment and require my attention. Of course you have no idea what I'm talking about, but once I've told you the whole story, this opening will make sense.

I had got as far as our arrival at the station. As I wrote, this was an extremely difficult moment. I kept looking around me to see if there was any chance of escape, but there wasn't. Hundreds and hundreds of people filled the platform, nothing but familiar faces, of course. All the bosses! Imbach, head of the Emigration Division at Lijnbaansgracht; Heynemann, head of the Westerbork office; Van der Reiss, head of the Food Division; Henri Gomperts, head of JV4;[1] etc., etc. The wagons were unbearably hot. And we had to sit on the floor, of course. Now this matters little to me, but imagine the elderly people. Besides, people kept fainting, while some suffered panic attacks and others had their hands trampled on so they were bleeding. It was a pitiful sight. The train was interminable, and still more people filed onto the platform, huffing and puffing with

1 The Jewish Association for Care and Nursing, a division of the Joodsche Raad.

159

their heavy luggage. Some, elderly people and parents with young children, sat on top of their luggage on the platform, waiting for someone to help them onto the train. Just like migrants.

Many were in tears, naturally, while others just sat there staring. Children were wailing, there was screaming and shouting, but also some jolly greetings, such as "You here as well?" from spirited youngsters. I found a fairly acceptable wagon that wasn't quite as jam-packed as the others because it had all the bigwigs. We also had a decent black policeman (every wagon was escorted by a member of the black police), who kept the connecting doors open to give us (and himself) a little fresh air. The transport from Central Amsterdam had consisted of passenger trains deporting 2,800 people. This transport, however, was made up of cattle trucks deporting 2,400 people. The train left at three, and was extremely slow because, of course, the engine had trouble pulling this long train. The pregnant women suffered most. There was one in our wagon, and considering the special care these women require and seeing them trodden on, jostled and thrown about, and thinking how this will affect these women, you realized just how low we had sunk. The train stopped hardly anywhere, only in Zwolle, where the station staff treated us very well and filled our canteens with water. As I mentioned before, I didn't have anything with me, but everybody shared with me. The journey went well, and at around nine o'clock we arrived in Westerbork.

I forgot to tell you that in Amsterdam the people were standing on the roofs of their houses, with binoculars, watching us go. A fine spectacle indeed! And while we were sitting there on the floor of that sluggish train, passing the beautiful forests and places such as Bussum and Hilversum, where we used to spend our holidays in such completely different circumstances, I did feel a bit sorry for myself. But I kept thinking: Don't dwell on it, just wait and see what happens next. Others went through all this a year ago.

When we got off the train at nine o'clock, we thought we'd seen the worst. But this was only the beginning. The first familiar person to call out to me was Juul. Although she wasn't allowed to approach the new arrivals, I did hear and see her. A moment later I spotted Father and Bob, who weren't allowed to come near me either. I joined an endless queue for the *Registratur,*[2] where we had to be registered. And we waited... There I spoke with Blüth, who said: "You don't look right, you should be looking sad." "So far I have no reason to," I said. At the *Registratur*, I had to hand in my identity card and ration card as well as my food coupons, but I pretended not to have any. You had to state your name and date of birth countless times. Actually, I have all but forgotten the many authorities we filed past, but the long and the short of it is that I ended up with De Vries, who submitted a so-called *Antrag,*[3] which meant that I would be held in Westerbork on the basis of my Palestine papers. I believe I have already written to you about this Palestine issue. It's important here, much more important than you might think. The *Antrag* was submitted and recorded on the *Lagerkarte*[4] I had received by then, and which serves as Westerbork's identity card, and off I went.

Outside I met a former colleague, who offered to keep my money for me until I'd been to see Lippmann-Rosenthal, which confiscates all the money.[5] To be absolutely safe, I also gave him my fountain pen, because you never know if they will confiscate it after a body search. And then — it was night by now — we had to wait again, for hours and hours on end. In open country, on damp soil — it was quite chilly at night — sitting, lying, half-sleeping in the dark. Again, bearable for me, but an ordeal for the elderly and sick. Many were carried away on stretchers.

After several hours I decided to join the queue, or my turn would never come. I came across many of my colleagues, among

---

2   The Registration Office.
3   Request.
4   Camp card.
5   Representatives of the Lippmann-Rosenthal Bank in Westerbork, the bank that was under German control, confiscated the money and valuables of the Jews that arrived at the camp.

Westerbork camp work card issued to Mirjam Levie, 2 July 1943
Author's collection

them Lex W. At long last, we found ourselves in a small building again — they're all wooden barracks — first at the JC, which took your money, counted it, returned it and gave you a receipt saying how much money you had. Then back to waiting and to Lippmann, where there were no Jews, of course. It was quite simple in my case. I gave them ƒ0.75 and when they asked me why I had so little, I told them that I'd been picked up off the street. But others were shouted at and searched, stripped, etc. When we were done there, we had to go to the quarantine section, where we had to undress and were checked for lice. It was embarrassing, to be sure, but there would be worse to come in that respect. At around five in the morning, we were taken to a barracks. Meanwhile I had come across a friend, and as she had been assigned to the same barracks we agreed that, if at all possible, we would stay together. By the time the beds were allocated, I'd lost sight of my friend, Jenny Spits (married now and going by the name of Jenny Sanders), but the person allocating me my bed was a former colleague and now a barracks leader here. She promised to reserve the bed next to mine for Jenny. I was given a good spot, next to the window. A barracks is a large, rectangular wooden building with windows. Alongside the windows and in the middle are beds, three-tier bunk beds, some in pairs, like twin beds, others individually. The bed frames are made of iron, with a base of intertwined iron slats. Add a straw mat and you're done. But let me assure you, I clambered into bed — I was on the second tier — and fell asleep at once. I took off my slip, covered myself with a blanket that Liesl Chevalier — the barracks leader I just mentioned — had given me, and slept. Up early and washed, with some borrowed things, in the washroom. At the end of every barracks is a rectangular area that has been partitioned off, with a metal trough in the middle and taps on either side. This is where you wash.

There's a flushable toilet as well, which may only be used at night and which is indescribably filthy. In the middle of the barracks is a kind of corridor and on the other side is a similar ward. In other words, there's a small corridor, called the kitchen — which is to say that the food is distributed there — a big ward on either side and at either end of those wards a washroom with 20 taps and a lavatory. Finally, both wards have a few tables near the kitchen.

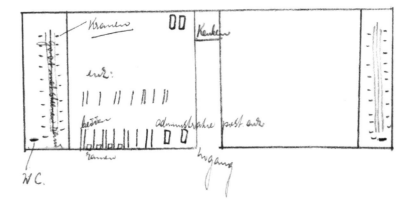

Let me now give you a technical description of the camp. From the small town of Hooghalen, a paved road brings you to the camp.

To the right of it runs a narrow railway spur, built after the camp had already opened. The transports come and go along this spur. In the old days, people had to walk from Hooghalen to the camp, carrying their luggage. It must have taken at least an hour. Nowadays, the train pulls into the camp itself. Whenever a wagon-load of parcels and the like arrives, it continues to the far end of the camp, to the barracks where they're registered and distributed. From there, the parcels are taken in wheelbarrows to the appropriate barracks. A list of recipients is pinned up, and they can then claim their parcels at the barracks' administration desk. Sometimes they're given a green ticket, which they have to take to the luggage barracks where they can collect their parcel.

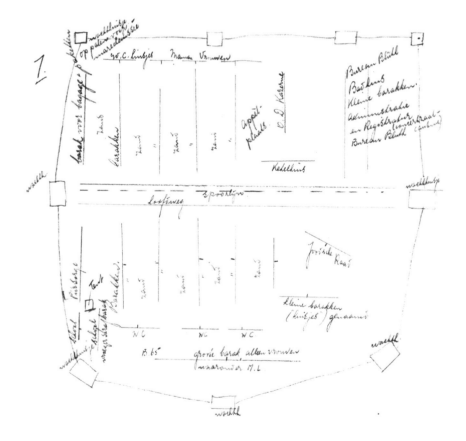

The transport train pulls into the camp on Mondays, and stays on the main thoroughfare for the rest of that day and night. We then clean and prepare the train for departure. The barracks are situated to the left and right of the main thoroughfare, most of them at right angles. I've already described the structure of one such barracks. They are completely symmetrical in that opposite the entrance is another door, so that, should you wish so, you could have the entrance on the other side. However, most of the barracks are paired, with their entrances facing one another. At right angles to the barracks, which are made of timber, are the latrines. These are small, red brick structures, built on the same principle as the barracks: the entrance in the middle and either side identical. Some of them belong to the barracks next to them, in which men sleep on one side and women on the other (here they call it "living," which still sounds odd to me, although it is actually more appropriate than "sleeping," for you really do live in them). One side bears the inscription "NUR FÜR MÄNNER,"[6] and the other, "NUR FÜR FRAUEN."[7] My barracks is a women's barracks and has its own small structure, "NUR FÜR FRAUEN." You enter and then, on your left and right, there's a single, large timber "box" with holes in it, eight holes on either side, without a lid and without a door. Some have wooden partitions between every two holes, others don't. These are commonly known as "egg stands."

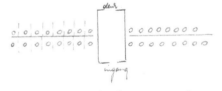

You enter and check what's free. So everybody is sitting there in plain view and everybody's noises are clearly audible. At first you're dead embarrassed, but you know you have to get used to everything, so you try to get over the shame straight away. And these lavatories are always filthy, because people don't want to sit on them and miss the hole when peeing or doing other things. Think

6 "Men Only."
7 "Women Only."

of diarrhoea...! I'm giving you a rather vivid description here, but this is our everyday reality. These lavatories are truly degrading, at odds with any sense of human dignity.

The entire camp is enclosed by barbed-wire fences and a ditch, and at regular intervals are small watchtowers on posts, made entirely of glass, from which a military policeman, who oversees part of the camp, ensures that nobody escapes. All the same, apparently once in a while somebody does escape, but when that happens everybody is terrified because they threaten us with firing squads. Usually, some extra punishment cases are put on a transport. On the whole the military police are decent, and peeved at having to work under the Germans. Right next to the camp is the house of the commandant and other Hun officials, whose numbers are few here. Monday is the only day of the week when this place is swarming with green police, the transport escort.

I've already described the transport train. But I should add that at the front and at the rear are cars with passenger compartments for the German guards. In addition to the big barracks there are small ones, or "little houses." These are built on the same principle, only they have partitions to create rooms, a proper lavatory and a kitchen in the hallway — in short, a "mansion" compared to the so-called "large barracks." To the left and right of the railway spur are the barracks of the JC, the *Registratur*, which doubles as a concert hall, the bathhouse, the boiler house, with a few taps outside where you can fetch boiling water throughout the day, the laundry, Blüth's office, the quarantine barracks, the smithy, the saddlery (for the Huns' horses), the carpenter's workshop, the hospital barracks, the outpatients' clinic, the storeroom, the kitchen, a separate kitchen for potato peeling, etc., etc., etc. At the entrance, there's another watchtower on posts and also a small timber hut on the ground, with military police. *That's all.* I cannot give you the size of the barracks, as I have no sense of dimension, but our barracks, which is one of the "large barracks," holds around 1,000 people, so you see they're huge, long things.

Thus far, my broad sketch of the camp's structure. Behind the boiler house is a large, open space, the *Appellplatz*, the roll-call area. This is where people must report for transport. I hope I'll never be able to tell you about the procedure, because it would mean that I had gone on a transport myself. When there are no transports, those on outdoor duty must report here as well. I'll tell you about "outdoor duty" some other time.

On to our daily routine and other technical details. At half-past five in the morning we hear: "Ladies, rise!" Our barracks has 1,000 women, i.e., 500 on each side. Only women, with their children. Most of the barracks have men in one ward, women on the other. No tables, no chairs; you eat, live and sleep on your bed. And unless you live on the third tier, you cannot sit up straight without hitting your head against the tier above. Besides, the beds wobble badly every time somebody climbs in or out, causing you to spill food, for example. And again, none of this matters much to me. I'm agile and quick enough to avoid accidents. But think of elderly people who are stiff! Not to mention the noise of all those hundreds of people. And to collect food you have to queue in the narrow corridors, etc.

Shabbat, 17 July 1943

I'm on the train from Zwolle to Assen[8] at the moment, hence this wonderful handwriting. But I want to write you a few lines, just for the curiosity of it, now that I'm back from holiday. That's right, I had a proper holiday, in Amsterdam. I even managed to write you a Red Cross letter. This train is jolting too much, my writing is "all over the place." I'll bring my story up to date soon. With lots of kisses, as soon as possible.

---

8   The capital of the Drenthe province in north-eastern Holland, not far from Westerbork.

19 July 1943

Today is Monday, the day before the transport.[9] Let me try to convey the atmosphere we live in here, although I already know that is impossible.

On Shabbat, I arrived back at around eight in the evening after a bumpy ride in a truck. Father and Freddy were waiting for me at the camp's entrance (or let me call it exit here). I didn't even feel all that miserable. In the old days, whenever I went back to Beverwijk,[10] I used to feel much worse. Anyway, I turned straight to Freddy and told him that he would get a travel permit for Amsterdam. He replied: "It's too late." I couldn't believe my ears. "What do you mean?" I said. "The Palestine List is *geplatzt*."[11] Bang, there it was. I'd been expecting it all along, and even discussed the matter in Amsterdam, but everybody there thought the Palestine List was a cast-iron certainty. But every time they said so, I would respond: "But surely the transport quota must be filled somehow!" So now the time had come. Father and Freddy told me that in the afternoon an announcement had been read out in the barracks to the effect that the people on the Palestine List should prepare for possible deportation. Father was still safe, because he was on the list of people with confirmed Palestine certificates. Exactly a week ago we had received a Red Cross letter confirming this. The question remained whether this also included Bobby, but it was bound to, because the Red Cross letter said "and family." As for my own status, I wasn't really sure, but I wasn't too worried. Father and I sat down on a step and I told him a few things. Later we moved down inside the

---

9 The transports to Auschwitz and Sobibor left every Tuesday.
10 See p. 76, fn. 101
11 "Collapsed." The camp commandant, SS *Obersturmführer* Albert Konrad Gemmeker, ordered the inspection of the Palestine applications, because there were not enough people for the planned transport to Auschwitz of 20 July 1943. Those who possessed a "numbered certificate" would be allowed to stay in Westerbork.

Het Nederlandsche Roode Kruis

No. **290424**

g. H C a.

➡ Formulier, na invulling, in te zenden aan het CORRESPONDENTIE-
BUREAU van het Nederlandsche Roode Kruis, Jan Pieterszl Coen-
straat 10, Den Haag, Tel. 770517.

VERZOEK
door tusschenkomst van het Duitsche Roode Kruis aan het
Internationale Comité van het Roode Kruis te Genève om inlichtingen.

ANTRAG
durch das Deutsche Rote Kreuz an das Internationale Komitee
vom Roten Kreuz in Genf auf Nachrichtenvermittlung.

1. Afzender   E.Bolle-v.Praag,
    Absender   (naam, voornaam en adres)
              (Name, Taufname und Adresse)

       N.Keizersgracht 62, Amsterdam.

       Verzoekt aan
        Bittet an

2. Geadresseerde   Leo Bolle,   P.O.B. 1085,(David Building)
    Empfänger   (naam, voornaam en adres)   Jerusalem
             (Name, Taufname und Adresse)   Palestine.

       het volgende mede te deelen :
        folgendes zu übermitteln:

(ten hoogste 25 woorden uitsluitend persoon-
lijke en familieaangelegenheden betreffende)
(Höchstzahl 25 Worte nur persönliche und
Familienangelegenheiten betreffend)

     Hartelyk gefeleciteerd verjaardag Hopenlyk
     volgende samen met Mirjam Levies op Wester-
     bork staan op veteranenlyst twee
     Je schoonmoeder woont by ons
     Houdt goeden moed   Veel liefs

     12/7'43.   Handteekening
                                  Unterschrift

3. Geadresseerde antwoordt aan ommezijde :
  Empfänger antwortet umseitig

A Red Cross letter from Els Bolle to Leo, written on 12 July 1943, in which
she sends regards on his birthday: "Warm wishes for your birthday. In the
hope that next year you will be together with Mirjam. The Levie family in
Westerbork is on the veterans list no. 2. Your mother-in-law is living with
us. Be strong. With love, Els and Father"

Author's collection

camp. Spirits were leaden. Everybody I knew looked terrified and I was almost afraid to say hello to them, because I was still safe and had just had a pleasant week. Wherever you went, you heard the words "Palestine" and "certificate." Whenever you met somebody and asked "How are you?" you'd hear nothing but "bad" or "dire." When you think that there are approximately 2,000 people on the Palestine List, virtually all friends and acquaintances, you can imagine what it must feel like to see all these people go into the unknown on Tuesday.

That's when I heard about the Heertje case, which gives you something of an idea of the intrigues and *Schiebereien*[12] here. Heertje is my uppermost boss, a young man and a true gentleman, who put a great deal of effort into organising the school system nine months ago, under insane circumstances, which I hope to explain to you in person, because they would be impossible, and I mean impossible, to describe. More later. It's a quarter-to nine; I'm going to hit the sack and want to continue writing in bed. Heertje is a Dutchman, and suddenly received word that his red stamp, earned on merit, had become invalid. It turned out that he had been accused of anti-German campaigning. A Dutch woman who had her eye on his job was said to have brought this story to the attention of the German-Jewish authorities. They investigated the matter at once, with the result that after nine months of hard work he will be put on a transport. The *"alte Kampfeinsassen"*[13] have now complained to Schlesinger,[14] the Jewish camp leader, and a report is on its way to the camp commandant. It means that Heertje will probably

12 Shenanigans.
13 The old or established German-Jewish camp inmates, who had been in Westerbork since before the war.
14 Kurt Schlesinger had fled Nazi Germany and had been in Westerbork since 1939. When, on the orders of the German occupier, a comprehensive Jewish camp leadership consisting of 12 divisions was set up, Schlesinger became the camp leader. The camp leadership had to draw up weekly lists of 1,020 people for deportation. The most important positions in the camp were occupied by German refugees.

not have to leave this week, but it depends on the commandant's response to the report. Either he leaves, or somebody else does. This is how it goes. One Jew condemning another Jew to deportation. We have sunk low. The background to all of this will have to wait until some other time. Now I'm going to hit the sack.

20 July 1943

Preparations for the transport are underway again. I'll tell you a bit more in the meantime. Leo Seeligmann just came to see me, and gave me the names of those who are going on the transport. Tiny van der Heyden, Izak de Jong, Rabbi Vredenburg, Rabbi Maarsen, the scribe Joune Norden, Mia Cohen-Mendelson (who has been here for months and has done extremely well), Meyer Pinkhof, Leo Pinkhof, Elie Ichenhäuser, Daniel Klein, A.T. Kleerekoper, Ro Hartog and parents. In short, almost everyone. I had wanted to tell you about yesterday, about queuing at the JC for hours on end to try and learn something or get something done, about the enquiries, whenever you meet someone, knowing full well that the JC is powerless, but you have no other connections and besides, they would be powerless, too. But I'm too preoccupied with the transport.

You see the lights come on at around three or four o'clock in the morning (as it happens, I had a bad cough last night, which kept me awake), and then the barracks leader yells: "Attention please, ladies!" And then it begins. Everybody whose name is called out must respond "Yes." Some, most, respond with a firm "Yes." Others cry. And even when you know your name isn't on the list, you still break out in a cold sweat, with your heart pounding furiously. To hear all those familiar names! And you only hear the names of those in your own barracks. You don't hear the others until later, since you're not allowed out of the barracks until the transport has left. Only those with valid stamps are allowed out after seven in the morning, as the people are making their way to the train. It would be impossible to mention every single case. Below me (i.e., on the bunk below mine) "lives" a woman whose only daughter, who is 17, has gone to Poland, and who has only one wish: to see her again. She doesn't worry about the transport at all. Another woman they forgot to call up, and her husband is waiting in the roll-call area. For at least there's one consolation: Husbands and wives, indeed families, leave together. What happens at the border, nobody knows. The dying, the infirm, children (the scarlet fever barracks was among those deported today). In a word, the leitmotif is this: I can't describe it.

And the mentality of those who stay behind! Like vultures, they swoop on the things people had to leave behind, because they may only take rucksacks, bread-bags and blankets. People end up taking pretty much everything, but they all leave the odd thing behind. On the other hand, it has to be said that everybody helps packing, and many give away their own things, if necessary. But then there's also the mentality of those in mixed marriages who are allowed to return to Amsterdam for possible sterilization, which is simply sickening. Leo Seeligmann just told me that he overheard one saying to another: "Aren't we lucky with our *shiksa*."[15] The people who are deported are, on the whole, very brave. Last week, one wagon sang *"Hatikvah,"*[16] the Jewish anthem; another, *"Houd er de moed maar in."*[17] I take my hat off to those people.

Let me tell you what a wagon looks like. It's a cattle truck, without light and usually bearing the inscription: 8 *chevaux*, 40 *hommes*.[18] In it are: a barrel with a tap, containing drinking water; an upright bucket covered with a square, wooden board that serves

15 A derogatory term for a non-Jewish woman, from the Yiddish. The source is the Hebrew word *shikutz*, meaning loathsome.
16 "Hatikvah" means hope. Since 1907, it has been the anthem of the Zionist movement; today it is Israel's national anthem.
17 "Keep your spirits up," a popular Dutch song.
18 8 horses, 40 people.

as a lid; and a sand bag. *C'est tout.*[19] And instead of 40, at least 60 people are packed inside these wagons, for at least three days and three nights. The sick are crammed together in wagons with mattresses on the floor. Every wagon has a Jewish *Zugführer,*[20] and at the front and rear of the train are carriages with some green police. I can't vouch for the accuracy of that last sentence, because luckily I haven't been through it myself yet. As the train pulls out a shrill whistle is blown, and what goes on in your mind at that point...

And imagine — Mrs Van der Heyden-Jacobson, the daughter of an extremely wealthy man, is off, without a destination, without knowing whereto, dressed like a tramp (the people look ridiculous, because they wear all their clothes for fear they'll be taken from them). Even if the conditions are no worse than in Westerbork, the uncertainty, being away from the Netherlands and being part of the immense Jewish problem in Poland, would be enough to drive you mad. But you know, don't you Leo, that when our turn comes, I'll be strong. At least we still have the good fortune to have you in *Eretz Yisrael* and to have a certificate waiting for us. I remain hopeful that this will get us out soon, as long as we can get hold of a postage stamp for a letter to you. But perhaps even this is too optimistic.

Before I stop, I want to tell you briefly about Freddy. Things were looking bad for him, because he hadn't received confirmation from Palestine. He had shown Marinus Kan your Red Cross letter, in which you'd written about his appointment as a youth leader for potential children's transports to Palestine. Kan had inadvertently taken it to Amsterdam, and when I was there last week, I asked for the letter back. It was delivered in Westerbork by courier (Kan couldn't find it while I was in Amsterdam), was recognized, and Freddy exempted on the basis of it. Sheer luck and coincidence!

19 That's all.
20 Train leader.

Write in Block Capitals

In grossen Druckbuchstaben auszufuellen

WAR ORGANISATION OF THE BRITISH RED CROSS AND ORDER OF ST. JOHN
Postal Message Scheme

From:

To:
Comité International
de la Croix Rouge
Genève

P.O.B. 1085,
David Building,
Jerusalem,
PALESTINE.

ENQUIRER
Fragesteller

Name _____ Bolle

Christian name _____ Leo
Vorname

Address _____

c/o P.O.B. 1085
JERUSALEM.

PALESTINE.
PASSED BY
CENSOR

Message — Mitteilung.
(Message not to exceed 25 words, family news of strictly personal character).
(Nicht über 25 Worte, nur persönliche Familiennachrichten).

JEUGDCERTIFICATEN HOLLAND. JEWISH AGENCY
JOU, FREDDY JUUL ALS BEGELEIDERS ERKEND,
MIS JOU ONTZETTEND . BID VÜRIG ONZE
VERLOSSING EINDELIJK ZAL KOMEN. VOLGEND
JAAR IN JERUZALEM

Date _____ 12. IV. 43

ADDRESSEE
Empfänger

Name _____ Levie

Christian name _____ Mirjam
Vorname

Address _____ Muidergracht 29
Amsterdam/Holland

4 MAI 1943

50000—28.8.42—G.C.P.

Red Cross letter from Leo to Mirjam, written on 12 April 1943: "Youth immigration certificates [for] Holland. [Via] the Jewish Agency. You, Freddy [and] Juul are needed to accompany them. I miss you terribly. I fervently pray that you will finally arrive at our redemption. Next year in Jerusalem." Due to this certificate, Freddy was not sent to the east.

Author's collection

If you had written that letter a fortnight later, if I hadn't gone to Amsterdam… The opposite happens, too. An acquaintance called me on Shabbat morning in Amsterdam to say that she was on her way to collect a registered letter for Mr Birnbaum. The letter came from Bern, and when I told Birnbaum in Westerbork he was overjoyed, for these would be the entry visas for Honduras, on the basis of which they would be exempted. The parcel didn't reach Westerbork in time and the family was deported. Perhaps the visas will arrive tomorrow. Fate, fate, fate. Bye my darling, more tomorrow.

21 July 1943

Let me continue with our daily routine now. As I mentioned, at half-past five, somebody yells "Rise!" and then the ward leader shouts: "Anybody sick?" This is when you report sick if necessary. You get up and wash in the washroom, and when it was still very crowded here you have to be quick or the water runs out. Wash, dress and eat. There's coffee in the morning, or something hot, anyway; I never know whether it's coffee or tea and I hardly ever drink it, because I was never in the habit of drinking in the morning and therefore don't need it. What I miss most is the water. The water here tastes of metal, contains iron, and is said to be bad for people who aren't used to drinking it, although it's quite healthy in itself. Eat bread. At seven o'clock, all the women aged 16 to 40 must assemble outside the barracks from where they're taken to the roll-call area, to do outdoor duty. The camp has various work commandos, so-called *Dienstbereiche*.[21] Outdoor duty is one of them, utterly pointless work, lugging pails of sand or carrying turf. It was introduced to stop people from wandering idly round the camp, to create the impression of a labour camp. I

21 Work divisions.

also spent a morning doing it. I was still with Jenny at the time. We had to assemble in the roll-call area and hand in our camp cards. I didn't have mine with me, so I could have sloped off if I had wanted to. It was ridiculous; they didn't carry out any checks. A foreman was in charge, telling us what to do. We were taken some place and given a wooden pail and a plank, and then we had to go to a sandy area to fill the pail with sand, but not too full or it would be too quick. Then two of you carry the pail and saunter through the camp to another place where the pail is emptied into a minuscule puddle. Back again, and 15 minutes to recover from your efforts. That morning the men had to carry turf, and they looked ridiculous as they sauntered past, each of them with a piece of turf under their arm like a briefcase. But what's really wretched is that all of these people wandering about here used to do such useful work.

But when the *Untersturmführer*[22] puts in an appearance, the work is done at a furious pace and the pails must be brimming with sand. Then it's an extremely arduous task, of course, from a quarter-past seven until half-past twelve, and from a quarter-to two until half-past six. You know I'm prone to back pains, and although my pails weren't full, my back did bother me. The next day I asked for a note for the outpatients' clinic, and told them the saga of my slipped vertebrae and the plaster cast.[23] The doctor who examined me was quite decent, said that he didn't doubt the veracity of my story and that I was certain to suffer here as well, but that he couldn't declare me *dienstfrei*[24] or unfit for outdoor duty as long as I wasn't stiff. When I argued that it would be too late then, that I would have to lie flat on my back for weeks on end, he said: "Certainly, but there's nothing I can do." A fine attitude, don't you think? I'm sure there was nothing he could do. Duty is duty. On the other hand,

22 The first commissioned SS officer rank, equivalent to a second lieutenant.
23 At the age of 15, Mirjam took a fall in a gymnastics class, and as a result spent 10 months lying in a plaster cast.
24 Exempt from work.

27.6.43   Fur die Baaackenleitung
von 65

Hierdurch teile ich Ihnen mit,
Levie, Mirjam, 20.3.17 fur die
Schule bei der Arbeitseinteilung an-
gefordert worden ist und von heute
ab in der Schule arbeitet.

Gruppenleitung
i.A.

Notice pronouncing Mirjam's placement in the school at Westerbork, 27 June 1943
Author's collection

there are doctors who, when you ply them with cigarettes, declare you unfit at the drop of a hat. The following day I was genuinely sick, with diarrhoea and lots of vomiting, and the day after, when I was still *dienstfrei,* one of Jenny's connections got me a job helping the secretary of the school administration. This is where I am now, typing silly notes (scraps of paper with one or two lines) and doing nothing most of the day. That explains why I have a typewriter at my disposal and I can write to you. The working hours are short, too; starting at eight instead of seven, and finishing at five. And it does not ruin your clothes the way outdoor duty does.

Well then: Out of the barracks at eight o'clock. The women aged 40–50 have to assemble in front of the barracks at half-past seven. They go to the potato kitchen, and spend about four hours peeling potatoes. Women with small children and women over 60 need not work. I have already mentioned the *Dienstbereiche.*

There is also indoor duty, women keeping the barracks clean, and the *Ordnungsdienst*, acting as police and stretcher-bearers. Every *Dienstbereich* has a *Gruppenleiter*[25] and a *Stellvertretend Gruppenleiter*.[26] These people are always *alte Kampfeinsassen*. I've mentioned their bitterness before, but I never imagined that their feelings ran so high. They have all become psychopaths, unable to see beyond the narrow confines of the part of the camp they control, and oblivious to the real world out there. They're filled with such hatred that they sent Imbach, the head of the JC's former Emigration Division, on a transport, because they thought it was his fault that so many were unable to emigrate.[27] They get away with it, too, because of course the commandant doesn't care who goes on the transport, as long as he can fill the quota required by Berlin and The Hague, respectively. The *Registratur* (where only *alte Kampfeinsassen* work) draws up the lists, so if anyone has a "connection" among the *alte Kampfeinsassen* who is prepared to help, can get his name crossed off the transport list. Needless to say, he will be replaced by somebody else. It's sickening, this cronyism. It's just like it was in Amsterdam, with the difference that in Amsterdam nobody said, "I want this or that man to go to Poland," which is what happens here, but only "This or that man must *not* go to Poland" (so another had to go in his place, of course). A very subtle difference.

Home at half-past twelve, pick up bread on your camp card for the next day — I have a hot meal at the school — potter about for a bit, and back to school. If your shoes need repairing, you can report this in the barracks. If you have no money you don't have to pay, which is rather odd at first (you can, if you have an account with Lippmann, cash up to 30 guilders a month). You can also apply for a laundry ticket and have your laundry done (once

25 Group leader.
26 Deputy group leader.
27 Imbach, a German Jew, was himself interested in leaving Holland, but did not succeed.

every couple of weeks). Women also receive a smoker's card, unlike in Amsterdam, and there's a canteen where you can buy cigarettes and lemonade and even under-the-counter butter, but the place is always so packed I haven't set foot in it yet. There are concerts every night, which is rather sinister, and even a revue. Thankfully, there's no concert on the eve of a transport. The commandant has a taste for these concerts, you see, and he insists on people attending them. He seems to have quite a soft spot for culture in general. He often listens in on singing lessons at the school, always with a large entourage. The conductor Hans Krieg is here, and he teaches the children songs, some of them in Hebrew and some in canon, and the sound of those hundreds of children singing is marvellous.

Once every couple of weeks you can have your hair cut. All these are special privileges reserved for people with a stamp. Once every two weeks you're allowed to write, either two postcards or a letter. There's censorship and you're not allowed to write about the camp's internal affairs, i.e., not about outdoor duty or about the transports and who has been deported. Naturally, some letters get smuggled out, e.g., by carpenters on the odd visit to the camp, military police, etc. On the eve of transports, we have a so-called *Notbereitschaft* (NB),[28] also "jokingly" known as the Nebbish Brigade,[29] and a *Fliegende Kolonne* (FK),[30] which must help carry luggage and is also recruited from long-term inmates. Finally, there's a *Fürsorge*[31] department, where you can go and ask for food or luggage if you can't obtain them any other way. Practically everything I own right now (remember, I arrived with nothing) comes from the *Fürsorge*. This is a story in itself, for although this "Fou" is extremely well stocked, thanks to all the luggage and food left by people who have already been deported, it will only give hand-outs after

28 Emergency Squad.
29 "Nebbish," from the Yiddish, means pitiful, ineffectual, meek.
30 Flying Column.
31 Welfare.

much begging, because when its supplies dwindle, its staff may be reduced, too, and they're scared to death of losing their job. Again, these are *alte Kampfeinsassen*, who fear that when their turn comes they will be the first to go if they have no — or less important — work. The people who expect to go on a transport, and find out on Monday that they have no, say, handkerchiefs, can't actually obtain any during the day and have to wait until Monday night, because there is always the chance that they will be released at the last minute.

I've given you just about all the technical details now. This leaves me to say that cigarettes open all doors. Everything here is corrupt to the core. I told you about the Heertje case, but intrigues are rife and I'm simply not cunning enough to understand it all. The fact is that a handful of German Jews are in charge and are the uncrowned kings of the camp.

My story has become rather muddled. And of course I have forgotten things. With so many new impressions it would be impossible to remember and record everything. I hope the time will come when I can tell you in person. "Speedily in our days, Amen."[32]

23 July 1943

My darling,

Freddy is going back to Amsterdam!!!!! We can't quite believe it; it's too good to be true. It has left me completely distraught. Of course it's wonderful for him, but for me it's very difficult to come to terms with, because he means so much to me. Freddy and Juul were in a real state themselves. Last week they were about to be sent to Poland, this week to Amsterdam. They're leaving tomorrow!! You're torn between such extremes of sorrow and joy here, you need a cast-iron constitution to cope with it all. Salomon Eitje is going back as

---

32 Quote from the Jewish *Amidah* prayer, the Eighteen Benedictions.

well, whereas his son Elie was sent on this week. A very bitter pill indeed. Freddy and Juul don't know yet whether they can return to their old apartment; it has been put under seal, but will probably be released now. It's odd, and perhaps difficult to imagine, but I'm completely devastated. And to make matters worse, just now somebody told me that Churchill is said to have spoken of 1944 or 1945 as the end of the war. At any other, level-headed, moment, I would have said: "He tells us something different every week, but never the truth," but now I can't bear it. The strange thing is that, now that we've lost our house, I don't have such a strong desire to go back. And yet, I'm devastated at the thought of having to stay here for many more months. I hope I can go on leave about once a month and that Mother will receive an *Ausweis* that will allow her to stay in Amsterdam, so Father can return there and they can be billeted together somewhere. Well, let's wait and see what happens. The only solution that remains: peace. This alone will lift the weight that presses down upon us in the most literal sense of the word. But please don't think that I'm always moping and that I'm never happy. I am, believe me, but I haven't been able to breathe freely or sigh with happiness for years now, not since the day you left. Let's hope… I'm starting to repeat myself. I'm going to eat now. It's Friday and *shul* is at a quarter-to eight. Bye, my dearest, I simply had to pour my heart out to you. I desperately need your comfort, my sweetheart.

24 July 1943

I'm over my rotten mood again, since so much has happened in the meantime. Yesterday evening I received a letter from your father telling me he'd had a Red Cross letter from you, in which you expressed the hope of seeing me soon. That was just what I needed. I was already sick with longing for you, only to learn that three months ago you wrote to say you were expecting me soon.

Yet another failure. But at the same time I think to myself: Perhaps sooner or later I'll see Leo again.

Saw off Freddy and Juul this morning. I wasn't nervous anymore, nor was I yesterday evening, when they came to say goodbye. They left at seven o'clock.

And now Bobby is going home!! Goodness knows how this came about. When I was in Amsterdam last week, nothing was being done on her behalf, and yet this afternoon she received a letter saying she'll be released on Monday! The most bizarre things are happening here. Just now, a transport carrying 800 people from the JC arrived from Amsterdam, and they say the rest are coming tomorrow. It had people, e.g., my friend Jenny, who returned to Amsterdam on Shabbat last week, because either they or their spouse had received an *Ausweis*. And now they're back again. The Huns are playing with us. We're glad now that Mother didn't get the *Ausweis*, so at least she's not on that list.

Imagine: At half-past twelve Freddy and Juul arrive in Amsterdam, and at three o'clock 800 people leave for Westerbork. This transport took place in decent passenger cars. And it's strange: I no longer yearn to go back. But I should like nothing better than to go on leave again. A lot of people from the transport are filing in now. I can no longer write in peace. I hope to catch up on the typewriter tomorrow. You can't say that our lives are dull. In fact, I wouldn't mind if they were a bit duller. Something different every day. Palermo and Orel have fallen[33] and there's fighting in the Strait of Messina... *who knows*. Goodnight, my darling.

---

33 On 10 July 1943, the Allies invaded Sicily; the city of Palermo was occupied on 22 July 1943. The town of Messina in the north-east of the island was conquered on 16 August 1943. At the Orel enclave (north of Kursk) near the Soviet Union, fierce fighting took place between 10 July and 18 August 1943, during which the Germans retreated from the entire region. The Soviets occupied Orel on 5 August 1943.

Sunday afternoon, 25 July 1943

My darling,

Something new every day! Bobby isn't going to Amsterdam. A great disappointment. This morning, it turned out to be a mistake. Isn't that a pity? She was very disappointed, naturally. And I'm particularly sorry for Mother, although she knew nothing of this saga. We never mentioned it to her, or she would have been doubly upset by Bob not coming. They had simply sent the discharge letter to the wrong person. She's almost over it. I'm going to give you the rest of my report now, and then it's back to taking daily notes and writing once every couple of days.

There are several exemption lists here. Among them are the *alte Kampfeinsassen*, approx. 1,700, who will stay here until the very end owing to their red stamp, and who, as I mentioned earlier, are in charge. Some red stamps are awarded to others on the basis of job status. There are only very few, for you usually need some kind of Z[34] on your camp card in order to secure a job. You can only do it the other way around through connections, and even then it's quite rare. Then there are the green stamps, also awarded by the commandant on merit. These stamps were declared invalid a few weeks ago, and the people who had them were put on a transport. There was also a list of parents of *Expositur* staff who had green stamps and went on a transport. People here call this *platzen*.[35] When the transport quota isn't met on a Monday, the commandant decides that some exemption list or other will be cancelled. Finally, there's the Puttkammer List. And last week the Palestine List collapsed. The people on this list had blue stamps and were exempted on orders from The Hague. I mentioned this before. Approx. 300 had the right papers. But for how long? It depends on whether there will be any more transports. The camp commandant, Gemmeker, has a vested

---

34 The first letter of the German word *Zurückgestellt*, lit. to stand back, or to be deferred.

35 The collapse of a list.

interest in the camp's survival, or he'll be sent to the eastern front. But it all depends on Berlin's wishes. Last week, Gemmeker showed a commission round the camp. Apparently, there are plans to reorganize the camp, as if it's to become permanent. There will be a café with a string orchestra, a cinema, a dance instructor! Madness taken to the extreme. Gemmeker is rumoured to have said that this will become a labour camp, and that if we have to work hard, he will provide us with recreation. You need to be here to believe it! And with all our worries, we're really not in the mood for any of this, but once you're there, you do have a good time. I went to the revue this week, with Ehrlich and Chaja Goldstein (!), and did enjoy myself. Ehrlich pokes fun at everything, refers to Schlesinger as "*Seine Majestät*"[36] and even dares to make insinuations in his songs:

Immer langsam, immer langsam	*Always slowly, always slowly*
Immer mit Gemütlichkeit	*Always with good cheer*
Wir hab'n noch lange Zeit	*Still so long a time to wait*
Es ist noch nicht so weit.	*The end is nowhere near.*

But it's bizarre to see someone like Juul in the audience, whose parents were sent on two days earlier.

Let me go through the last few items I jotted down. In the hospital barracks here I saw little children from Vught, so thin and quiet and lifeless, that the sight of them brought tears to my eyes. There are some who came here all by themselves, without parents or family, and whose names are not even known. It's not until you see these children that you realize how great a tragedy has befallen us.

A few days after we arrived here, a transport from Vught arrived, and that's why I know a bit about Vught. There was a group of men who had worked in Moerdijk,[37] without a star, because the others were not to know they were Jews (which of course they

---

36 "His Majesty."
37 A village in the province of North Brabant, not far from Rotterdam.

knew), and they had been quite comfortable there. When they came to Westerbork and were sent on to Poland (transports from Vught are always sent through straight away; they're so-called transport material), absolutely everything was taken away from them and they were given just a suit (they had worn uniforms for work and their own clothes had been taken from them). According to the labels, these used suits came from Greece — filched from Jews over there, the way things are filched over here. Vught itself is said to be a model camp, with avenues lined with flowers, central heating, modern dining rooms and dormitories. The truth is, they got no food, but were beaten and bullied instead! NSB girls had been enlisted to bully the women. So they were targeting the women there, too. I think I prefer the mess here. I know of a girl whose father, aged 42, died as soon as he arrived from Vught, and whose mother and aunt were sent on that very same night. A week later she was also called up for transport, but then withdrawn again. Somebody recently said: "We're suffering enough for generations." It's true. And yet, we do laugh! For example, there was this little old man who snuck into the women's ward, one evening, just as the women were about to undress. He wanted to have a peek! The barracks leader was rather rough with him and a fight ensued. One of the women, sitting on her third-storey bunk, took off her shoe and set about whacking one of the people fighting on his bald pate. In one of the barracks, all the inmates have to catch 50 flies a day and hand them in to the barracks leader. No kidding!! (We're plagued by flies here.) I'll stop now. More tonight, when I hope to go through the last few items.

I've already written to you about the transport nights. We never had one as bad as this week, because all our acquaintances went. A few weeks ago Lex W. also left, a week after his entire family, parents, future in-laws and his girl, had gone. It's awful to see families torn apart. And some people really go to seed. Looking at the camp, it could actually pass for a gypsy encampment. Some, like Father, bear up well, whereas others, like Lex, have their spirits crushed. I believe I forgot to tell you that approximately two weeks ago, the NIZ was cleared out — luckily Mother had just been discharged — and everybody sent on. Grandmother, too, and she went straight to Poland. At the age of 89, imagine!

As soon as I arrived here, I wrote to Eitje that he should try to secure me a travel permit on the strength of the fact that I used to handle the work permits for the German Jews. Blüth then showed me a letter from the National Employment Office, such a gem! Amsterdam wouldn't survive unless I came back to take matters in hand. I said to Blüth (who was to present this letter to the commandant): "Even if I don't get the permit, I'd like to have this letter as a keepsake." I never expected to get the permit. But on Monday, 12 July at half-past six, I received a letter granting me leave until 17 July. Isn't that great? That evening, the eve of transport, would you believe it, I granted an audience, as it were. I was asked to pass on a lot of messages, and, illegally, took a few letters and jewellery for friends. The following morning, I stood by the exit. To my left was the transport train, to my right a truck carrying people in mixed marriages, Fritz Grünberg from the JC, a courier, a few other people going on leave, and myself. I'll limit myself to one funny incident during our trip. Compartments had been reserved for Westerbork, because of all the luggage. In Assen, the train became packed. (There are far too few trains.) Fritz called the train leader, who went and stood in front of the compartments with "Reserved for Westerbork" signs and said: "Out please, gentlemen." And filing past us we saw… some Employment Service bigwig from the Dutch Welfare Ministry (the bigwigs there are all NSB) and a Dutch SS officer in uniform! They ended up holding on to a strap a bit further down, where they could curse the Jews with the comfortable seats. Isn't that great?

Arrival, reception committee, your father, Els, Eitje, Jo Pronk. To no. 62. A beautifully laid table, a saucer with sweets from Miss Roos, an egg! Had a few lovely days. Talked and talked until I was hoarse. I must tell you one more thing: When I saw all those beautiful mansions and compared them to our filthy barracks, I could have cried. I'm going to stop. I have to leave. I promise to bring my story up to date tomorrow. Only one more item on the agenda.

22 August 1943

It's Sunday afternoon, and I've been longing to write to you. Yet now that I have the time, I don't have much to say. Since I last wrote to you, I've been put on outdoor duty. All the young people have to work the land to bring in the harvest, and on Tuesday evening I also received a call-up. I wanted to give you a detailed description of my adventures as a woman farmer, but Father just appeared at the window. He's coming in now, so nothing will come of it. I'm not really in the mood either, and because tomorrow is letter-writing day I still have to write some postcards. So I'll stop now and continue this evening, after a couple of visits to the hospital barracks. Bye for now, my darling.

24 August 1943, 9 o'clock in the evening

In very high spirits! I'll probably be discharged from outdoor duty and go on leave — probably, that is — to Amsterdam for a couple of days. I intend to play truant tomorrow and write to you.

25 August 1943, evening

I never got around to writing today, because in the end I was working. The weather was lovely, so I didn't play truant. But let me tell you how I ended up doing outdoor duty. Late on Tuesday evening, I received a note saying I had been put on outdoor duty.

Upon inquiry, I learnt that practically all the women between 16 and 40 have to do outdoor duty for a couple of weeks to help bring in the harvest — the bulk of which, three-quarters I believe, is destined for Germany — before they can go back to their old jobs. I didn't mind, providing I could go back after a short while and providing the weather is nice. I'm a fine farmer, don't you agree? I asked my boss, who assured me that he'd call me back as soon as possible.

Wednesday morning: Rose in the middle of the night, put on some old clobber, got to the roll-call area at a quarter-past seven. In the meantime it had begun to pelt with rain, and I had to go back inside. An hour passed. Then several groups were lined up in the roll-call area and with all the yelling and calling out of names — chaos. The new recruits all had to work for Bauer, an Austrian Jew who's a cross between Puss in Boots and a fairground operator, a vulgar man who shouts a lot, but wouldn't hurt a fly. We were counted, lined up in threes, and marched out of the camp. I was wearing wooden shoes, would you believe it! I never got around to telling you that I nearly always wear wooden shoes here, to spare my shoes. Very few can do it and I'm extremely proud I can. I have calluses on the top of my feet. In the evening and on Shabbat, I wear regular shoes.

The camp is set in stunning surroundings, beautiful heathland, and yet I was extremely downhearted, because I was thinking of how we used to cycle here and enjoy the view, whereas now we're prisoners, gawped at by the occasional passer-by. There are a few houses outside the camp, among them those of the commandant and the military police, and the entire staff there consists of Jews. Kitchen maid, butler, gardener, etc. Just like the black slaves in the southern states of America. I tried to cheer myself up by bearing in mind that it wouldn't last forever and that I'm healthy and strong — almost everybody here has something, e.g. diarrhoea, angina, lots and lots of infections — but it was difficult all the same. I think the slavery hits you much harder outside the camp. Although strenuous, the potato harvest itself isn't so bad. The worst thing is the dirt. You can't imagine it. When I come home I'm as black as a chimney sweep, and my whole body is covered in dust. I need at least an hour to get clean again. And I have to work on Shabbat as well. I struggled to overcome my dejection and I would have loved to have been comforted by you. My *"Anschmiegungsbedürfnis"*[38] is greater than ever, whereas in Amsterdam I used to be quite upbeat. My only comfort is that it affects everybody. Everybody is saying, many of my acquaintances anyway: "I don't want to think, I just let things wash over me." Besides, we haven't had any political news recently, and hardly any mail is coming through. It's all extremely depressing. I have written many times that here you're either *himmelhoch jauchzend* (an exaggeration, of course) or *zum Tode betrübt*.[39] On Sunday we had a children's craft fair, organised by the school. The commandant, accompanied by Aus der Fünten, visited and inspected every table with great interest. If I hadn't seen it with my own eyes, I would never have believed it. Taking advantage of the commandant's good mood, my boss tried to get us discharged from outdoor duty. Apparently it's not all that easy, but the matter is still being considered. I played truant today, even though it's really too risky, and now I'm lying on a dirty stretch of land, writing to you. I intend to cover, in telegram style, a few more things I have jotted down and then call it a day.

a.   Spoke to Sluzker about my leave. Will probably work out.

b.   The women here whose husbands are still working for the *Expositur* in Amsterdam are going back home, so Jenny is leaving again.

c.   All the while I've been here, I haven't had my period. Most women haven't. It's said they put camphor in the food.

Another transport left last night, mainly the elderly, sick and punishment cases, and another one is planned for next week. I'm expecting the worst.

---

38   The need to snuggle up to somebody.
39   A quote from Goethe's *Egmont*: On top of the world, or in the depths of despair.

Westerbork, 2 September 1943

Dear Juul and Freddy,

This heading is nonsense, but I'm writing in the school with a big crowd of people around me. I have jotted down a few points and although I may have covered them last time, I'm too lazy to check. So I'm going to work my way down the list.

Let me begin by telling you how my discharge from outdoor duty came about. It was such a miracle, I still don't understand how it all happened so quickly. You should know that scarcely anyone ever gets out. I'd had enough, because the weather was turning bad, that's to say, I'd been caught in a downpour and because it's all open country there's nowhere to shelter. I was dry again in a jiffy — isn't that a funny word? — for it was only a shower, but I thought to myself: Let me try and get out of this now, so that by the time the weather becomes really nasty, I'll be out. So one morning I stayed in bed, obtained a *dienstfrei* note — I hope to be able to show it to you one day — and went to the outpatients' clinic. I heard that Dr Elzas was one of the doctors on duty and asked to be seen by him, because he's a brother of Frits Elzas, whom I know well and who had asked me to pass on his regards when I was on leave. I never did, because I think it's very odd to walk up to somebody I don't know and tell him: Your brother sends his regards. Especially when that person has some influence. Very pushy.

Well, I went in and passed on his brother's regards. We had a very nice chat, for he had just received his Palestine papers and I told him the whole plaster saga. He examined me briefly and then handed me a note for the head of the outpatients' clinic, in which he recommended I be exempt from outdoor duty and be given time off until 15 September. I laughed myself silly, for all I could think was: Is he serious about all these wonderful Latin terms he has written down? To cut a long story short, the head of the clinic gave me a note for the employment office: "*Wegen Wirbelsäulekrummung aus dem Aussendienst zu befreien.*"[40] Great, don't you agree? You see,

40 "To be discharged from outdoor duty on account of curvature of the spine."

```
Lager Westerbork,      26.8.      1943.
Frl. Levie, Mirjam Sophie Bar.:  65
Sie sind wieder der Schule zugeteilt
zugeteilt und werden ersucht, sich
-em- sofort        -um-        Um- in der
Bar. 35 Dienstleiterbüro  zu melden.
                    Verwaltung
               Arbeitsc...
Ros.
```

Administrative notice from 26 August 1943, pronouncing Mirjam's placement
once more in the school

Author's collection

that's an order, not a request. In the afternoon, the employment office re-assigned me to the school. *Schluss.*[41] Ten days' holiday, gorgeous weather and now back to work again. Bial, the head of the employment office, didn't sanction the two weeks' *dienstfrei.* It would have been too much, and besides, I didn't even like it, because I wouldn't have known what to do with myself. I'm quite healthy, I don't need sick leave. You have no idea how good I look. I have never looked this good in all my life. Rosy cheeks, very short hair, lots of ringlets at the back; in a word, I believe you'd fall in love with me if you saw me. I tried to have my picture taken to show you later what I looked like in Westerbork, in long trousers, but I couldn't get it done. A great pity, but it can't be helped. There are worse things. There really are.

Another funny anecdote. By the time I was released from outdoor duty, I was filthy, of course. I had cleaned my hands as best

41 End of story, that's that.

as I could — they looked decent enough — and for once I wanted to have my hair washed at the hairdresser's. I can easily do it myself because it's so short, but I was free and wanted to have it done properly. But I have no smoker's card, because I only arrived here on 20 June. The people who arrived before this date and have the right stamp get a smoker's card — which doesn't happen in Amsterdam — and this smoker's card allows you to have your hair washed once a month. So off I went to the hairdresser and asked what I should do. "You can come between five and seven," I was told. So I went. Somebody else received me and told me: "No, impossible, you need a note from Schlesinger." I can't remember whether I told you that Schlesinger is king here and unbelievably powerful. "But I don't know Schlesinger," I said, cheekily. "To *Verwaltung* II."[42] After some verbal sparring with a rude lad, I learnt that Schlesinger was out. So off I went to the barracks and washed my hair myself, but I did go to Schlesinger the following morning. I wanted to see for myself. And indeed, I was given a note saying that I was entitled to have my hair washed once a month. One for the archive. It's akin to asking the Secretary-General for permission to wash your hair. I'll have to explain to you in person how daft this is, or try to anyway, for it's impossible to give you an idea of the relations here. They are so idiotic that somebody who has always lived a normal life can't possibly comprehend them.

Westerbork, 2 September 1943

Dear Freddy and Juul,

This is a continuation of the previous letter, but again the heading is just for show. Now, alas, some less pleasant news. Last Tuesday another transport left, and despite initial reassurances that there wouldn't be one this week, another is scheduled. Gretha and Ies have gone, with Gretha four months' pregnant. And Marianne

42 Department II.

van Stedum volunteered to go with her sister, even though she had been assured by the *alte Kampfeinsassen* and Schlesinger that she would always be exempted. Among the many transport cases was a woman who was having a miscarriage. She was allowed to stay, but her husband had to go on the transport. She decided to join him, and was carried to the train on a stretcher.

It's striking how rarely people cry. They're numb and unable to think. I had an *Ausweis* that night that allowed me to go out, and I ran errands for lots of people. I went to see Gretha and Ies as well, and said goodbye to them. I can't tell you how eerie it was, the pitch-black night, not cold, but wet and windy, the dark barracks and the train. Now and again I sank down in the mud or found myself wading through a puddle — luckily I was wearing wooden shoes — and I had a terrible headache because I was coming down with the flu, which I have since fought off with every possible means. One of the errands took me to the industrial barracks, where people were working for... the revue. There I learnt that the cobblers were also working for the revue, and that their request to help the people who had to go on a transport that night had been turned down. The commandant has a soft spot for revues, that's why... It truly beggars belief.

I'm approaching the end of my material. One more thing. I believe I have already told you about the 60 employees who were sent back to Amsterdam, were rounded up once more, and are now allowed to return again. Yesterday evening I learnt that these people are indeed allowed to return to Amsterdam, but that in their place 60 other families of JC staff still in Amsterdam must be dispatched to Westerbork and that these will probably be sent on. And the Professor actually agreed to this trade in people! The *Sperre* of the people who are still here — the 60, that is — expires on 15 September. If the others haven't arrived from Amsterdam by then, these people will be sent on! It's unbelievable, and that's gradually becoming our second leitmotif.

Let me stop now, my dear boy, on a cheerful note. For the moment, the people who keep kosher can get meat-free food. I doubt it's kosher, but of course I eat it. If there's kosher, why would I eat the non-kosher? Today the kosher food was late, so we sent somebody to ask why it took so long. That person was a baptised Jew, asking about the kosher food! Isn't that funny? Well, Leo, this has been another detailed account. I may go to Amsterdam next week, *who knows*, and then I'm bound to have a lot to tell you again.

One more thing. This week a young boy came to see me in school, and he had to give his date of birth and address (i.e., his barracks number). His barracks number was 65, the same as mine. I said: "Hey, I'm in that barracks, too!" "Oh yes, Miss," he said, "I know you. I've seen you plenty of times in the washroom." More or less naked, that is. He sounded so innocent. I'm really stopping now.

6 September 1943

My darling,

It's "Monday before transport" and this afternoon everybody has time off to pack. The mood here is indescribable. What happened is that last Friday the commandant informed the *Dienstleiter*[43] that the camp will be dissolved around 1 November. Four transports are earmarked for Auschwitz, and the *Obersturmführer* announced that people from other camps would also be going to Auschwitz. One transport to Theresienstadt, one to Vittel. The one to Theresienstadt in cattle-trucks, too. Barneveld[44] to Theresienstadt. Vught to be dissolved, too. In other words… the liquidation of the remnants of Dutch Jewry. A consequence of Himmler's decision to clear Western Europe of Jews.

And now the news that beats everything else. The remainder of the Palestine List (approx. 300 people with the right papers) is

---

43 Duty officer.
44 This refers to a group of prominent Jews, mainly intellectuals, who were housed in a castle in the village of Barneveld. The group, which had been deported to Westerbork in September 1943, was indeed taken to Theresienstadt. Most survived the war.

going, along with the baptised, Ecuadorians, Paraguayans and what have you, to *"Mitteldeutschland."*[45] Whereto remains uncertain.

My darling, I don't have the peace of mind to tell you how I feel, because everybody is watching me, curious about all this writing. Today is writing day and you're allowed to write only two postcards or one letter. I've already written my postcards, so this letter doesn't make sense to them.

A funny incident. A Polish Jew went to the registry, where his official documents are kept, to have a look at his papers. "What kind of papers do you have?" "Paraguay." They searched and searched... but no trace of Paraguay. The entire registry was turned upside-down. At long last they found his papers... they were Ecuador papers! The man had actually forgotten what nationality he had [bought].[46]

Westerbork, 13 September 1943

My dearest,

I really ought to write you a letter when all around me is dead quiet, so I can concentrate and gather my thoughts, but this is impossible in the barracks. Since hearing of my departure, I set out to write to you a hundred times and even thought of phrases to express my feelings, but meanwhile I'm feeling completely different again. As I've been telling you over and over again, one moment you bear up quite well and the next it's all too much. On Shabbat morning I received a letter from my boss, which I'll treasure. I went to pieces, because at that moment I had a very clear vision of what it really means to go away, into the unknown, not knowing whether you'll be hit by a bomb or, when the Germans are facing defeat, be destroyed some other way. And yet I still believe that we'll hold

---

45 Central Germany.
46 A number of countries, including Ecuador and Paraguay, sold passports to Jews who had the financial means.

out the short while it will take. But afterwards... how much time will pass before their lordships will have decided our fate? And regardless of whether you're interned in Central Germany — they say the Palestine people are going there — or whether you'll be put in the *Auschwitzreservaat*,[47] when the war is over it will take months to get out again. It means I'll have to wait even longer to be reunited with you. And when I think that the war may be over a week after we have gone... And much more importantly: When I'm gone and the war is over and I manage to get hold of a postage stamp to inform you of my whereabouts, I still have every hope that you can get me out. But Father and Mother! Of course Father is incredibly lucky to have his certificate, but even if he went to Palestine, his life would be ruined, because he wouldn't be able to look after himself. But if he remains in Westerbork, nothing will be lost. I told you that the furniture is in storage, his position at the office is open, clothes etc., have been hidden. All he needs to do is go to the office, rent a few rooms, and that's that. And the situation is really such that we could see a change any week now. The coasts are being bombed, Italy has defected... any minute now, transports to Germany could become impossible. I'm writing relatively calmly now, because this morning I learnt that the Palestine List has a few weeks' reprieve. And although I know perfectly well that such rumours and announcements are meaningless, I cling to them, because a few weeks can make all the difference.

And then there's the question of Mother. If internment were definitely on the cards, it would, of course, be better for Mother to join us, because she has nobody to protect her in Amsterdam and it would be awful if, say, a week after we had left, she ended up in Westerbork all by herself. I have written to Amsterdam about the matter and have put it to Eitje, Freddy and your father, who all agree with me. I also put the case to one of the bigwigs here, and expect to have a response soon. When I do, I'll let Eitje know when

47 Auschwitz reservation.

we'd like to bring Mother over. I believe I forgot to write to you about my leave. I have been running to the JC for weeks now to find out what's going on. Last week, it emerged that I wasn't eligible at all. Again, I passed it on to Eitje at once. But last Shabbat, Grünberg said I would be among the next group to go on leave. We'll have to wait and see if it's true, because I no longer believe a thing. Of course, it would be absolutely delightful, not only to take care of the hiding issue, but perhaps also to come back with Mother.

I must admit that I'm not yet free enough from material possessions not to mind that I may never see my beautiful trousseau, silverware, etc., again. Being here has made me see how much it means to me, although it's not essential, of course. And I'd like to tell you a bit about our Friday evenings here. During the first few weeks, we weren't settled enough to organize anything of that nature. Besides, without tables, it was completely impossible. But now we have tables and benches in the barracks and although it remains difficult — you mustn't forget that there are regulars at these tables who you can't really chase away — I couldn't bear to see Father adrift. Now, we have been quite lucky as far as the people at our table are concerned. They're out most of the time, so we have the place to ourselves. A sheet serves as a tablecloth, two potatoes as candlesticks, and although we usually have no treats, I do prepare something every now and then. Once I made a bread pudding, which I was allowed to bake in the central kitchen, and last week, when I didn't have enough sugar for a cake or a pudding, I roasted very thin slices of bread on the stove and sprinkled them with butter, sugar and cinnamon. They were quite tasty, actually. I also made some sandwiches with a kind of fish paste. A piece of white paper with a fringe cut into it as a *challah* cover,[48] and some more scraps of white paper to put the sandwiches on. It was primitive, of course, but pleasant enough. And Father loves it. He's bearing up

---

48 A cloth used to cover the prescribed two *challah* loaves on Sabbaths and holidays.

extremely well. We have a regular group: A couple that "lives" at this table, Liepman Prins, who is here without his wife, and Cohen de Lara and his wife who, when they saw us, asked if they could join. All in all, quite a big group. There's also a kind of Zichron Friday evening for people who don't live in one of the small houses and therefore can't mark Friday evening — which strictly speaking includes us — but I went once and found it so tedious that I have no intention of ever going back.

My darling, I'd better leave it at this for today. I haven't been able to explain how we feel. Perhaps because we feel different from one minute to the next. Yesterday evening, there was a puppet show for the children. I went with several from our barracks and enjoyed myself immensely with the children. A cute little girl sat on my lap throughout the show. I kept thinking how wonderful it would be if the two of us had such a little girl. Last week I went to see the revue, which I told you about. Quite extraordinary by Westerbork standards. It's a curious sensation, the feverish excitement of people who know that within a week or two they will be plunged into the unknown. It's *unheimlich*[49] and although I laughed — you know me too well — I couldn't shake that feeling.

My very dearest, I'm going to leave it at this. Perhaps a miracle will happen, although I very much doubt that the war will end in time now that we're in imminent danger. History takes its course without any consideration for us, for you and for me. Bye, my love, I keep hoping — against my better judgement.

Westerbork, 4 October 1943
My dearest,
I'm writing in pencil because I'm in bed. A great deal has happened, Amsterdam is well and truly empty now, but let me tell you everything from the beginning. Two weeks ago today, I woke up

49 Sinister.

with a headache and a sore throat. I'd better stay in bed, I thought to myself, for if I fall ill now and I get my leave, I won't be able to go. I only missed half a day at the school, because I had the afternoon off because of the transport. So I reported sick, and later had my temperature taken. I didn't ask how high it was, because I didn't think I had a fever. I washed in the washroom and went back to sleep until the doctor turned up, examined me and told me I was running quite a temperature. "How high?" I asked, taken aback. 103.6. That was at eight in the morning. To cut a long story short, he suspected scarlet fever and had me admitted straight away. Father was alerted, a terrible consternation. I felt sorry for him: Yet another thing to worry about. Not to mention my leave…

On a trolley to the scarlet fever barracks. I couldn't help but laugh, for it was like watching my own funeral. I was completely wrapped up in oilcloth, put on a two-wheeled trolley, with Father and Jenny bringing up the rear. In the scarlet fever barracks they said I didn't have scarlet fever, but diphtheria. So off to the diphtheria barracks. There I was put in an isolated section and given all kinds of injections and jabs and the best possible care. Three days later it emerged that I didn't have diphtheria, but angina. I was then taken to the regular hospital barracks, which is where I am now. I was quite ill, had a terrible rash from the injections and a kind of inflammation of the jaw, which was so bad I cried with pain. I hope to be allowed to get up today and for the whole thing to be over soon.

Something funny now. We have discovered that I have a secret admirer. Well, he's no longer "secret." The school porter, around 40, and with a voice to scare little children off to bed. Apparently everybody knew, except me. Fancy that, he sent flowers first and then came to visit. Only the top hat is missing. It would be hilarious were it not for the fact that he visits every evening and I'm already growing tired of it.

And now the big blow! On Tuesday night, the whistle was blown. At first we thought a fire had broken out, but a moment later we learnt that part of the OD and NB (= *Notbereitschaft*) had to go to Amsterdam, because everybody would be coming here. And indeed, the following day, luckily in passenger cars and in wonderful weather, the remainder of the Amsterdam contingent arrived, including Eitje, Asscher, Cohen, Van Tijn and Sluzker, who have all been housed in the regular, big barracks and not in the small houses. A few escaped and have gone into hiding, e.g., Brandon. Max Plotske was caught straight away. Karel Hartog made off as well. Gien[50] has just given birth to a second daughter and is at the CIZ,[51] the only Jewish hospital not to have been emptied; its future hangs in the balance. Of course some people were overlooked again, but their numbers are so few that this marks the end of the final chapter of the persecution of the Jews in the Netherlands. I forgot to tell you the "trifling fact" that on Wednesday, the whole of Barneveld also arrived here. There is great uncertainty about their fate. There is talk of a transport of 2,000 people. Tomorrow! Miss Slottke, Rauter's secretary in The Hague, is here again today, so the blue stamps are likely to be decimated again.

Mother looks reasonably well, your father less so; he's so fastidious, he has trouble adjusting. Bye, dearest, I'll write again soon to tell you the rest of the story. Only I see no more opportunity to smuggle these letters to Amsterdam, which is a pity.

24 November 1943

Dear Mies,

This heading is nonsense again, as on previous occasions, but although I'm alone right now, a crowd could come marching in any moment, hence this opening. It has been a long time since I last wrote, because nothing even vaguely worth mentioning happened. I managed to smuggle my previous letters to Amsterdam. Meantime,

---

50 The wife of Karel Hartog.
51 *Centraal Israelietische Ziekenverpleging* — Central Jewish Hospital.

Verwalt'ing, Bar. 34.   No.

Name: Levie

Vorname: Mirjam

geboren: 20.3.17   Bar.:

Familienangehörige:

Ihr Antrag vom:
Entscheidung:

Sie werden zwecks Palaestina Austausch in
ein anderes Lager ueberstellt. Die ein
gereichten Unterlagen anbei zurueck.

Datum: Kontrolle:
18.11.1943   DR. ? Verwaltung

1.Anl.

"Decision: You will be moved to another camp in preparation for your exchange
to Palestine. Attached are the application documents. Signed: Administration,
18 November 1943"

Author's collection

I wasn't at all in the mood to write, and life was one long succession
of boredom and apathy and despair, because there was no end to
the interminable waiting. The transports continue, and although
I have never had any real cause for concern, I can see it drawing
closer and closer. And on top of everything else, this wretched
winter, so dark and cold and miserable.

But then suddenly a change! Last week all the people with foreign papers were summoned to appear before Miss Slottke, and we were told that we would be exchanged to Palestine and that, in anticipation of this exchange, we would be going to Celle, near Hanover in Germany. This announcement unleashed a flurry of excitement as never before. It was the sole subject on everyone's lips. It was quite an event. Initially, only the people on the first and second lists of veterans were called up, as these are the only two lists to have been approved by Berlin. But after a few days, the third and fourth lists were also passed, which meant that your father, Eitje and Freddy would be coming along as well. We were to travel by passenger train, be allowed to carry up to *f*250 and the camp would be under Red Cross administration. The latter isn't official, but the first part is.

A leaving party was held on Saturday evening. We were scheduled to leave Tuesday evening at six. And lo and behold, on Monday morning a passenger train pulled in, decent third-class carriages and a luggage car. During the course of the day, it was loaded with apples! Cigarettes! Sausages! In a word, too good to be true. Indeed, too good to be true. Monday night — we had already hosted a leaving dinner, everything was packed, the laundry was done, we had showered and washed our hair, etc. — at half-past twelve, I was woken up by noise on the ward and I heard that people had to hand in their papers. Liepman Prins, who works at the registry, was there, and he told me the transport had been cancelled. And indeed, yesterday evening the train left again, empty. So far, everybody is still in the dark.

Curiously, rumours of another *Austausch*,[52] have surfaced now. The Weinreb List,[53] which I must have mentioned before, has

---

52 Exchange.
53 The Weinreb List was an imaginary one. Weinreb claimed to have high-level connections with the Germans, and disseminated permits to the Jews (most of them for *f*100 per person) that led to the delay of those Jews being transported from Westerbork, until his plan was exposed and the lists "collapsed." After his

come into force again, after 800 people on this list were sent on. Weinreb himself spent time in prison and came out without a Star of David; his family was discharged from Westerbork today,[54] and now the people on his list are rumoured to be sent to Portugal, where they will be exchanged with Germans in Brazil. The whole camp has gone mad. As for ourselves, we don't know whether to be disappointed or glad. It's certainly a nuisance, for we had wired to Amsterdam for provisions for the journey, and received them, so now we have to eat them without knowing whether we may still go tomorrow or the day after tomorrow. It's too ridiculous for words.

We have been dealt yet another blow, i.e., we heard that Father's business has been seized. Think of the consequences! If Father were in, say, England, he could return to Holland after the war and walk straight back into the office. But if the business has been dissolved! His whole life is gone. Besides, part of my trousseau is in the depot, my diary — i.e., my letters to you — as well as furniture, linen, parcels, etc., belonging to Father and Mother. Just what we needed! Luckily, we received word today that everything is more or less all right again. You have no idea how it wears you out, being torn between hope and fear. I daren't hope that I will see you again soon, and yet I have the feeling it may well happen. Do you know what they call this transport? *Austauschwitz!*[55] Isn't that funny?

ruse was discovered, Weinreb collaborated with the Germans (which gave him and his family protection for some time until they went into hiding). After the war, he was sentenced to six years' imprisonment. Presser wrote in his defense, casting doubt upon whether it was indeed necessary to try such a man, since the judges could not understand the terrible plight of the Jews during the war. De Jong and Moore are based on the checking committee of the Rijksinstituut voor Oorlogsdocumentatie (RIOD — the State Institute for War Documentation) from the 1970s, that declared Weinreb to be guilty. See Michman, Beem and Michman (eds.), *Encyclopedia of Jewish Communities: The Netherlands* (Heb.), pp. 109–111, 138–139.

54 Weinreb was relased from prison (and his family from Westerbork) after he agreed to collaborate with the Germans, who were looking for the "high-level Germans" with whom he worked.

55 A play on *"austauschen"* (*austausch* = exchange) and "Auschwitz" (*witz* = joke).

At any rate, I have the impression that the people on the Berlin-approved lists won't be sent to Poland. I'm on the first, Father, Mother and Bobby on the second, and your father on the third list. **Let's wait and see**. On the eve of the transport, Els suddenly fell ill, though luckily not seriously. She has pneumonia, but it might have been worse. Your father has aged a great deal here, mentally as well.

A big crowd is filing in now. I wasn't in the mood and I had little patience, but perhaps it won't be long now until I can embrace you and devote every minute of the day to you.

24 December 1943, Friday

Last Sunday was six months since we've been here. I'm writing this with the help of a few notes I made, but without much detail, because as usual time is too short and I don't have the peace of mind to write a decent account. On the one hand, these six months seem to have flown by, while on the other I feel as if my leave, for example, happened years and years ago.

The symbol of poverty used to be the day labourer, who eats potatoes with a bit of mustard. We have now reached that level. Luckily we received some more parcels, and somehow I always manage to scrape some extra food together, but one time I had to make do with potatoes and I kept thinking how low we had sunk. You should bear in mind that we were eating this from a bowl, sitting on a wooden bench at a wooden trestle table, surrounded by all manner of people walking, talking and eating, with water dripping from the roof. You see, it was very cold outside and although the barracks is scarcely heated and we keep our coats on, the air inside is still warmer than it is outside. It rises up to the timber beams, where it condenses and comes down again in big, dirty drops, sometimes splashing on our heads, sometimes on our table or in our food.

As an antidote to the above tale of poverty, I would now like to tell you about a "feast" I rustled up, because your father and Freddy are both without their wives at the moment. Juul and Els are both in the hospital barracks and your father, in particular, always mopes about, so I invited him and Freddy to dinner in my barracks on Friday evening. On the menu: soup, made from a sausage I was given once and had saved for a special occasion. It contained: vermicelli, also put aside, two small tins of mixed vegetables, rolled oats, potatoes and some fresh carrots, *geschnorrd*[56] from the kitchen, and broad beans, which Mother had "organised" (= stolen) at work. She has been assigned to the bean-sorting unit, you see. Potato latkes, made with fried onion, some butter, tomato ketchup, a bit of cheese spread, some broth made with a stock cube and rolled oats and baked in the domestic science school. A delicious pudding, made with two litres of milk, which required seven trips to the *Tischlerei*,[57] where I know someone who gives me milk. The people there are given milk because they inhale a great deal of dust. And also semolina, pudding powder and surrogate coffee. I didn't get the milk until Friday afternoon, when the stove was no longer hot, so it took an hour — literally — for the pudding to be done. And then it had to be cooled down in cold water. But the end result was terrific and delicious. Spread some slices of toast with tinned fish paste. Coffee (surrogate, that is). A quarter of an apple.

You have no idea, Leo, how much planning, running around and worrying went into this "feast." It looks simple enough on paper, but it was an insane amount of work. That said, it was divine, and your father loved it and had plenty to eat. But you must remember that the meal served eight people: the four of us, your father and Freddy, a girl from our barracks who is all alone, and Jenny. We didn't start until quite late, because otherwise there's no place at the table, and since I had to finish cooking by half-past four, the food

---

56 Scrounged.
57 Carpenter's workshop.

had to be kept warm. And because our pans aren't big enough, I had to cook two separate portions of soup. See here, just a glimpse of the difficulties, but I managed fine.

There was an article in the newspaper about the bombardments in Berlin, reporting that people there have stopped smiling. Do you remember that I wrote to you about Hitler saying "We shall wipe the smiles off the Jews' faces"? We have indeed stopped smiling, but so have they! Still, we're trying to make the most of things.

This week, in broad daylight, hundreds of aircraft flew towards Germany. It was an unforgettable sight. A beautiful blue sky with small white clouds and big, white, parallel lines, with one aircraft at the head -----†----- a bit like this, five on either side and among them, as in an aquarium, slender white trails: the fighters, flying across and between them. The roar of hundreds of aircraft, with more and more appearing in the background. Truly indescribable. The entire camp came out to watch, and now the commandant is in such a foul mood that a new *Lagerorder*[58] has been issued, of which more later. Somebody here joked: "It's so busy up in the sky, the birds have to walk."

Last Sunday, the Huns celebrated their *Julfest*[59] and behaved like such pigs that one of his lordships had to be bandaged in the hospital barracks. This is absolutely true and naturally it got around the camp at once. As a result of this, and the commandant's foul mood, a new *Lagerbefehl*[60] was issued. We had organised a great *Hanukkah*[61] celebration for the children, the same for every barracks. At two o'clock on Tuesday, the first performance took place in Barracks 61. It was a great success. The children were all

---

58 Camp regulation or camp order.
59 The *Julfest*, or Yule, is the ancient Germanic winter festival. The Nazis tried to replace Christmas with the *Julfest*, but were unable to push it through.
60 See above, footnote no. 58.
61 An eight-day holiday to commemorate the rededication of the Second Temple in Jerusalem, in 165 BCE. The festival is observed by lighting candles in the Menorah: one candle on the first evening of *Hanukkah*, two on the second, etc.

seated by the barracks' entrance, each with a bowl and a cup, at tables covered with white sheets, and we had a puppet show, choir, dances, sketches, the best essay on *Hanukkah* was read out; in a word, it was wonderful, it really was. But a couple of hours later, the *Lagerbefehl* was issued, banning all gatherings. *Schluss.* Each of the barracks had also organised its own evening for the adults, with recitations, speakers, etc. The *Lagerbefehl* ruined everything. I'm telling you all this to illustrate the difference between the *Julfest* and *Hanukkah.*

But this only serves as a guide for everything I want to tell you in person, for I know full well that I'm incapable of giving you a written account that comes close to conveying the actual situation. In person it will be equally impossible, because there are no words to describe things as they really were. I also gave the children at my table in the barracks little presents, things I had "organised" at the school, e.g., boxes of crayons, exercise books, erasers and pencils. All individually wrapped, with string, as pretty as possible. We also lit tea lights, one light for every evening.

In Amsterdam, all the people in mixed marriages have been called up. They had to come forward. Men under 45 will be put in labour camps in Holland; those over 45 have to work at Boschplan in Amsterdam.[62] The children from mixed marriages have to go to Germany. Apparently, last Monday Groningen was hit by a bomb, which left us without light and water for half a day and a night. It meant a loss of 7,500 working hours, as well as many other difficulties, of course.

Time to stop, my love. I've covered all my items now. Again, this is just a kind of agenda and I hope to tell you everything in detail. We'll need years to talk about everything we've been through.

---

62 Between 1928 and 1945, the *Amsterdamsche Bosch*, the Amsterdam Forest, was designed and planted as an employment project for unemployed people.

Bergen-Belsen

18 January 1944

My dearest,

We're in Celle![1] And I have such an awful lot to tell you, I simply don't know where to start. I'm also struggling to concentrate again, for even though it's not very crowded, people are talking loudly so you can't help but be distracted. I have a few more notes from Westerbork. Let me copy these first before I begin.

1. At the beginning of January, German citizens were evacuated to Assen. They arrived without luggage, without anything. The Jews (from Westerbork, of course, for there are none left elsewhere) had to prepare everything for them. They were quite surprised to find any Jews left in Holland.

---

1   The Bergen-Belsen concentration camp was located near the town of Celle (not far from Hanover) and was in operation from 1940 until 1945. Until 1943 it was a POW camp, mainly for Russian POWs. In 1943, a part of the camp was taken over by the SS. This part was supposed to house mainly Jews with foreign papers for exchange with Germans. Bergen-Belsen was divided into a number of independent sub-camps, including the "camp for prisoners," the "camp for special and neutral cases" and the "Hungarian camp." The so-called "*Sternlager*" (named after the yellow Star of David that the Jewish prisoners wore on their civilian clothes), in which Mirjam lived, was the biggest camp, with some 4,100 prisoners earmarked for exchange. After March 1944, Bergen-Belsen became a regular concentration camp and absorbed a great number of prisoners from other camps. As a result of over-crowding, many prisoners died of disease, malnourishment and exhaustion; approximately 35,000 people between January and April 1945. When British troops liberated the camp on 15 April 1945, they found some 60,000 survivors, of whom 13,000 died in the following days and weeks.

2. An example of the corruption in Westerbork, of which we got only the occasional glimpse, because we weren't really in a position to see what was going on behind the scenes. Helga Klau is a clothes horse, her face always painted, even on transports. She's the sweetheart of one of the German-Jewish bigwigs, who is baptised, works for the JC and therefore lives in a small house, together with a few others, Hetty Brandel among them. One day Helga was off work, and found Hetty's mother in the house. She wasn't best pleased to have one of these old women in the house on her day off. Hetty said her mother could come whenever she wanted to. The following day Helga turned up with a note, signed by the baptised bigwig, Todmann, and the king of the camp, Schlesinger, saying that on her days off only those people she wanted to receive would be allowed in the house.

3. A woman from the Barneveld List escaped. She left her husband behind. The repercussions: 20 people from the Barneveld group to the punishment barracks, their heads shaved, etc. Among them, the parents of the late Paul Denekamp,[2] Houthakker and Betty Prins, who lost her child in Vught.

On Friday, 7 January, Lea arrived, rounded up after somebody was murdered in her neighbourhood. Three weeks in Scheveningen prison, where she received Red Cross parcels. Extremely sad, the more so because at that point we were already fairly certain that we were leaving. We contacted her through the *Antragstelle*[3] and spoke to her at length. And just before our departure, I went to see a "connection," my only one in Westerbork — and one I never used, because I never needed him and because I fell out with him once when he tried to kiss me. He's the head of the metal workshop and he promised me that, if at all possible, he would keep Lea in the camp. He could probably do something for one person. I was extremely glad about that.

2 An officer in the Dutch army, killed in action in 1940.
3 Office that submitted applications to the camp leadership.

This marks the end of the Westerbork chapter and the beginning of Celle. I had already mentioned that there was talk of a transport. Just when I'd begun to comfort myself with the thought that there wouldn't be any more transports and we'd be able to buy ourselves a Westerbork-Amsterdam ticket after the war. *Es wäre zu schön gewesen.*[4] Opinions differed. Some said yes, others no. But the word from "official quarters" was: Yes. So we had to start thinking about packing again.

On Saturday evening, we received a note: *"Sie können mit Transport rechnen."*[5] So still not entirely certain: *"können"* rather than *"müssen."*[6] The entire camp was buzzing again. In spite of all the preparations, many refused to believe the transport would actually go ahead. Rumours were rife: Celle was supposed to be good, under Red Cross administration, with a recent exchange of 1,000 people. Aus der Fünten was rumoured to have called it *"Das grosse Los,"*[7] the journey there in a passenger train!

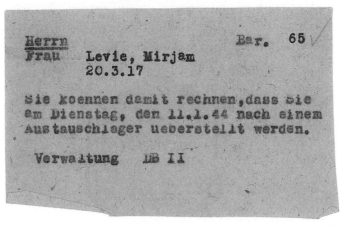

"You may take into account that on Tuesday, 11 January 1944, you will be transferred to an exchange camp. Signed: Administration"

Author's collection

4   It would have been too good to be true.
5   "You may expect to go on the transport."
6   "May" rather than "must."
7   "The lucky ticket."

Monday: Packed, prepared fish patties, received a bread-bag from the *Fürsorge* (!!).[8] Tuesday: Continued packing, said our goodbyes, and at two o'clock we were all packed and ready to go, with a rucksack, bread-bag, my blanket bag, Mother's rucksack, bread-bag and blankets, large bread-bag with provisions. My handbag, Mother's shopping bag, my shoulder bag. And that was without the luggage of Father and Bobby, who were coming to our barracks, so we could set off together. To the train at approx. three o'clock. We had dropped off Mother's rucksack with all the non-essential items as luggage, but we wanted to hold on to the rest because we didn't want to lose any of it. So I set off carrying an enormous rucksack on my back, a bread-bag over one shoulder, a small shoulder bag over the other, a handbag in one hand, the blanket bag in the other... Well, I got heart palpitations after only a couple of steps. Luckily, those who were staying behind and who were allowed out helped us with wheelbarrows. The train was already chock-full, but the four of us did manage to find a compartment, near the lavatory. The main road was full of people shaking hands; all the "bigwigs" were there. Lots of talking, laughing, shaking hands, in short, quite a jolly affair. But gradually the road became quieter until only the OD was left.

But that was just the beginning. We were already fairly cramped because of the luggage. Bobby and I were sitting on top of the rucksacks, which we had put on the seat. But the girls from the FC (Flying Column) arrived with a truck full of suitcases and began to fill up the compartments, so we could barely see one another. It was freezing but, we said to one another, it will warm up as soon as the engine gets going. All this time, more and more luggage kept arriving: the luggage we had dropped off as "freight." The corridor along the compartments was crammed with suitcases, rucksacks, blankets, hampers, etc., blocking access to the lavatory. We sat hemmed in by suitcases, on top of the rucksack, with our

8 Welfare division.

Auszug a.d.Kennkarte - Uittreksel u/h Persoonsbewijs.

Nummer v.h.Persoonsbewijs: A.35 / No 591056

Naam: Levie--

Voornaam: Mirjam Sophie--

Geboortedatum: 20 Maart 1917

Plaats en land van geboorte: Amsterdam - Nederland

Nationaliteit: Nederlander

Gehuwd met:

Gesch.
―――――― op:
Overl.

Laatste beroep: /Kantoorbediende/ Secretaresse Joodsche Raad

Laatste woonadres: Amsterdam,Pretoriusstr 20 I

Signalement: Man/Vrouw - Kenmerken:

Uitgereikt op: 5 November 1941

In Gemeente: Amsterdam

Voor uittreksel conform,

Lager Westerbork,den 10 Januari 1944.

Voor den Burgemeester van Westerbork,

De chef van de hulpsecretarie

"Lager Westerbork"

(B.T. van Donselaar)

Part of Mirjam Sophie Levie's identity card, issued in Westerbork, 10 January 1944,
signed by a representative of the mayor of Westerbork

Author's collection

feet wedged between other luggage. We didn't know the people in our compartment, but they turned out to be very friendly.

At half-past five, the train pulled out of the camp at a snail's pace and came to a halt just outside the camp. We did our best to create some order in the chaos, put the rucksack on the floor, a suitcase on the seat and then one of our travel companions and I sat on top of it. Quite comfortable at first, but later the two wooden straps around the suitcase began to hurt. The train left at a quarter-past six. Slowly. It was cold, the train unheated, a beautiful, clear night — it was Tuesday, 11 January. Meanwhile, we had discovered that our provisions hadn't been loaded onto the train, and I was particularly sorry about the delicious fish patties. Fortunately, Father and Bobby had bread and butter with them, Mother had nougat and liquorice in her bag — carefully saved all these months — and I had mints, so at least we had something for the journey. Still, a shame about the jam, butter, oats, peas, sugar, etc., we had so carefully kept back from our parcels for the "transport." And as for the marvels they had promised us — cigarettes, sausages, apples — we never saw any of them. The train went terribly slowly, kept stopping, and I tried to absorb the fact that we were crossing the border, into the unknown, but nothing sank in. I was neither sad, not even for Father and Mother, nor hopeful — only a little curious. We crossed the border at Nieuweschans, and passed Leer, where we saw the first German houses. The train stopped frequently and didn't go very fast. We chatted, ate and laughed, and every now and then our neighbours needed the lavatory and clambered over our suitcases, etc. Otherwise, the journey passed without incident. The train was unlit, because it had no black-out blinds,[9] so we had an excellent view. As I said, it was an exceptionally clear night. The only thing worth pointing out is that nearly all the stations in Germany were brightly lit, whereas in Holland you couldn't see a thing.

---

9   Trains were a sought-after target for British and American pilots. Turning on lights on a train without black-out blinds would have drawn the attention of the pilots.

And then... Bremen. We rode past a deserted heap of rubble! Deserted, obviously, since it was night. But the streets of large, large neighbourhoods — the train spent several minutes passing them — were strewn with rubble, with collapsed houses or houses without roofs or one or two floors missing. Through the occasional gap you would glimpse collapsed or subsided houses, and the houses that were still standing without windows or doors. Some neighbourhoods were relatively unscathed, and would still have a tram, for example. But there, too, lots of houses without windows. Bremen made up for the entire journey.

At three o'clock we stopped. Where, I still don't know. We tried to get some sleep, although we were uncomfortable, and dozed a little. At approx. six o'clock we continued, moving further and further from the civilized world. No more houses... heathland, now and then some woodland. In a word, the sticks. Until we reached a tiny station somewhere... Celle!! Somebody said: "So far, they haven't duped us. We aren't in Poland, but in Celle." Indeed. In Celle we drove up and down for a bit; apparently we had to get onto another track. Then, it must have been around half-past eight, it was certainly completely light by now, the train began to move again, slowly. And when it inched past a small platform, we spotted a column of greens — my neighbour said: "*Waffen-SS*" — marching onto the platform. A moment later, we saw how the platform on either side of the train was cordoned off, with a fellow with a rifle and a bloodhound positioned at approx. 30-metre intervals. We looked at one another... Then the train came to a halt and the compartments were opened. "*Raus! Raus!*"[10] Then I knew what time of day it was. We pulled the luggage out onto the platform, and schlepped it to a waiting car. Then we walked to the camp. The weather was gorgeous, and we were happy to be moving our frozen feet. We walked along a beautiful, hilly avenue — the Adolf Hitler Strasse. I never thought I'd be walking along one of these — past

10 "Out! Out!"

lots of decent-looking army barracks. After walking for an hour or so, we came to a barrier that was lifted. In we went. On either side, small wooden barracks, green, dilapidated, squalid. We saw a lot of people in overalls, with a red cross on the back, who looked wretched and clearly had to work extremely hard. Who these people are, I still haven't figured out. Some appeared to be Russian, judging by their faces. We passed a small field that had a sign with a skull and two bones, by way of a "no trespassing" sign.

On and on we went, past barrier after barrier, until we identified some Jews by their Stars of David, and we recognized someone who had left on the Theresienstadt transport last September. So he didn't go to Theresienstadt, but to Celle. At that point, we didn't yet know that the entire Theresienstadt transport had ended up here; we thought the Palestine people from that transport had been sent from Theresienstadt to Celle. But now we know they never went to Theresienstadt, none of them. We had to line up in ranks of five in a large open space. Behind us three small stone buildings, the latrines, without partitions, just as in Westerbork, although these had lids to cover the holes. In front of us the pathetic little wooden barracks.

There we stood, in ranks of five, being shouted at. But not manhandled. After we'd been standing there for a couple of hours, a green — I'll make some enquiries as to who or what exactly they are[11] — clambered onto a bench and started calling up groups of people, in alphabetical order, for registration. Money had to be handed over — we had actually been allowed to take *f*250 with us — but we were *not* searched!! Then off to the barracks. Men and women separately, divided by barbed wire and a gate that can be locked. Small barracks. A dining area, leading straight to a dormitory. Small wooden bunk-beds, two tiers, with a straw

---

11 The "greens" mentioned by Mirjam in this letter — and from now on — are SS guards in the Bergen-Belsen concentration camp. They are not the *Orpo* policemen who wore green uniforms.

bag — not a straw mattress — and a straw pillow. An overcrowded room, with narrow aisles, three lights, a lavatory. A dining area with large wooden tables and benches and a few small, narrow cupboards. From there: collecting the luggage. All the luggage lay strewn haphazardly over a large field. Lots of frantic rummaging, and people crying because they couldn't find their things; I nearly did, too, because my blanket bag had gone. Luckily I found it, as well as the provisions! Schlepped everything back, for it was already getting dark. The elderly were at their wits' end, because people only thought of themselves. Schlepped it all to the barracks, the men to theirs, and then the gate was locked! Made the beds and then we ate. Some kind of cabbage, I believe, I can't quite remember. We had good spots, Bobby and I on the upper tier, below the light, Mother on the lower tier. To bed. Scared to death of falling out, didn't sleep a wink, not knowing when to get up.

Suddenly the order: "In front of the barracks!" In pyjamas, with a cardigan and coat on top, fur mittens, scarf, socks and shoes… outside the barracks door. Told Mother to stay indoors, with fear in my heart, not knowing how the Huns would react, although so far they had been fairly decent. Standing… an hour to be counted and counted again. The little children were crying and shivering with cold, and still it didn't add up. Two men from Theresienstadt are more or less in charge here, that's to say, they act as intermediaries between the Germans and the Jews. Back inside, food, porridge I believe, not sure. Some of our luggage had to be taken to a depot, the rest in the cupboards — five people share a small cupboard in which they can keep their coats and tableware.

I'd been appointed administrator and was preparing a list of all the people in the barracks — I'm in Barracks 19. How this appointment came about, I don't know. We had only just arrived in the barracks when Mr Katz, the husband of our *Barackenleiterin*,[12]

---

12 Barracks leader.

approached me and said: "*Sie sind die Assistentin meiner Frau.*"[13] Food — cabbage soup and bread, I believe — and to bed. Slept better, but was woken up at midnight, because the Germans turned up with a list of people whose nationality they wanted to know. Woke those people at six o'clock, enquired after their papers, took the list to the appropriate barracks, washed — I hadn't washed the previous day — roll call. Stood for another couple of hours. In the afternoon, I wanted to draw up a table plan. You know we share the barracks with people who have English papers. Most of them are rather rude people, and they already had a bad name in Westerbork. We also have the Nordheim, Lissauer, Mossel, Pinkhof and Simon de Jong families in our barracks.

More next time, my love. It's getting too dark and I need to go and help. Perhaps this evening; if not, perhaps tomorrow. Everything here is so uncertain you can't plan anything in advance. Bye, my dear. When I arrived here amid all the squalor, I felt completely cut off from you and that it was all over for us. But hope springs eternal.

20 January

I'm continuing my account amid an infernal din. In chronological order, because I don't have the peace of mind to provide you with any commentary. I intend to give you the story so far and save a more detailed reflection on events for later.

In the meantime, I got called out to schlep *gamellen*.[14] You're rushed off your feet here. But I'll write about that when I've had a chance to think about it.

The table plan was a complete failure and spoilt our Friday evening. After dinner we all sat at a table together, recited *Kiddush*[15]

13 "You are my wife's assistant."
14 Iron food barrels.
15 *Kiddush*, which means "sanctification" in Hebrew, is a blessing said to sanctify the Sabbath or a Jewish holiday.

and sang a little. It was rather forced, naturally, as we weren't at all in the mood for singing, but we put on a brave face for the children's sake. Halfway through... the lights went out. Air-raid warning! I can't tell you how eerie it was. In the pitch-dark, with all these women who started bickering out of sheer nervousness. A green stormed in and barked that it was strictly forbidden to burn candles, because an attack would leave us all dead. Later, we were allowed to light a small candle. The children were afraid, some were crying. We then had another little sing-song in the pitch-dark and told stories. As the evening wore on, the children fell asleep in our laps. We took them to bed and, not knowing what to do with ourselves, eventually went to bed as well. The lavatory in our barracks was out of order, but we weren't allowed to go outside, so we had to wee in a bucket (approx. 140 women), in jam jars, saucepans, etc. I haven't told you yet that our barracks has no washroom. The barracks opposite us has a single washroom — so far it has always been out of order — in which *all* women are expected to wash. A detailed description of the camp will follow. But not of the entire camp, which is said to go on for miles, and of which we know nothing.

Nothing special to report about Shabbat, except that it passed unnoticed. The men worked a little less, as they do across Germany, but because you're rushed off your feet here, the men could still only spend a very short time with the women. We spend every waking hour schlepping iron food barrels and everybody has to be in by seven o'clock, the men in their separate barracks. The gate is locked behind them. It's getting too dark now, I have to stop.

21 January

I'm continuing my letter in the men's barracks. You're never really relaxed here, for you can always be called away for some job or other, carrying food barrels, etc. On Sunday, roll call was very brief. Only 15 minutes. The Huns themselves were clearly keen to get back inside. But Monday was a day I'm not likely to forget. The numbers didn't add up, and they were so bad-tempered that they kept us standing until after our midday meal. The men who had gone to the *Entlausungseinrichtung*[16] were forced to line up as well, and were sent back to work without food. And the men who'd been labouring had to line up, too, covered in dirt. Then there's a peeling commando to which Bobby has been assigned. Everything is supervised by the Germans. And the men have to schlep wood, cut trees, etc.

Now on to the *Entlausung*[17] of the women. From the waiting room you enter another room, where the racks of clothing have been returned. You go there starkers. The clothes are nice and warm, because the clothing racks have been pulled through hot air. You dress, wait, get counted and off you go. This is about all that happened in the past few days. Next Tuesday or Wednesday,

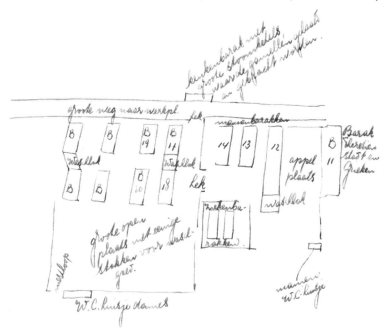

16 Delousing facility.
17 Delousing.

the Theresienstadt transport is finally going to Theresienstadt (at least that's what they're told), raising our own hopes of getting out. People say we're in the best camp in Germany. And yet this camp is far worse than Westerbork in terms of hygiene, freedom and lots of other things.

It's time to stop, my love. Shabbat Shalom, my dearest, and I hope that sometime soon I can prepare you a wonderful Friday evening. Bye, sweetheart. Yesterday was six years since you left, by train, for Palestine. I don't know how I've borne it, but I had to.

23 January

From now on, I'm going to try to write a couple of times a day, a little at a time, so I have less to write each time and I can go into a bit more detail and give you a better idea of what we're going through.

At half-past five, the lavatory guard rings a bell. Every night, five people keep two-hour vigils beside the only lavatory in our barracks to ensure the women don't throw in any paper or sanitary towels, etc., because the thing doesn't flush very well. The mothers with children, who have a lot to do, get up. The others stay in bed a little longer. At six o'clock, Albala — the Greek Jew who mediates with the Germans and who, as far as we can tell, grovels a great deal — enters the barracks, blows a whistle and shouts: "*Auf, bitte!*"[18] At approx. a quarter-past six, I get up. My towel and washcloth are on a little rack, which I fashioned from a hanger and some pieces of string. I take soap, toothbrush and paste from my sponge bag — it's in a small box on the beam — put on a coat, which hangs from a nail in the ceiling, and embark on my journey. To get to the women's washroom, we need to cross a large field. But throughout the time we've been here, the women's washroom has been out of order.

18 "Get up, please."

222 • *Letters Never Sent*

Most of the women fetch water in pots and pans the day before and use this to wash in the morning. We do the same for Mother. But Bobby and I wash with the men. I'm not prudish, and if I ever was I'm now well and truly cured. But you can't have a proper wash with the men, at least not naked. One "advantage" is that there's only a tiny dimmed light, so you can barely see.

The journey there is simply a nightmare. It's pitch-dark, and this morning it was very wet and windy. I trudge through the mud in my socks and shoes. Within spitting distance, by the fence, I hear the voices of the men fetching barrels of coffee, but I see nothing. One of my shoes gets stuck in the mud. Through the gate to the men's barracks, straight on to the men's washroom. Swarming in the semi-dark. I don't know what to do with my coat, then decide to hang it on the door to the men's dormitory. I wash, as best as I can. Journey back. Continue dressing, combing my hair. A few boards fell out of my bed this morning; it happens all the time here. The bottom of the bed is made up of loose boards and because they're a bit too short, they keep falling out, onto the downstairs neighbour — Mother. Fetch coffee, without milk and sugar, but nice and hot. Breakfast. Bread and a bit of synthetic honey (from our provisions). Then to the latrines, again quite a trek. But at least now it's a little lighter.

And now I'm writing here while the ward is being cleaned and full of people who aren't at work — women over 60 and mothers of children under four. The light is abominably bad. At half-past seven, the workers make their way to the roll-call area. Some time later, we see a column of men and women walking to work along the main road, in ranks of five, silent. Greeting isn't allowed; somebody who did got a stone hurled at his head. But we do greet furtively. I have to stop, my table is being cleaned. More after roll call.

Roll call was awful. I already wrote to you that the weather is vile, wet and windy, and the terrain is one big pool of mud. Our barracks leader didn't join us so she could search the barracks for stolen goods while everybody was out. I had to take her place.

Because of the beastly weather, we had left as many people as possible in the barracks, i.e., elderly women, children under 10, in short, bent the rules as much as we could. We made our way to the roll-call area and, after a couple of minutes, the Hun who always does the counting turned up — we call him Wilhelm Tell[19] — and I had to "report," that's to say, each barracks leader has to give the number of his or her barracks, along with the number of people who have turned up for roll call. The others are counted inside the barracks, but the leader must also know their number in case the Hun asks for them. Hence: Barracks 19 — *vierzig Personen.*[20] Still in the barracks were six mothers, 20 children under six, 15 children between six and 10, 14 sick and four bed-ridden people. We noticed at once that Wilhelm was in a foul mood. And indeed… after a few minutes, everyone who had stayed in the barracks came hobbling out. Little children, old dears, in a word, everybody. I lined them up in ranks of five, separate from those I had already reported. But the sick from all the barracks had to stand together. I walked back over to create some order in the chaos, so they wouldn't be shouted at again, but I was ordered to stand with the people of my own barracks. So back I went. At that point we were allowed to march off, but the elderly and sick had to stand to attention for an hour. It was awful. Mothers cried because their children had to stand there for an hour while they were allowed to go. We slunk off.

A little later: schlepping barrels from the kitchen to the distribution area. Back. Gave Mother a sandwich, while I had some rolled oats and sugar, uncooked. Who would have thought? After an hour the others returned, soaking wet of course. We sat them down by the stove and gave them coffee. Then: food. A spoonful of carrots mixed with turnips and four small potatoes in their jackets each. Another big row, because one reckons she has less

---

19 After the famous Swiss hero. A play on words, from the Dutch *"tellen"* = "to count."

20 40 people.

than another. We're now introducing a system whereby we call people according to their bed number whenever we have a little "extra," i.e., whenever there's a little left over after the food has been fairly distributed. In this way, everybody will have their turn. After the meal, I chatted briefly with Chelly Nordheim and Ro Lissauer and studied Hebrew for an hour with Riwka Mossel. And now I'm talking to you again. But I ought to do it a little less openly, because everybody wants to know if I'm writing a diary. Only I don't know how, because everything you do here is public. Everybody literally knows whether you're doing a wee or a poo. Degrading.

I won't have much to write in the next few days, because the days are all alike. On the one hand, it's quieter this afternoon because we can't be called away for work — today is Sunday and an official day off — on the other hand, it's much busier because everybody is "at home." And I have already told you about the calibre of people here. Absolutely disgraceful. Last week I saved my potatoes, and then in the evening fried them and shared them with Mother. The whole table sat there staring and you could hear them think: I bet she took ours. Ro Lissauer told me how they're watching in the evening to see if we're taking bigger helpings. It's awful, the people are like hyenas.

Let me tell you what the rest of the afternoon will probably be like; that way there's less to write tomorrow. It's a pity, because writing is my only pleasure here, but the risk of people finding out is too great. I'll keep it short. Riwka Mossel lent me a book. A bit of reading, and then we get our rations of bread, margarine (30g per person per week), a spoonful of jam per person and *kürbis*.[21] Between six and seven I'm on lavatory duty in the barracks across the road, where fortunately the washroom has reopened. Appoint and instruct tonight's lavatory guards in our barracks. Fix the boards that have fallen out of my bed again and to bed! The best time of the day, thinking and dreaming of you. Officially, we have

---

21 Pickled pumpkin.

to be in bed by eight o'clock, but it's usually a little later for me because I often have things to discuss with the barracks leader.

24 January

The above must be corrected. We received no margarine. The Greeks pinched it from under our noses. Perhaps we'll receive some tomorrow evening. We received no *kürbis* either. This morning we could wash in the women's washroom for the first time. I now take pleasure in something as simple as that. It's a bit lighter now as well. Otherwise, the programme was the same as yesterday. Coffee (yesterday afternoon we had mint tea), bread, synthetic honey (from our provisions). Roll call. Almost everybody had to line up outside and it was over after 30 minutes. Prepared a list based on bed numbers, schlepped barrels and distributed food. It's my job to record who has, and who hasn't, received an extra portion.

25 January

I was extremely busy yesterday evening. The food rations were wrong, so lots of fuss and bother. We had bread, *kürbis*, jam and margarine rations. It's a lot of work, the more so because we were short of eight portions of margarine and had to take a little from each of the available portions to make up for the shortage. A mess! We also had a kind of watery gruel, which I made into a pudding with our last packet of pudding powder. Our cupboards, in which we're not allowed to keep leftover food, were inspected yesterday. And apparently too few people reported for work. As a punishment, the others had to work until eight o'clock, and today we had to send 15 extra women, so even the women between 50 and 60 had to go. If it happens again, the penalty, we were threatened, will be a withdrawal of food rations, an hour's marching around the roll-call area (after work), and standing to attention for three hours.

We had no roll call this morning, because the Theresienstadt people are leaving tonight. They've been assured that they're really going to Theresienstadt and that their journey will take three days. They will be given decent food rations, but travel in cattle trucks. Of course, that will be the last we hear from them. I'm going to stop. More later.

26 January

There's so much to write about every day and I forget such an awful lot every day that I really ought to write much longer accounts. You still have no idea about all the mad rushing around or the indignation over the fact that elderly people have to work while the mothers of children under three, i.e., young women, are free. For example, I forgot to tell you that every evening after seven o'clock, the greens march in to check for men in our barracks. Sometimes they crack jokes; at other times they're in a foul mood. I also forgot that we have air-raid warnings nearly every night, and that we have grown so used to them that we can clear our beds, undress and go to bed in the pitch-dark. Dormitory inspection, with different briefings every day. First they tell you to tuck the blankets in, then to fold them, until nobody knows what's what anymore. It's called *Bettenbau*.[22] The songs the children sing: I don't know them all yet. In Westerbork, the punishment barracks used to march to the following song:

We are the fine young lads
From the S-Company
We work like dogs all day

22 Bed-making, literally bed-building.

But never shed a tear
We'll never give up hope
However long it takes
The time will surely come
When we're back in Amsterdam.

(to the tune of *Turnlied*)[23]

The children here sing to the same tune:

Right early in the morning
As we are getting up
The soldiers come a-marching
To do their totting up
They count and count and count
A hundred times or more
And if it doesn't tally up
We stand until we're sore!

There's another ditty to the tune of the *Turnlied*, but I'm not familiar with it.

Otherwise there's nothing special to report about yesterday. We received bread, curd cheese and a nice soup. But as I said, people were quite agitated. The Theresienstadt transport has left and rumour has it that a transport of 2,000 people will be arriving from Westerbork tomorrow.

This morning we had a shower, which was lovely, because it meant we didn't have to show up for roll call. The weather was beastly and the others spent three-quarters of an hour standing outside and another half-hour inside. This afternoon I washed some clothes — we ate turnips + carrots + four small potatoes in their jackets — and then at three o'clock roll call again, soaking wet

---

23 A popular Dutch song, lit., "Gymnastics Song."

and cold. As of today, the barracks leader has to stay inside while the *Stellvertreterin*[24] — that's me — has to report the numbers in the roll-call area. Schlepped food barrels afterwards and now I'm writing to you. But I have to stop again, because it's getting too dark. Yesterday afternoon I chatted for about an hour with somebody from the men's barracks. And this morning Dasberg came here for a list of the children. They want to try and set up a school. And this evening I have to hand in yet another list of the working people. All in all, plenty to do. I'm going to stop. More tomorrow.

I forgot to tell you about the establishment of a kind of Jewish Council here, with Eitje, Kan, Gelber, Weiss, Ahlfeld and Andriesse, as well as with Albala (the Greek), as an intermediary between them and the Germans. Whether something will come of it remains to be seen. These people don't have to do any of the regular work.

27 January

After an extremely upsetting midday meal — white cabbage + four small potatoes in their jackets — because there was very little food, a quick note from me. The weather is vile again. Word had it that roll call would be inside the barracks and, if it went well, we would do this every day. We already got our hopes up... but no, a moment later the greens came to fetch us and we had to make our way to the roll-call area after all. Luckily, the numbers tallied after 10 minutes. Blatant bullying; they might as well have done it inside the barracks.

The transport from Westerbork didn't arrive. But this morning the rumour went round that we will be exchanged in two weeks' time. In the meantime, I got called away to *schlep* coal. *Sehen muss ich.*[25] But the mere thought of it takes my breath away. And I keep thinking about what I'm going to eat. Prosaic, don't you think?

24 Deputy.
25 Seeing is believing.

Yesterday somebody told me they thought I was 19, 20. I'm very happy to know that I have retained my youthful looks for you, despite everything we've been through.

28 January

It's Friday again today. Every day is the same, with one indistinguishable from the next. Yesterday evening we had bread, *kürbis* and a kind of rhubarb soup. Another air-raid warning and to bed in the dark. I forgot to mention that I have a very bad cough and I haven't slept for several nights. It was so bad, I was scared to death it might be pneumonia. And there are no medicines here. "*Es gibt nur Leben oder Sterben*,"[26] the commandant has said. But fortunately I slept soundly last night, and I'm coughing much less. My feet are always cold and wet, because I walk in and out of the barracks all the time. Luckily we still manage to keep clean. I have a more or less proper wash every morning and a shower once a week. In Westerbork I also had clean underclothes, because we could take our things to the laundry every now and then. We can't do this here and have to wash everything ourselves and then hold each individual item up to the stove until it's dry. You can't put anything down or you lose it. Last night I lost another jar of *kürbis* and a knife. Filched from my cupboard. One of the worst things about being here is that the Palestine people aren't together, but distributed across various barracks. The people here are awful. It was already notorious in Westerbork. It occurred to me this morning that I wouldn't be able to write to you about roll call in the dark, which takes place every morning at seven for the outdoor workers. But today we were told that tomorrow there will be two roll calls, at seven and at nine, for everybody. In honour of our Shabbat!

26 "There is only life or death."

I'm going to stop, my love. We just saw a group of people marching along the main road, with luggage. Apparently, they're Russians moving to the prisoner barracks.

This place is full of surprises. This afternoon, we all had to attend roll call, except the children under 15. Many who've been on indoor duty until now will be moved to the shoes (the *Schuh-Kommando*).[27] I managed to avoid it, as *Stellvertretend Barackenleiterin*,[28] but I felt ashamed when I saw the others leave.

One other thing I forgot. I mentioned the corruption in Westerbork. I can't write to you about corruption here, for I know nothing about it. Only that the Greeks are said to have white bread and butter lying openly on the table. What happens is that children up to age three and their mothers receive some extra rations, i.e., butter, milk, sausage, white bread, and the Greeks simply filch some of it. And these are the *Jews*. Words fail me.

29 January

My dear boy. Today is Shabbat, although you wouldn't know it. And because I do nothing but write (for work and other kinds of *Chillul Shabbat*),[29] I can't resist the temptation to write to you and have a quick chat, even though I know I shouldn't. We did have roll call at seven o'clock this morning. It was the usual selection for the various work commandos. One of the greens has a powerful torch, and uses it to shine at everybody in the face to take his pick. Like cattle.

Albala is a rotten bastard, as I told you. This morning he yelled at the barracks leaders again, such that people started jeering. Albala approached the group doing this and yelled: "Who did that?"

27 The shoe commando, the barracks where workers took apart old shoes to salvage usable parts.
28 Deputy barracks leader.
29 Violations of the Sabbath.

When he got no response, he called for... the *Oberscharführer*,[30] who fortunately pretended not to hear. Yesterday, he moved a woman from the potato kitchen (comparatively pleasant work) to the shoes, only because he wanted a Greek woman in the kitchen. The Russians I mentioned yesterday have left, the women anyway. To Vittel they say. They also say that the Greeks are leaving shortly, and then it will be our turn. I daren't get my hopes up.

Yesterday, we suddenly saw on one of the beds: *"Die letzten Juden gingen nach Auschwitz zur Vergasung (tod)."*[31] Nobody knows who wrote it. It's very grim and what exactly it refers to, nobody knows. Perhaps (G-d forbid) we'll find out later.

It's odd how quickly people forget. In Westerbork, everybody groused and longed to be back in Amsterdam. Here everybody grouses about Celle and talks about Westerbork as if it were paradise. And nobody talks about Amsterdam anymore. Hopefully, we'll never have it so bad that we long to be back in Celle. Every now and then, when you think about how much people must be suffering, it seems a miracle that we're bearing up at all. One woman, a bit older than most, lost her husband in Westerbork and is here on her own. Her life seems so meaningless to me, without any promise of happiness. Another woman is here with her husband who's almost completely blind and thus dependent on care. One time this man was dragged out to work, and when they realized he was genuinely unable to see, they left him out in the rain all day. He wasn't allowed to go back. A young woman's husband is in a concentration camp and she doesn't know whether he's dead or alive. Everybody has his own sorrow and I believe we haven't yet grasped what has befallen us.

It's afternoon now, and we just had another *Arbeitsappell*,[32] that's to say, everybody had to go to the roll-call area for selection of

---

30 A commissioned SS officer, equivalent to a sergeant.
31 "The last Jews went to Auschwitz to be gassed (death)."
32 Duty roll call.

the work commandos. For the record: This afternoon we ate turnips and potatoes in their jackets again. Yesterday evening we had bread and a broth. This evening, bread + sauerkraut salad.

I have nearly completed my round-up of the week's events, sweetheart. I'm vain enough to believe that this diary may be found hundreds of years from now and serve as an important source of information. That's why I included all the trivial things, because they may provide an outsider with a more vivid picture. After all, I'm so caught up in all this that I can't put myself in the shoes of a person who isn't going through this himself and therefore knows nothing about it. Perhaps one day our children will read it. (I feel just like Glückel von Hameln.)[33] But as soon as I'm back with you, it's *schluss*.[34] From now on, I intend to limit myself to writing notes instead of such lengthy sagas.

30 January

The train has pulled in, and now we're in Celle
With all the yelling and beating, life here is hell
The Huns torment us with their endless roll call
Keeping us standing till well after nightfall
And look, there's Albala, a whistle in hand
In ranks of five we are told to now stand
And if the numbers don't tally then he'll be irate
He'll raise his voice, shouting: You people just wait!

(to the tune of the *Turnlied*)

Punishment tomorrow, because people organised (= stole) wood. Work an hour longer.

---

33 Glückel of Hamelin (1646–1724) was a Jewish woman who kept a diary. Written in Yiddish, her life-story was originally intended for her children.
34 I will stop writing.

31 January

Last night, 83 Jews arrived from Benghazi, Darna, Tula.[35] Dual nationality. They look wretched, almost naked. Have been through seven camps.

Worked in the shoes this afternoon to relieve somebody else. Proper slave labour.

2 February

No roll call. Transport from Westerbork on its way.

8 February

The transport from Westerbork arrived, 900 people, and they've already settled in. They didn't bring much news; one transport left Westerbork for Poland and another for Theresienstadt. Little news on the war. I'm not really in the mood to write. It's too busy here for any kind of coherent thought. No more word on our departure. Last week everybody claimed that the people with English papers would be leaving on 11 February, but now, with the 11th rapidly approaching, nobody believes it anymore. Yesterday somebody said: "When I wake up in the morning I cry because it's the break of day, and when I go to bed at night I wish the night would last forever." It's true. We're used to this place now, it's bearable and could be even worse… but the only thing that keeps us going is the hope of getting away. That said, I personally don't expect a camp in Sweden or England to be much better; the only thing that matters is that they're not in Germany. For if we're here when the war ends — true, the end is still nowhere in sight — it could take ages for their

---

35 Benghazi and Darna are towns in Libya. Tula is a village in Sardinia.

lordships to decide our fate. I'm going to stop, my love, because I'm just stating the obvious. Let me try to give you a very rough sketch of the sharp contrast between then and now.

The JC in "normal" times, i.e., not too busy. It's two o'clock on a Friday afternoon and I'm sitting opposite Eitje, taking notes. Halfway through a letter, he says: "I'm going home early this afternoon, Shabbat starts at five." He finishes dictating the letters. "Type them up quickly, for I need to go." At four o'clock, he's gone. A handshake and a smile: "Good *Shabbos*, love, and see you at my house at eight o'clock tomorrow evening (to work)." "I'm visiting tomorrow afternoon." "Oh yes, that's right. Well, see you then." And off he goes. At a quarter-to five, I cycle over to his house to get the letters signed. The maid shows me into the room and tells me that Eitje will be down shortly. And indeed, a moment later he appears, freshly bathed, shaven and dressed to the nines — white shirt, black Shabbat suit, you know what I mean. The maid leaves to set the table, the candles have already been lit, he signs in a hurry, snaps the mail folder shut and I dash off. The next day, I come for a visit. He's wearing a tail-coat now. The table is covered with a white cloth. Eitje sits in front of one window; his wife, in a dark-blue dress with white lace, in front of the other. On the table are a few silver platters with biscuits and the like. We talk: about the Committee, about all kinds of things. Other guests arrive and there are introductions. Eitje admires my suit and my large hat and talks about which of my clothes he likes and dislikes. He shows me out and thanks me for my visit. I walk down Sarphatistraat and go to no. 62 [Nieuwe Keizersgracht].

Last week's Shabbat. The weather is awful. I have discussed a few matters in Barracks 11 and squelch through the mud back to my own, dressed as a tramp (no exaggeration), with downright filthy shoes and stockings (and you know how smart my shoes and stockings used to be), cold and miserable. Close to my barracks, a few men are trying to drain the soil a little bit, with long shovels and spades. One of them is Eitje, dressed as my opposite number, wearing a cap. This is what we have come to. I've tried to convey how somebody like Eitje used to treasure the Shabbat, what painstaking preparations were made, how he spent the day... and what has become of Shabbat here. And perhaps it will be all right in the end, but it does give you an idea of our general decline, both materially and culturally.

10 February

This morning I was terribly down, because I missed you so much and I'm so sorry that the years, which we could have spent so happily together, are just slipping by without any meaning. When I saw my filthy underclothes, I could have cried, and suddenly everything seemed unbearable. Sometimes, e.g., when I see something clean, I have visions of a quiet, tidy house, which is clean and full of beautiful things. I'm not asking for much, just a cosy room with all the pretty things we already own. I'd better not think about it, or I'll never stop dreaming. During the war, the first few years anyway, I bought a great deal; after all, money had become meaningless and I had enough. I'm in better spirits now because... we had no roll call! It's bitterly cold, with an icy wind and a thick blanket of snow mixed with mud. We were dreading the prospect of roll call. We counted the people inside the barracks and lined them up, and the whole troop had just walked out of the building when a green marching along the main road signalled: no roll call. We jumped for joy inside the barracks. That's why I'm in a much better mood. We're off to have a shower.

12 February

In a hurry. Yesterday was a dreadful day. Roll call from a quarter-past seven until half-past ten, and from half-past eleven until a quarter-past three. *Angeblich,*[36] because two barracks had reported late in the morning, but probably because the Germans were annoyed by the constant air-raid warnings the day before yesterday and at night. When a woman fainted and people asked to take her back to the barracks, the boss said: *"Lass sie kaputtgehen, bei uns gehen so viele kaputt."*[37] I didn't have to go, that's to say only in the morning, but it was upsetting to know that Mother had to stand all day. In the afternoon we brought in some benches, and the children, who had been allowed to stay inside, visited their mothers. Fortunately, they were allowed to wander around and didn't have to stay in line. I made a big jug of hot *lemon secco*[38] and secretly passed it round in the roll-call area. But it was awful, all the same. And the people in the work commandos weren't allowed to come back and had to work all day without food. We, too, received our rations when the others did, i.e., we fasted for a day. That brings you up to date, sweetheart.

16 February

A transport from Westerbork arrived unexpectedly today. We were not expecting it until next week. We have no news yet, as they only just arrived and will be completely isolated from us until they've been through quarantine. A total of 770 people: Palestine, 120.000 stamps and South American papers. Last week, a transport left Westerbork for Auschwitz; the entire hospital barracks, irrespective of *Sperrung,*[39] was deported. Only a handful of Palestine people were spared. I may know more tomorrow. Before I forget, the African Jews [from Benghazi, etc.] will be leaving soon. To Vittel, they say, with Palestine scheduled for 1 March. So... fresh hopes. Rereading

---

36 Allegedly.
37 "Let her rot, so many of our men are rotting."
38 Powdered surrogate lemon extract.
39 Exemption.

the above, I see that I forgot to tell you that on Monday we were counted twice again, because the numbers didn't tally. But today, due to the transport, no roll call. Yesterday we had apple sauce, gone off a bit, but still tasty. We also received washing powder, clay soap and toilet paper. Astonishing!! But roll call remains dreadful, especially with all the snow, wind and hail we've been having. On the other hand, we must count ourselves lucky that it's not utterly freezing cold. And every day brings us closer to spring, to peace and... to you! Isn't that a beautiful, poetic way to end?

19 February

Not much to say. It has been bitterly cold of late, with snow and a nasty, biting wind. Luckily, roll call didn't last very long. The day before yesterday, the African Jews did indeed leave. Of course, this was immediately followed by rumours of all of us, including the English, leaving soon for Palestine. The sooner the better. 1 March or 3 March, they say. You know, darling, a while ago Zadok Mossel and I were talking about you. Mossel was wondering whether we might celebrate the *Seder* together. And suddenly I could see myself at some table or other... all by myself. I felt sick with despair. Admittedly, it doesn't look as if, should we still be here, we can celebrate the *Seder* — no men, no *Haggadot*,[40] no *matzot*, no light — but from time to time, I do see myself sitting by your side and listening to your voice.

Charles Polak died yesterday; you know him, the secretary of the Zionist League. He had been married for seven years, and leaves a wife and small child. He caught pneumonia here. Dead within days. It's the very, very worst that can happen, quite irrevocable. It's even worse here, because nobody can do anything for his wife;

---

40 Plural of *Haggadah*, the religious text featuring the story of the Exodus from Egypt and the ritual of the *Seder*.

she has to report for roll call as usual. The corpse is collected with a dung cart to be cremated, and nobody is allowed to escort it. Their little boy was sick, too, and was admitted to the hospital barracks so he wouldn't have to attend roll call. They wanted to put him in the bed where his father had just died! I'll leave it at this, my love. I'm looking forward to rereading your letters this afternoon, for the umpteenth time. Somebody came up to me yesterday and said I would make a good mother, because the children are so fond of me. Wonderful!

21 February

My spirits are soaring! Mrs Katz, our barracks leader, just asked Albala whether we're leaving, whereupon he replied: "*demnächst.*"[41] Imagine: We may be fortunate enough to get out. I was in such a bad mood yesterday. It was freezing cold, the barracks was scarcely heated, and I had that sinking feeling again. But today it's milder and I'm feeling a bit better. A *hesped*[42] for Charles Polak was held yesterday. Herzberg[43] spoke, not in his usual, rhetorical fashion, but very unaffected and good. He cried a great deal when he also commemorated Paul Denekamp, and I suspect that he was really crying for himself and for all of us when he said: "I can still see them walking together." So I see them in my imagination, two young, well-dressed people. And now... It was remarkable, though, that we could have this kind of meeting at all. Enough for today. They're saying: Friday in a week!

41 "Soon."
42 Eulogy.
43 Abel Herzberg was chairman of the Dutch Zionist Organization.

24 February

Seventy people with English and Palestinian papers who had been interned in Italy arrived today. They're from North Africa. And five people here received parcels from Holland. I believe it bodes well that we're actually receiving the parcels. Everything was searched, loaves cut open, but nothing stolen. It's bitterly cold, but very bright and sunny. I'm going to stop now. Not in the mood today. Yesterday I was brimming with optimism, but today I'm much gloomier.

25 February

Just for the record, a few items I forgot to mention. Now that it gets light earlier, our working hours have been extended. Roll call takes place as early as a quarter-to seven and the work commandos only return after six in the evening. This week it has been 12 degrees below zero every single morning.

The Africans who arrived here yesterday travelled for five days. The camp they were in came under the administration of the Red Cross, which also provided food for their journey, kosher no less.

The people here live on photographs and memories. On their Sundays off and in the evenings they show them to one another and get immense pleasure from the beautiful clothes or, when taken indoors, the beautiful interiors.

I'm so anxious, all I can think of is the *Austausch*. And the faster Friday, 3 March approaches, the more pessimistic I become. When I think we might be liberated, I struggle to hold back the tears. Isn't that odd? I expect to be in floods of tears during my first few weeks with you. Yesterday, I told the children a story about what we will be doing next week. Packing and the like and then on the train, past Vienna, Budapest, Bucharest, and then on the boat... taking us to Turkey where we're going to visit the Sultan. From there, on camels to Palestine. And then I'll get married to you and the children will all come and stay with us and there will be lots of delicious food, especially oranges. And the house will be beautifully furnished. In a word, a fairytale. I gave my imagination free rein and enjoyed it even more than the children.

Half-past one in the afternoon. They were in a foul mood today and kept yelling. One man was hit because he didn't take off his hat quickly enough. The barracks leaders were sent back to the barracks twice to check the number of women who had stayed behind, because we were one short. When I came back the second time, I bumped into the green who had just hit that man. "*Sucht doch gut nach, denn sonst bekommt ihr wieder kein Essen. Es muss doch stimmen,*"[44] he said kindly. Would you believe it? They left us standing until the others came back from work. Home to eat, and at three o'clock we had to line up again. Apparently, the error lay with the *Schuh-Kommando.* So hopefully it won't take too long this afternoon. But when they're in a foul mood, they'll think nothing of leaving us outside in the freezing cold all afternoon. Very simple. Goodbye, my love. Shabbat Shalom.

One more thing. The people on outdoor duty are made to work extremely hard. They even serve as horses, i.e., four or five men walk between the shafts of a cart laden with wood, soil, stone, etc., while others push. I call them *Stellvertretende Pferde.*[45] The exertion is too much for many of the men and they faint, while some twist their ankles. Yet they still have to join the procession (consisting of a couple pulling, a couple pushing and a German SS man bringing up the rear), either leaning on another man's arm, or in-between two others, just walking back and forth. And for this the Huns have mainly picked on intellectuals, among them Chief Rabbi Schuster, Jaap Meijer, Jo Melkman. Pure sadism.

---

44 "Please check carefully, otherwise you will go without food again. The numbers have to add up."

45 Substitute horses.

26 February

I'm listless and irritable today. I have diarrhoea and incredibly sore muscles (every morning before roll call we do gymnastics in order to warm up) and I no longer believe that we're leaving on Friday. That's the worst. Let me finish yesterday's story. There was one too many at the *Schuh-Kommando*. Their (German) boss knew this, but didn't report it, or he would have been punished for miscounting. A fine attitude, don't you think? On the way back, he let the man go through a different gate, and told him to fall in with the others coming back from roll call. That's how scared this man (a *Scharführer*[46] or *Oberscharführer* or whatever these fellows are called) was of his superiors. But we paid the price. Luckily, the numbers tallied immediately in the afternoon.

A woman was sent here from Vittel, all by herself, because there was a problem with her papers. Yesterday morning she was suddenly told that her papers are fine now and that she should pack; yesterday afternoon, she went back to Vittel. Like a bolt from the blue. It raises my hopes a little, but otherwise I'm useless today. I should like nothing better than to go to bed and not speak to another soul. Bye, dearest, I hope to be more cheerful next time.

29 February

Again I feel "*himmelhoch jauchzend, zum Tode betrübt.*"[47] The tension is unbearable. I have constant diarrhoea, brought on, I believe, as much by the cold as by nerves. Either way, it leaves me awfully weak. Rumours are rife. A wood commando guard claims he has been appointed as an escort for the transport to Ankara,

46 A commissioned SS officer, equivalent to a corporal.
47 See note 39, p. 189.

which is said to leave on 3 March! The *Oberkommandant* came back from Berlin on Sunday evening, and apparently there will be several transports between 3 and 13 March. When he was in the luggage depot, the commandant is rumoured to have said that everything had to be in the right place, so it could be collected without delay, for we were all leaving. The kitchen's *Oberscharführer* said: "*Nachher erzählt ihr, dass ihr nicht genug Essen bekommen habt.*"[48] (Which is more than true.) At the same time, more and more people are being assigned to work commandos. Father has also been assigned to the shoes, and your father to the wood commando.

Meanwhile, Mrs Maykels has been to see me. We talked for quite some time. And just now a relatively reliable source told me that the transport has been put back by four weeks because of the cold, and that there will be a change of leadership here, with better treatment. Oh, Leo, I just can't bear it any longer. Another four weeks and G-d knows what will happen in the meantime. I would like to go to bed and cry. When will these torments, this agonizing delay, ever end?

1 March

And like so many times before, I'm already over the worst of it. But from now on, I shan't believe another word. Besides, perhaps it's better for Father and Mother and for your father, because they'll be able to go straight back to Holland.

As of yesterday, Bobby has been working in the SS kitchen. Extremely hard work, starting at a quarter-to six, staying over in the afternoon, and back in the evening (I don't know what time yet). But the food is excellent. Yesterday they had white cabbage with potatoes and gravy, so filling that even the men couldn't manage a second helping. Our wasted, starving men — that's

48 "Later you will say that you did not get enough to eat."

saying something! Apple sauce, pudding, in a word, anything they fancy, they get it, but *nothing* may be taken home, their clothes are searched. I'm stopping now, sweetheart. I still have bad diarrhoea and feel poorly today, but I'm over the worst of the disappointment. How many more blows will come our way?

The prisoners-of-war who were held here have left.[49] People are saying that the camp's leadership will be replaced and that we shall receive better treatment. I'll believe it when I see it. I have learnt my lesson.

6 March

Was ill for a few days. Have no peace of mind right now, for I'm sitting next to a woman I don't trust and who, if she knew what I was doing, might well give me away.

10 March

I'm over the disappointment again. Not least because I was extremely busy for a couple of days. We organised a *Purim*[50] party for the children! I took care of all the preparations for our barracks and I'm extremely proud and pleased, because it was a great success and the children liked ours best of all the barracks.

We had put aside curd cheese, taken a few potatoes out of our rations for a few days, and asked all the parents for a slice of bread for each of their children. A man on outdoor duty was asked to bring some fir branches, which was quite an undertaking actually,

---

49 Probably referring to the Russian prisoners-of-war in a separate camp at Bergen-Belsen.
50 The festival of *Purim* commemorates the deliverance of the Jewish people of ancient Persia, as recorded in the Book of Esther.

for you're not allowed to take any wood. But the man I asked approached his *Scharführer* and explained what he needed it for, and then he was given permission. Even so, his mates were worried. When he marched into the roll-call area in the evening, carrying half a forest, there were German visitors! Luckily, they didn't say a word.

I had brought a few sketchbooks from Westerbork, which I used to make a lot of little drawings and then wrote the name of a child on each of them. Two women had been punished and received one less margarine ration each this week. We should have returned these two rations, but we secretly kept them. And by a miraculous coincidence, the canteen had some biscuits, but too few to sell to the camp as a whole. The leaders then clubbed together and bought them, so each barracks had some biscuits for its children. A girl from the barracks also made some drawings.

On Wednesday we fried small potato latkes (we have approx. 40 children + a few little brothers from the men's barracks — they had no party). Yesterday I made dough from potatoes, sweetener and curd cheese, shaped it into biscuits (without baking them), made a small indentation and put a dollop of jam on top. They looked lovely! Toasted slices of bread on the stove, spread them with jam, topped with a slice of bread with curd cheese and a dollop of jam. Pushed three tables together, covered them with a sheet and two small tablecloths. Plates and bread boards with the treats. Put the drawings with the names where the children were sitting, with a fir twig beside each nameplate and more twigs around the dishes. It looked lovely. All the children were smartly dressed, so I felt obliged to put on a frock (I'm always in trousers here), which the children loved. We read the *Purim* story, sang and played games. And we ate, of course. It was tremendous. And everybody had a wonderful time. Albala, Kan, Andriesse, etc., came to have a look. Given our circumstances, it was quite exceptional. Hans Krieg sang, and when all the children were singing *Hatikvah*, all the grown-ups began to cry. Except me, of course. Mrs Mossel did an excellent job hosting the celebrations.

On to our private party. Up at half-past four in the morning, distributed soup, got to Father's barracks at seven, where I made pudding on the stove. The ingredients came from Leo Reichenberger, who's in Father's barracks and who's extremely kind to him. Cocoa, powdered milk, a tiny bit of sugar and potato flour. The cocoa was ancient and we didn't have enough sugar, and yet the pudding was tasty! Our standards have changed; we like everything now. Then roll call. A long one. Afterwards I made a spread of our saved-up potatoes and sweet curd cheese, which Bobby had "organised," so to speak, lightly toasted four slices of bread on the stove, put on the spread, traced a criss-cross pattern with a fork, a dollop of jam on top... and took them to your father and Freddy/Juul. Handed out the food and had some myself. Took the spread to Father's barracks, where Leo Reichenberger's little boy had toasted the slices of bread we had brought over in the morning. Put the spread on, topped them with a bit of jam, and also made some biscuits + pudding. Had a pleasant meal together, something we hadn't had during all of our weeks here. Back to the barracks. Had a kip. *Schluss.* It's afternoon now. I don't have much other news, except that duty roll call starts at six o'clock these days, which means that we're woken up at a quarter-to five. It's a long day, it really is.

Bobby works in the kitchen that prepares food for the American Jews, who don't wear a Star and don't have to work. And when you hear about the vast quantities of food the SS still receives, e.g., real butter, lard, apples, etc., and how much is thrown away, you get the feeling the war will never end. In fact, without any more war news, you wonder if it will go on for another 10 or 20 years. It's awful. There are plenty of aircraft though, and last week we had a terrible fright when a bomb exploded in the middle of the night.

15 March

A ban on wearing mackintoshes over coats and galoshes during roll call. Another *Austausch* rumour. New bed-making instructions every day.

18 March

Westerbork transport arrived. At a quarter-past twelve, we learnt that they would arrive at half-past twelve. (Last Thursday.) They travelled for 36 hours, approx. 200 people. Izak de Vries, Elie Dasberg, Mrs Van Tijn. And Karel and Gien Hartog's children, completely undernourished and neglected, without clothes. All have diarrhoea. Extremely monotonous diet. Obsessive craving for good food. Hungry faces, especially the men, like in a film. Soldiers with trench coats and rifles. Reminiscent of films from Siberia.

22 March

It has turned wintry again, with snow, hail and freezing temperatures. I have nothing to say, except that punishment with bunkers, i.e., prison cells, is rife at the moment. Similarly, people are often forced to stand by the gate, without food. And they're driving us mad with incessant bed inspections. I had a miserable birthday. I'm so old, and all our years go by, waiting. I'm not in the mood today, I'm talking nonsense. Better luck next time. I didn't even have time to reread the letter you wrote for my 21st birthday. I got round to it only yesterday. I was extra busy, because my "manageress" was ill and I had to do everything on my own.

23 March

I've found myself really tiresome of late (like before), and that's why, from now on, whenever I'm not quite in the right frame of mind, I'll only make notes. The curious thing is that, despite all my fairly faithful descriptions, I still haven't been able to give you an impression of what's going on here and how we live. It may not seem all that bad, but it is.

Let me tell you briefly what happened yesterday. The Germans have been obsessed with inspections in recent days. The beds, the cupboards, the number of people at work, etc., etc. We had heard that the *Arbeitsführer*,[51] the head of the shoe commando, was planning a tour of the barracks. And in the afternoon we saw another green, who always does morning roll call, entering the barracks across the road. So we had been warned. A look around the barracks. Bread off the stove (toasting isn't allowed), the children were playing with benches — quick, back in their place. A look around the dormitory. And back to doling out bread. The children were standing in front of the windows. They're coming, they're coming! *"Achtung!"*[52] (The barracks leader must shout this when they enter.) Everybody rises. There they were, three of them, the *Arbeitsführer*, the roll-call man and the man responsible for the camp's cleanliness, commonly known as the king of turds, because he inspects the lavatories, + Albala and the Jewish work supervisor. And Albala promptly said: "Watch out they don't escape through the dormitory." The rotten bastard. If it doesn't occur to the Germans, why should he remind them?

Mrs Katz, the barracks leader, accompanied one to the dormitory for inspection. And I accompanied the *Arbeitsführer* through the ward. He points at somebody. *"Wie alt?"* *"Vierzig Jahre."* *"Was machen Sie denn hier?"* *"Ich bin schwer asthma*

51 Work detail manager.
52 "Attention!"

leidend."⁵³ Contemptuous laughter. "*Ach was, asthma. Ist das auch schon zu schlimm, um bei den Schuhen zu arbeiten?*"⁵⁴ My response: "*Die Frau ist wirklich schwer krank.*"⁵⁵ (The woman suffers from stress-induced asthma. When she's nervous — and who isn't? — she gets the most frightful attacks. Her shoulders go up and down and she gasps for breath.) He asks no further questions, and continues. Points at me and many others. He has the name taken down of a young woman who has been assigned to cleaning the barracks so she can stay with her young child. I tell him what she does, and he says: "The old women can do that; after all, they had to run their own households back home." He yells, because these people can't talk in a normal tone of voice: "*Wollen Sie mir etwa sagen, was die Frauen zu tun haben? Dann können Sie auch zu den Schuhen gehen.*"⁵⁶ As he continues, we give the women who haven't been inspected surreptitious signals to join the women who have. They steal across behind his back, so eventually there's nobody left on the other side.

Meanwhile Mrs Katz has come back with the other green, who mutters: "*Es ist mir zu viel Betrieb hier*"⁵⁷ and disappears. "*Wie viele Barackenleiterinnen sind denn hier eigentlich?*"⁵⁸ the *Arbeitsführer* barks. "Two," Albala says in a conciliatory tone, although there are three of us at the moment. Yelling, ranting and raving, the procession makes its way out, whereupon the entire barracks erupts in nervous cackling. Three women were put down for work and this morning, when they reported for duty roll call, they were sent back again because they were too old. That's the well-oiled German system for you.

53 "Age?" "Forty." "Then what are you doing here?" "I have bad asthma."
54 "Oh, I see, asthma. Since when is asthma an excuse not to work in the shoe commando?"
55 "The woman is really very ill."
56 "Are you trying to tell me what these women should be doing? Then you can go to the shoes as well."
57 "It is too busy here for my liking."
58 "How many barracks leaders are there here, anyway?"

27 March

Yet another new notebook. How much longer? Again, just a few facts; I'll unburden my heart later. Last Thursday something awful happened here. A man was shot dead. Allegedly, he came too close to the barbed wire. There's a watchtower on posts, with a soldier in it, and a sign somewhere that says: "ES WIRD OHNE WARNUNG SCHARF GESCHOSSEN."[59] The man must have missed the sign, or perhaps it wasn't even there, and the soldier on duty must have been glad to shoot a Jew. He didn't aim for the legs, but hit him in the lungs. The man died half an hour later, 40 years old. I keep thinking of the death notices from Mauthausen: *"Auf der Flucht erschossen."*[60] He had surgery and everything was done to save him, and I have the impression that the soldier overstepped the mark. A detailed protocol was drawn up... but for his wife, the war is lost.

On Friday afternoon, Rabbi De Vries suddenly passed away. He was fine when he arrived here. His wife, who had been ailing for years, died here after about a fortnight. He himself died after a sickbed of only two or three days. Pneumonia. And you should know that Izak de Vries and Elie Dasberg,[61] are in quarantine in the camp and aren't allowed out. Burials are not possible here; corpses are taken out of the camp on a dung cart. The Rabbi wasn't in the hospital barracks, but in the so-called *Altersheim*,[62] a special barracks for men over 70, women over 65, and those certified unfit to work by the German doctor. These people needn't attend roll call. His remains were taken to the hospital barracks and, together with another body, carted off the following day.

---

59 "We shoot to kill without warning."
60 "Shot whilst trying to escape." The Germans often used this terminology when reporting on the killing of a Jew; for example, in the death notices from the Mauthausen concentration camp and the Amersfoort concentration camp in Holland (where many Jews were murdered together with members of the Dutch underground).
61 The son and son-in-law of Rabbi De Vries.
62 Old-age home.

An aircraft was shot down here on Thursday. We saw it catching fire and the crew parachuting out. A memorable sight.

About your father. I already mentioned that he suffered a dizzy spell last week. He's in the hospital barracks and Freddy, who works there, spoke to the doctor, and isn't very positive. His eyes, hands and feet are all swollen, and Freddy says he's a wreck and even fears he won't pull through. When I was with him yesterday, he complained of 'flu, although I thought he didn't look as bad as a few days ago. I don't have much good news, my love, and I know how much all of these things will upset you. Now that I have to tell you this about your father, I'm reminded of the letter I wrote to you when your mother fell ill. How different our circumstances were back then! In those days, even the best and dearest wasn't good enough, whereas now we can't give him anything other than a slice of bread with jam, margarine or curd cheese, and a bit of soup or turnips. Still, I believe Freddy is a bit too gloomy.

All manner of rumours are doing the rounds again. They say we're going to Theresienstadt or even back to Westerbork, and that 1,000 parcels have been put together. Besides, and this is a fact, a 1,000-strong transport is expected. *Häftlinge,*[63] or regular prisoners-of-war. I may be able to tell you more tomorrow. I take no notice of the rumours. They no longer cheer me up or get me down. As I said, seeing is believing. Only I hope Theresienstadt isn't true. The last time all these rumours went around, I had a beautiful ending to my diary, namely that nothing you read could ever be as upsetting for you as it was for me when I wrote it. After all, you would be reading it in the knowledge of a "happy ending," whereas for us this remains to be seen: Will we make it, yes or no? And finally, as my concluding remark, that in spite of all the misery (misery isn't the right word, but there's no word to express what we're going through), I'm glad to have been with Father, Mother and Bobby, because I have a feeling that without me they might have gone

63 Prisoners.

to Poland long ago, and because I have been able to alleviate the burden somewhat in all kinds of ways. And I understand how you must feel, my dearest, always anxious and uncertain about our fate. But, alas, these concluding remarks will have to wait, for our ordeal isn't over yet. Still… all is going well, as they say.

5 April

I have been utterly desperate again these past few days. The cold spell is finally over, which makes an enormous difference, but even so I'm worn out, my dearest. I don't have much news. On Sunday summer time began, and with duty roll call at half-past five we lost an hour-and-a-half of sleep. Later it emerged that half-past five was a mistake and now roll call is at six again. On Sunday, they made all the work commandos line up again in the afternoon. They had to march around the roll-call area for an hour-and-a-half. The weather was fine, so it wasn't so bad in itself, but it was yet another chunk out of the few hours of free time that people have. They're working 12 hours a day, with a one-hour break. Bobby works from half-past four in the morning until half-past five, six o'clock in the evening. Extremely hard.

Thank God your father is well again; that's to say, he's an old man and has now been admitted to the old people's barracks, but all in all it wasn't as bad as we had feared. He was released from the hospital barracks earlier today and I'll be visiting him later. Let me stop now, my love. More tomorrow. Friday evening is *Pesach*. It doesn't bear thinking about.

10 April

I can't believe it's only been five days since I last wrote to you. It seems much longer. My original plan had been to paint you a picture of our trips to the bathhouse. But in the meantime more important things have happened, so I'd better tell you about those first. On Wednesday last week, a transport with 90 people suddenly arrived from Westerbork. Not many acquaintances of ours among them, but there is talk of another transport. They're in quarantine in Barracks 10, and speaking to them is strictly prohibited. The guards have orders to shoot. That said, Father manages to speak to someone every now and then, because he works for the food distribution. Only 2,000 people remain in Westerbork now. Along with this group of 90, people were deported to Auschwitz, Theresienstadt and Romania.

I believe I forgot to tell you that some 10 days ago, seven Hungarian women arrived here. They had been in Theresienstadt, and were sent to the camp for foreigners here in Celle. Due to the occupation of Hungary (so that report is true) they had to leave that camp, which is a few barracks down from us, and now they're here. And a transport of *Häftlinge* arrived. They've also been housed in separate barracks, surrounded by thick reed borders with barbed wire. Last week, on our way to the bathhouse, we caught a glimpse of them. A lot of men, all packed together, in striped uniforms, with shaven heads. That was all. These people are said to be dying by the dozen of chlorine poisoning. Who or what they are, nobody knows.

And now *Pesach*. You know how I was dreading it. I would have liked nothing better than to hole up in bed. But as barracks leader (assistant, that is), I had no choice. Chief Rabbi Davids had issued instructions[64] — I kept them — and a special

64 From Chief Rabbi Davids' instructions: "Preparations for the *Seder*: Cushions for the person conducting the *Seder*. Instead of roast meat, baked potato, and instead of egg, some of the afternoon's vegetables. For *Kiddush*, tea (or thyme tea or surrogate, provided it is made of leaves) or milk. Time of the *Seder*: In view of the camp regulations, the *Seder* will commence Friday evening at seven o'clock (after dinner, when the young children are in bed), while text and commentary must be limited in order to finish within one hour. Given that work usually finishes early on Saturday, families can start the second *Seder* at six o'clock that day. Where necessary, there will be one *Seder* in Dutch and one in German. The children's *Seder* is on Saturday afternoon. For technical reasons, a meal will not be possible. Nonetheless, we shall follow tradition by singing the *Shir Hama'alot* (Grace after Meals) in the traditional fashion. Before the consumption of *chametz*

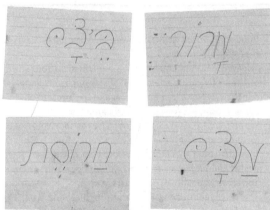

Names of the *Seder* plate components and their translation to Dutch with a short explanation. In the center of the note is an added sentence: "Under normal circumstances there would also be: *matzot*, a shankbone, an egg."

Author's collection

prayer[65] was written by Rabbi Abraham Levisson.[66] Considering the clientele here in our barracks, I didn't have an ounce of faith in proceedings. But it was a success! Contrary to all expectations! We faced nothing but opposition. The women refused to give up their places — we wanted to bring the Orthodox people to the front, so they could follow everything — and we only had an hour-and-a-half for everything. For the *Seder* plate[67] we had… nothing. On Friday evening, we got changed and the children especially looked very smart. Two tables (no, wait, we had intended to arrange the tables into a horseshoe shape, i.e., to push them together, but at the last minute the news came that this was forbidden). The Germans knew there would be *gebeten*.[68]

On the table, a cardboard box covered with a white towel. On it: saucers with dried vegetables, a mixture of raw carrot, beetroot and potato, salt water. All with a piece of paper, by way of a label, explaining what it represents. A jam jar for the wine. Tea surrogate for wine. Two cushions with covers. Tea lights for candles. *Schluss*.

Sitting at our table were Cantor De Jong and family, the four

(food containing yeast), the prayer (that Rabbi Levisson composed) must be meaningfully recited."

65 "Heavenly Father! You know it is our will to do Your will and to celebrate the feast of *Pesach* by eating *matzot* and abstaining from *chametz*! To our deepest regret, due to exceptional circumstances and the threat to our lives if we do not consume all the food apportioned to us, we cannot now obey these commandments. But we are prepared and take it upon ourselves to obey Your commandment that requires us to live and not die, and to obey Your counsel: Only take heed to thyself, and keep thy soul diligently! Therefore hear our prayer: Keep us alive, preserve our health and deliver us soon, so we can obey Your commandments, do Your will and serve You with all our hearts, Amen."

66 The chief rabbi of the Friesland province, and from 1942 also the Gelderland province.

67 Plate containing the various ingredients symbolising the Exodus from Egypt, such as the *maror*, bitter herb (horseradish), symbolising the bitter times suffered by the Children of Israel in slavery; salt water, symbolising the tears they cried; the *charoset* (a mixture of nuts, apples, honey, wine and cinnamon), symbolising the mortar that the slaves had to prepare for the construction of the pyramids; the *matzot*, the so-called "bread of affliction," etc.

68 Prayers.

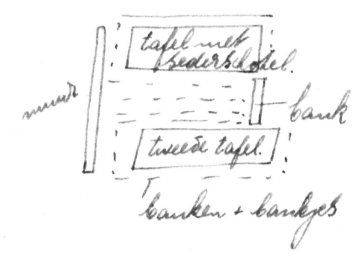

of us, in a word, quite a few. The same at the second table. And in between, the people were tightly packed. The Orthodox, who wanted to celebrate the *Seder*, come what may. I forgot to tell you that at first it looked as if we had to conduct the *Seder* ourselves, because men aren't allowed in our barracks after seven o'clock. But because of the extension of the working hours — until half-past six — the men are now allowed to stay in the women's barracks until five-to eight. Cantor de Jong's wife lives with us, which is why he conducted the Seder here, but he wanted me to read the commentary. There are 140 women in the barracks. The men, who always eat with the women, bring the number to close on 200 people. And what people! I was expecting the worst. But it went exceptionally well. First I told the story, very briefly. Then, that we have to celebrate the *Seder* as if we'd been through it ourselves, which we used to find difficult, but not at all now, because we're actually experiencing slavery. (I was thinking of the transport commando, the "*Stellvertretend*

Pferd" that passes our barracks day after day.) But that after this slavery we shall also live to see deliverance. It really hit home! And when De Jong started reciting the *Haggadah* (I delivered a very brief commentary on each section and sometimes only the literal translation: e.g., "from slavery to freedom"), the entire ward slowly gathered round us. And so we celebrated the entire *Seder* — omitting quite a few sections of course — and in conclusion, the children sang *"L'Shana Hazot bi'Yerushalayim"*[69] and we all sang *"Hatikvah."* Tears all round. But everybody was elated. So was I. But I was devastated when I thought of you. This is not what I've been dreaming of.

I had planned to go and see Mossel after work on Shabbat, to hear some *midrashim*.[70] After all, I couldn't really tell them the history of *Pesach* again. But it all took a different turn.

Early in the afternoon on Shabbat, we saw an aircraft shot down. And several hours later, a terrific noise! The camp was under attack! Everybody had to stay indoors. The aircraft swooped very close to the ground. We spotted two with very odd shapes, like sailing vessels. Everybody ran for cover, flat on the ground, under the tables. It was awful. And the noise was deafening. We saw the Huns speeding off down the main road. On bicycles, motorcycles and in small cars. The thought flashed through my mind: This is how they'll run when the time has come to capitulate. At a certain point, we saw smoke in the dormitory. A woman lay motionless on the floor. We immediately sent for a doctor, and a moment later she was carried away on a stretcher. She never regained consciousness and died later. Hand shot off. Dozens of bullets in the barracks, through the ceiling, through the walls, beds riddled with bullets. Miracles happened: Some people had just got up when their beds were hit, or the handbag dangling from the bed was riddled with

69 The *Seder* is concluded with the song from the *Haggadah*: "Next year in Jerusalem!" But in Bergen-Belsen the children sang, *"This* year in Jerusalem!" (*L'Shana Hazot*).
70 Stories based on Bible texts.

bullets. Father was outside; he lay face down on the ground, and, when it was all over, he picked up four bullets. I'm petrified. I know that what will be, will be, despite my hopes of getting out alive. But the thought that it may be all over for us and of the kind of life I will have had... without any meaning, makes me feel so miserable. Moreover, a Hun told us that these were reconnaissance flights, taking photographs, and that they'll be back... Perhaps we don't appreciate the gravity of our situation, because we're too subjective. A 37-year-old nurse died and, they say, 22 *Häftlinge*. We didn't celebrate the second *Seder*; I wasn't up to it. In fact there were no celebrations anywhere. Yesterday we had some more positive news about the war and the *Austausch*. I do my best not to harbour any more hopes.

14 April

I have nothing important to say. But what was important to us is that today, after three months, we were given something different to eat, namely a kind of potato and turnip soup. A great occasion for us, although I admit that within the context of world events, it's a matter of little importance. We're having constant air-raid warnings. This is nothing new, but in the past nobody in the camp took any notice. However, now the Huns are extremely nervous, and every time we have an air-raid warning, we're not allowed out of the barracks. It's particularly oppressive at night, and every now and then I think to myself: Why do we make such an effort to keep our spirits up and to not let them get us down? An outsider wouldn't give a penny for our lives, yet we can't help but hope. Yesterday evening I quarrelled with Albala, but it would take too long to tell you the whole story. These past few days we've had lovely spring weather, which really lifts your spirits, making you feel that everything will be all right. But the war takes no heed of our feelings. That's how I keep my optimism in check. Bye, sweetheart.

258 • *Letters Never Sent*

[At the end of April 1944, a commission from Berlin visited the camp. Names of people on the Palestine List were read out, and these people were told to stand to one side. Mirjam's parents and sister were called up, but Mirjam herself was not. She then approached the commission, her name was written down, and she was allowed to join the others. That very same day, this group of approximately 260 people moved to a neighbouring camp, where they didn't have to do any work and roll call lasted only 10 minutes.]

28 May[71]

What happened to us today beats everything else we've been through, and I'm still trembling as I write this. I'd stopped writing after hiding my notebooks. We'd heard that our luggage would be searched for papers upon our move from the old camp to this place, and because I so dearly wanted to take my letters to you with me, I had crammed them somewhere at the bottom, hoping for the best. I was so dejected; nothing seemed to be happening, and I began to doubt whether we would ever leave. Life here is quite bearable, especially so these past few days when the weather has been lovely, but we were terribly bored and the uncertainty, especially, wore us down. Every day, new IPAs[72] did the rounds, but I was determined not to believe a thing. And no one was expecting anything to happen today, *Eerste Pinksterdag.*[73] This morning, the first day of *Shavuot,* we had a Hebrew conversation lesson with Mossel, tremendous, followed by food, and I was just about to lie in the sun when the air-raid warning sounded. But strangely enough, people in the barracks pretended not to hear and therefore some of us were reluctant to go back inside. For want of anything better to do, I had climbed back

71 This letter was written after the move to the neighboring camp.
72 The *"Israelitische Presse Agentur"* or Israelite Press Agency; in other words, the rumour mill.
73 First day of Pentecost.

onto my bed and was reading *Les frères Karamazov*[74] (borrowed from Mrs Mendes da Costa), when suddenly the *Oberscharführer* stormed into the barracks. *"Alles raus, aufstellen, die Namen werden verlesen."*[75] That means: We're leaving. But... if names are being *verlesen*, that means not all of us are going. Who? Just then, we saw the commandant racing towards us on his motorcycle.

Lined up in front of the barracks. Names, more or less in alphabetical order, are called out. Meanwhile, the aircraft thunder overhead. The commandant has a pair of binoculars and all he does is peer up into the sky. The tension is... unbearable isn't the word. Enough to drive you insane. Levy Walter, Levy Katharina, Levisson... we're not on the list. What does that mean? Will there be another list later? Our card index is on the table.

The commandant has a red-bordered letter in his hand and one of us calls out the names on a list. Levie, Moritz... so we're on it after all. Father, Mother and Bobby. Not me. I step forward and, like before, tell them I'm part of the family. *"Dann werden Sie noch aufgerufen."*[76] That sets my mind at ease. I'm out of danger, I think to myself. I wasn't fully aware of the danger I was in. I'll tell you why in a moment.

Called up is Mindel Färber, Clara Asscher-Pinkhof's five-year-old foster daughter. She herself is not. Called up is old Mrs Pinkhof, who isn't even in our camp. Called up is Marinus Kan, who had earlier declined to go on account of his son and who is, in fact, not *transportfähig*[77] himself. Old Mrs Pinkhof is collected by Albala. They halt at the fence. *"Wollen Sie mit nach Palestina." "Ja." "Aber Ihre Tochter geht nicht mit."*[78] They talk briefly... she's coming along. I simply can't describe it.

Meanwhile, we've had yet another quick roll call to discuss

74 The French translation of Fyodor Dostoyevsky's *The Brothers Karamazov*.
75 "Everybody out, line up, the names will be read out."
76 "Then you will be called up."
77 Fit to travel.
78 "Would you like to go to Palestine?" "Yes." "But your daughter is not going."

luggage matters. Everything must be ready by seven o'clock tomorrow morning. So I'd better stop now. More tomorrow.

29 May

I'm writing this on my bed. We're having another air-raid warning. I reread yesterday's account and it sounds so awfully tame. The nerve-wracking wait, the scenes when Sally and Jo Pinkhof said goodbye to their mother, the moment it emerged that Abel Herzberg and Vromen weren't on the list. The commandant never stopped peering at the sky and then suddenly, when we got to the letter "P," everybody had to go inside. That meant uncertainty for the people after "P" and those who hadn't been called up. The Mossels!! Zadok, who has taught us every single day of our stay here, even on the other side, in the shoes. After a while, back in line and on we went. Then it was over. The commandant read out a few stipulations and asked if there were any people who, for some reason or other, didn't want to come along. He added that he had received this list, as well as a standby list, from Berlin. The others, who haven't been called up, have to go back to the other camp. What that means only we, who have been there, can understand. They had to pack and leave at once. We helped them. Oh Leo, in all these years I hardly ever cried; I did occasionally when I was alone, but never at times when there was really plenty of reason. But at that moment, I went to pieces. Mossel's wife, in tears, not for herself but for the children. And Vromen, giving me addresses with trembling lips.

After a while... another roll call! The numbers don't tally. Will some be struck off the list? No, there are too few!! Vromen Leopold, Vromen-Snapper E.!!! That feeling can't be put into words, never. The others left. And now we're all packed, the Germans will be weighing the luggage later and we're set to leave this week. I'll continue on the train.

31 May

If we stay here much longer, I'll end up with a huge bundle of paper. But I *have* to write to you, otherwise I can't bear it. Such an awful lot has happened in these past few days. After that terrible Sunday, once the others had left, we began to get excited. This week! The dreadful uncertainty — when — was over. And the preparations were continuing apace. Stipulations concerning luggage, while in the kitchen parcels were being put together. An announcement yesterday — be ready with luggage at half-past six in the morning. The luggage will be taken to a garage, together with one member of the family, searched, and then sent on to the station. Back to our barracks, and travel on Thursday. Great agitation. If everything is taken to the station, how are we meant to sleep or wash the night of Wednesday to Thursday? Answer: Everything must go. This morning at half-past five we began to take luggage outside in alphabetical order. Mayhem. We still had lots to do when the deputy commandant and another green approached on their bicycles: "*Alle Bagage zurück in die Baracke. Die Reise hat sich um etwas verschoben!!!!!*"[79] Whack! Like a blow to the head. Yet most people remained optimistic. *Etwas*, a little. Probably a damaged station. A matter of days. At ten o'clock, just before roll call, the commandant appeared. "*Er bedauert ausserordentlich, aber... die Reise ist auf unbestimmte Zeit verschoben!!!*"[80] Our mood is indescribable. Our nerves are so torn and twisted that we have lost all resilience. We're devastated. So once again... uncertainty. Unpack again, get used to this place again. We had already left in spirit.

I must mention one more incident. On Sunday a daughter had been called up, but not the mother. At first the daughter wanted to stay here too, but she let herself be dissuaded by the others. Then yesterday, one of the people on the list suddenly died in the hospital

---

79 "All luggage back in the barracks. The journey has been pushed back a little!!!!!"
80 "He is awfully sorry, but... the journey has been pushed back indefinitely!!!"

barracks. So another can go in his place. The daughter pleads for her mother, but there's still the standby list. One more person will be put forward by Berlin. If any other places become available then the commandant will be free to choose. That one person is... the mother. If you were to write this in a novel, people would say: too much of a coincidence. But these are the facts.

I'm in pieces, believe me. We don't know if anything will come of it now. And again, we have to get used to the misery, uncertainty, danger. There are air-raid warnings at least twice a day. Yesterday I thought to myself: No more fear in a couple of weeks' time. But what if we're still here when the war is over? Trenches are being dug. What's the purpose of all this? Will we ever meet again? I had so many plans. I was already thinking of our children. Bye, my very dearest.

7 June

Yesterday mail arrived here for the first time, not on a form, but proper mail, much of it from Switzerland. I'm trying to adjust to the idea of staying here until after the war, but oh, it's so immensely difficult. When we go to the bathhouse later this morning, we'll see the camp exit. Lying in the sun recently, I tried to imagine my feelings when the barriers will open. But now! Our future had seemed so bright and so close. More delays, more uncertainty. I'm tired and in pieces. My dear, if we ever read this story together, or if in 20 years' time we watch a play or, better still, a film about what has happened to us, we're bound to shake our heads and say: They did pile on the pathos. The most incredible things are happening. Believe it or not, we're back in the old camp!! Let me tell you the whole story from the beginning.

After the blow, we slowly picked ourselves up again. On Sunday evening there was a brief lecture on our situation after the war, followed by an extremely interesting debate. Of a very high standard indeed. It continued on Monday evening. The following morning the order came: immediate relocation to the other side!!!! Later we were told that it was a purely internal affair, that we'd stay together as a group in one barracks, that we wouldn't have to work and that we should leave our luggage packed because *"es jeden Moment losgehen konnte."*[81]

So now we're all crammed into Barracks 15, in the old camp, without a dining area, living on our beds, tightly packed together. We moved in a downpour that left our clothes soaking wet, but fortunately I could hang them out to dry yesterday. And when we arrived on the other side, we heard about the invasion of the French coast!! Again, words can't describe how we feel. It sounds so simple: We moved from one barracks to another. But what this really means is: A rush on beds, which you try to manage as best you can, not knowing what to do with your luggage, not knowing what to eat from, etc. I shan't go into any detail. Now all that remains are unanswered questions. Will we get away? What do they mean by invasion? How much longer?

Spoke to your father and Freddy, very down. I would have liked to join them for a bit of a cry, but they rely on me for comfort. My comfort arrived yesterday, in the form of a Red Cross letter from you! You can't imagine what it means to get a few sweet words from you. The letters were sent on from Westerbork. The Red Cross secretariat also sent me a response with regard to our marriage, which I didn't understand at all, but it doesn't matter anymore. I no longer worry about being without an identity. People know where we are and our names have been registered, a hundred times over, on the *Austausch* list.

81 "It could happen any moment."

10 June

We've already had another blow. Work. For the past two days, I've been working in the shoes. On Wednesday evening we were told to be ready for a shower at eight. At half-past ten in the evening, Albala came to say that we had to appear at duty roll call at a quarter-past six. I had already fallen asleep and the blow left me half-dazed. I imagined there had been a phone call from Berlin that evening: *Austausch* called off. I was completely devastated again. As I'm writing this I'm in fairly good spirits, but this morning, when I was extremely down, I could have given you a much better description of how I felt. And indeed, it was terribly difficult yesterday. Dirty, grimy work, from six until half-past eleven, and from half-past twelve until half-past six. You effectively end up working at least 12 hours before you're back in your barracks. But we have a pleasant table, are learning Hebrew, without books of course, and all in all things aren't too bad. Our *Austausch* prospects remain unchanged and we continue to live together. I'm prepared to believe it, just so I can bear it. As soon as we receive official word that the exchange has been called off, I'll have to stake my hopes on a speedy end to the war again (in which I have no faith). Admittedly, things are going well and it may only be a matter of months, but I do fear the end here. For now I cling to the idea that we may get our *Austausch* after all, because the *Austausch* commission has nothing to do with the war. The thought of having to waste many more months here…

Tomorrow afternoon, Sunday, we have roll call at half-past one ahead of our afternoon off. I'm now geared towards getting up, working, eating, sleeping. Sunday afternoon washing and taking care of my hands. And no thinking.

12 June

I would really like to give you a detailed account of the plight of the Jews in our camp, but I never have the time. We work from half-past six until approx. seven o'clock in the evening, and now I'm writing in bed. And although I don't work hard, the day is so long and life so hectic, that I'm extremely tired. I've told you about my despair, and yet I've depicted the camp in not altogether unfavourable terms. Still, we can't bear it much longer. Our men are skin and bones, ashen-faced with sunken cheeks and dull, hollow eyes. Even the once-portly women are thin, with baggy clothes, although they generally look better than the men. And everybody, without exception, is hungry. We eat too much to die, too little to live. From five in the morning until eight at night, we live on three thin slices of bread (dry), one litre of rice soup with leek and five spoonfuls of rhubarb each. *Schluss.* That was yesterday's menu. It does vary a little, but the portions remain the same. I forgot the coffee in the morning and evening and occasionally a few potatoes. I'm off to bed. I fear the worst if we're still here by winter. Not to mention Poland.

14 June

I could tell you the following story later, but by then I may have acquired so many new impressions that this will have slipped my mind. It's difficult to write with all this noise around me. But here we go.

"Ladies, rise, ten-to five." I stay in bed, wake up slowly, try to open my eyes. I manage after a few attempts. My first thought is: Let me sleep, another one of those endless days, I can't do it. Then

I realize what time it is and finally get up at twenty-five past five. What follows is a standard routine. Take soapbox, towel, stockings, shoes off the beam, and go outside. Lovely fresh air, a stroll to the latrines, then to the washroom, wash, back to the barracks, comb my hair, return everything in bed to its proper place, cover with a blanket (so the bed cover isn't aired, it's beaten in the evening), smooth everything — *Bettenbau, Scheisse*[82] — eat bread, three dry, wafer-thin slices. A whistle: "*Raustreten zum Appell*,"[83] and slowly we flock to the roll-call area. It's swarming with people. Everybody is walking up and down, talking. Another whistle: "Line up." The show begins. Everybody joins his own work commando: shoes, uniforms, linen, outdoor duty, etc. Men and women separately, in ranks of five. The foremen line us up. Lots of yelling and jostling. The Jewish head of labour (= slave driver) yells and struts about. Then several Germans come marching up the main road. One with a dog, followed by the bigwigs on bicycles. They stop at the exit. Then, after endless recounts, we hear and see the various commandos marching off.

At the gate, the Jewish foremen and the Germans are all counting like maniacs. Then we, too, hear: "*Frauen im Gleichschritt, marsch.*"[84] They're not allowed to say *Damen*.[85] And off we go, a long, long line, to the shoes. The shoe barracks is indescribable. Dirty, airless, dark, cold, everything you (don't) wish for.

I might as well stop, my love. I can't describe what it's like to sit there for 11 hours. Or the threat afterwards of having to stand by the gate until half-past nine. Still, there are some funny things too. The Italians with their animated gestures. The Huns yelling. Our lot, doing nothing all day, just pretending to work, etc. It's all like a film which, as an outsider, you would watch with horror — especially the men's emaciated, sallow faces — but which, if you're

---

82 Bed-making, taking a dump.
83 "Outside for roll call."
84 "Women in lockstep, march!"
85 Ladies.

in it yourself, is not too bad in some respects, but worse in others. Once in a while we're all down, but then we lift each other up again. We draw great support from one another. And you get to know the people as they really are. People who were ladies and gentlemen in Amsterdam can be like hyenas here, thieving and deceiving, but those with innate decency remain unchanged and even manage to care about the plight of others.

15 June

I completely forgot to tell you what we do in the shoe commando. Old shoes are sent here: in tatters, dirty, covered in dust, etc. We take them apart and sort the leather. The filthiest job there is, sometimes there is dog mess on the soles. It's all done with tiny knives (we had to hand in our pocket knives for this), although the toughest shoes, e.g., combat boots, may be put on a kind of saw, which is shaped like a guillotine and just as blunt as the knives. *Voilà.*[86] Punishments: Standing by the gate with bowed heads, having bread rations withheld, etc., etc.

I often think of a film about our lives (provided there's a happy ending), symbolizing the changing times. It would start with our engagement reception and end with me, in *Eretz Yisrael*, writing a letter to the film company with the request to film our story. After the close-up of our *chuppah*[87] in Palestine, there would be scenes showing Bobby in high school, learning about the silk industry in Lyon, and then, in a filthy barracks in Bergen-Belsen, cutting open silkworms. Perhaps it could earn us some money. It's intended as a kind of propaganda film for the solution to the Jewish question. Who knows? I have it all in my head. But will I ever get it done?

86 There you are.
87 Lit., wedding canopy. Here, Mirjam is referring to her wedding ceremony.

18 June

Today, Sunday, a year ago (20 June), I was deported to Westerbork. What will the next year bring?

20 June

On Sunday, the diamond workers were taken to the *Kommandantur*[88] and interrogated one at a time. Back at half-past two in the morning. Secrecy. The IPA claims they must choose: Delivering (and cutting) their (illegal) diamonds, or Poland.[89]

21 June

Air-raid warning at the moment. Wonderful, now we don't have to go to work. Yesterday we saw Hanover in flames.

23 June

This evening I'd like to write to you about the life of appearances we live here. We work in the shoes from half-past six in the morning until half-past six in the evening. That's to say, we don't work. To give you an example: I do nothing, perhaps two shoes a day, but I'm down for 35 pairs. This figure is passed down to Berlin via *Scharführer*, *Oberscharführer* and *Kommandant*. All have something to gain from high production figures, so each of them adds a little extra. I'm curious to know how high the figure will be

88 Commandant's office.
89 150–200 Jewish specialist diamond workers were forced to cut diamonds in Bergen-Belsen. A few of them lived to see the camp liberated.

in Berlin. When the guards walk in, you don't have to work, only pretend.

Enter a dormitory and it looks tidy. But the beds are full of damp and dirty towels, clothes, food, etc. Just so long as it looks tidy on the surface. All show. The cupboards are clean, bowls are clean, etc. But if you want to save some of the afternoon's ration for the evening (which is rare, nobody can stop himself from eating it all), you have to hide it in your bed, because you're not allowed to use the cupboard. The bathhouse — a smelly space, a dirty floor you walk across with clean feet, six to a shower. All show. And so it continues.

Something else. At the camp exit, en route to the work barracks, is a small hut, three by four metres. It has a bunk bed and two young men live in it. They do nothing all day, but aren't allowed out because they work in the crematorium and probably see too much. We pass it on our way to the shoes. Mrs Van Tijn, who craned her neck to see the young men, was clipped round the ear with the flattering words: "*Du, neugierige alte Ziege.*"[90]

28 June

In the course of the week a transport from Yugoslavia arrived, approx. 450 people. Today a couple of Africans left. Wild IPAs about us, but I don't want to get excited. Evening. IPA speaks of imminent departure because the Germans have demanded that our list be submitted this very evening. I believed it, but didn't let it get to me and tried to resist believing it for fear of further disappointment. At any rate, I had better hide this notebook again.

.

90 "You, you curious old goat."

30 June 1944

I'm on the train, and I still can't take it all in. I ought to look out of the window, since we're passing through a glorious landscape, but I want to tell you what happened. Briefly, in telegram style, because I really shouldn't miss this view. Besides, I do hope to see you in a few weeks, perhaps even a few days!

Yesterday, 29 June

Emerging freshly washed out of the washroom at a quarter-past five, I saw Lübke (a green) in front of Barracks 15 and people jumping for joy. Realized: We're leaving. Didn't stop to think, but acted. Ran off with towel under my arm, said goodbye to friends, realizing that there wouldn't be time later. Terrain cordoned off. From half-past six in the morning until half-past seven in the evening, four greens went through every individual item of luggage. We left the barracks at approx. half-past one (we = the women). Crossed the main road, *Leibesvisitation*[91] in garage. Didn't amount to much. Our luggage had to be left in the barracks. The men's turn at half-past seven. Saw the luggage taken away on carts. At three o'clock in the morning we marched off, the sick and the elderly in trucks. The moment the barriers were raised is one I'll never forget. It was still night (three o'clock), and I had a bit of a cry in the dark. (I wasn't the only one, I think.) At five o'clock, after an extremely tiring walk, we arrived at Bergen Station. Luggage a mess. Managed to retrieve a few things. At seven o'clock sharp, the train pulled out. Old second-class carriages, seven to a compartment next to open corridors, lavatories, in a word, everything we hadn't had for years. An armrest! Velvet seats! Nothing special in and of itself (e.g., no water, no sleeping facilities, the seven of us slept packed together ·

91 Strip-search.

à la sardine), but our standards have changed. The sight of shops, views of the countryside without barbed wire.

Our journey — magnificent doesn't do it justice. Through the Thuringian Forest, Hildesheim, Northeim, Göttingen. Mountains, densely forested and with a wide, sloping valley running through them. Sometimes with villages, sometimes with just a few houses. And with orchards. Every conceivable shade and shape of green, the bright yellow of corn, the red of poppies, the pink of clover. And now, the River Main, with a broad valley and the mountains, curving around the valley in a protective embrace. The train winds its way through, revealing new vistas all the time, so wide and peaceful and lovely that I really ought to write about them, but instead I keep looking outside. Until now there has been little to remind us of the war, except this: No men, and those you see are in uniform (mostly SS), and female workers at the stations. In fact: Very few people and no cattle in the fields. Notices at the railway stations: DIE RÄDER ROLLEN UNS ZUM SIEG, UNNÖTIG REISEN VERLÄNGERT DEN KRIEG.[92] On the train: VORSICHT BEI GESPRÄCHEN, FEIND HÖRT MIT.[93] *That's all.*

Würzburg. The people seem to know there's something special about us. At every station, people are leaning out of their windows to see the *Sonderzug*.[94] We're also given water and sometimes warm milk and warm water for the Hartog babies. Our transport guards are fairly decent. One in civilian clothes (wearing gloves for fear of contamination), two in uniform. But I still can't quite comprehend it; I can't quite take it in. It's all too sudden. Nuremberg. Not bombed very often, but fairly battered looking. Dead, dead quiet in the streets, six people at a giant station. Our guard, in addition to the man in civilian clothes, consists of two greens who, after each station, walk up and down the length of the train (I almost

92 "The wheels roll us to victory. Unnecessary travel prolongs the war."
93 "Caution while speaking, the enemy is listening."
94 Special train.

wrote barracks), counting. As if we'd run away. We're precious, you
know.

2 July

What we are experiencing is really worth recording in a diary. And
it's only now, now that we're returning to a more or less normal
society and we're slowly embracing the feeling that we've been
saved, that we realize just how low we had sunk. Slowly, for we have
such fear of disappointment that we daren't let ourselves go. Let me
continue my story. The camp had given us: One *Kuch*,[95] half a pound
of margarine per person and a tin of delicious, rich liver pâte to share
among five people. But my stomach had grown so unaccustomed
to food that yesterday, when we had to get off the train, I felt dead
nauseous. We arrived in Vienna (at half-past seven, I believe), where
we were met by about five greens. We got off, put our luggage on the
platform and waited. But because I wasn't feeling well, I returned to
the train and lay on the bench. "*Sie fahren als allerletzte*,"[96] the green
said kindly. "*Und bleiben Sie nicht in der Sonne liegen. Sorgen Sie
dafür, dass das Fräulein im Auto sitzen kann*,"[97] he said to the group
leader. Treated like a human being! We're not used to it anymore.
Really not. In a truck to the *Obdachlosenheim*.[98] A colossal building,
stone staircases, large, bright dormitories. Beds, not on top of and
right next to one another, but separate, with clean, white sheets. A
washroom with basins and hot and cold running water. And this
is relief for the homeless. Normally, we would have said: Looks
quite decent. Bare, of course. It was a palace to us. My hands hadn't
been properly clean in months. A shower when we arrived. Food.

95 Dark German rye bread.
96 "You will travel last."
97 "And please stay out of the sun. Please see to it that this young lady gets to sit in
    the car."
98 Homeless shelter.

Curried rice and a mug of soup. All plates, spoons, etc., belonged to the *Heim.* We all received a meal ticket, which is punched. As well as a ration of bread. And the people, the staff, extremely friendly. Last night, Taubes delivered a speech, saying that, thank God, the conversations about thick or thin food are now a thing of the past. And he's right. We're learning to laugh again, are kinder to one another — in a word, we're becoming human again!

We're continuing our journey today and will shortly, at the request of the Turkish government, be inoculated. Last night the transport from Vittel, which is to be exchanged with us, arrived.[99] They were tremendously spoiled, private rooms, a park, only the best. And in sharp contrast, a transport of Hungarians arrived yesterday evening, which is just now leaving for Poland.

Enough. More on the train, I think. We're escorted by a commission: One man from the *Auswärtige Amt,*[100] one man from the *Polizeipräsidium*[101] and one man from the Swiss Consulate. Thursday in Constantinople!!![102]

2 July, later

In Hungary now, in a Mitropa[103] train, second-class. Just ate in a *Speisewagen!!!*[104] Stars of David off. Finding it difficult to write. Just taking notes. Forgot that in Nuremberg we saw the *Halle* where Hitler gives his speeches. I never thought I would see this place.

---

99   In Vienna, 61 Jews from the Vittel camp joined the group of Jews to be exchanged from Bergen-Belsen.
100 Foreign Office.
101 Police headquarters.
102 Now known as Istanbul.
103 From the word *Mitteleuropa*, Central Europe: The company that provided restaurant and sleeping cars for different trains passing through the expanses of Europe.
104 Restaurant car.

274 • *Letters Never Sent*

3 July

In Vienna — soldiers. In Hungary — *puszta*.[105] A pity we're travelling through all these cities without seeing them. Budapest — suburbs in ruins. Three huge fires. We're in Újvidék [Novi Sad] now (border of Romania and Hungary). Original route was via Belgrade, but too dangerous.

Yugoslavia after all. Indescribable. Travelling hundreds of metres above the Danube. Trees up to their tops in the water. Meadows in the middle of the river. On the other side, villages and small towns built against the rocks. Poor, poor, poor. Sheep with shepherds and a dog. Small horses. Women with yokes and two round baskets. All barefoot. Men stripped to the waist. We're waiting in front of a tunnel, are about to set off again, I believe.

It is now a quarter-past eleven. The train has come to a halt. Bombardment. Columns of smoke wafting towards us. Have the tracks been hit? Half-past one: We're still stuck and, taking advantage of the situation, I carry on writing. Until Vienna we were treated well, i.e., we had comfortable seats and enough provisions. We had no water, but the journey was generally quite pleasant. From Vienna onwards it's all show, because this train will take us into Turkey. Hence... a Mitropa train, first-, second- and third-class (with apologies for the third class) — the train is slowly starting to move — two restaurant cars, one sleeping car — the train has come to a halt again — but: No luggage car, so the luggage had to go into the third-class compartments, no water, two cars short, so there are far too many of us in one compartment. One sleeping car, just for the Huns. The food is tasty (we like everything), but by no means sufficient. German Red Cross nurses don't do a thing, because we have our own nurses. All show. And they're really peeved at having to offer us this good life.

---

105   Hungarian plain.

Belgrade. Magnificent city. Very heavily bombed. Airport bombed to smithereens before our very eyes today. All the station clocks in Yugoslavia have stopped. Many people are barefoot. Shepherds and shepherdesses. German soldiers flirt with us: "*Es sind Juden, ihr bekommt Unannehmlichkeiten.*"[106]

4 July

Bulgaria. Rocks, caves. Armoured cars in front and at the rear of the train; fear of partisans. Cottages made of dung and straw. Population anti-German, shabby, poor, some in bearskin hats (in July). The most bizarre things happen here, things that are too crude and too improbable. This morning, at some poor, chaotic and picturesque little station, a string orchestra boarded the train, looking like they'd stepped out of a revue, with enormous moustaches; one man in German uniform (probably stolen) and barefoot, and the others in the most unlikely get-ups. So now we're travelling with musical accompaniment! There's no musical send-off for those travelling to Poland. A poignant contrast.

4 July, later

We travel a short distance and then the track is checked for bombs again. Between the cars we can see flames on the tracks. Sophia very heavily bombed. Half-past eight and pitch-dark. Sheep and shepherds. The Huns have already taken off their uniforms. Unrecognizable in civilian clothes.

---

106   "They are Jews, you will get into trouble."

5 July

We're stopped at the Turkish border. Yesterday evening we crossed a neutral zone. I'd never heard of it, but our commission had already changed into civilian clothes and the villages we travelled through were brightly lit; we hadn't felt so joyous and safe in a long time. Father had to sign a declaration saying that for the duration of the war, he wouldn't take up arms against *"Deutschland und seine Verbundeten."*[107] (All the men, of course.) It looks like we won't leave here before two o'clock, and won't arrive in Constantinople until very early tomorrow morning. The strange thing is that when, a couple of days ago, I was in bed and imagined being in Constantinople, i.e., in safety, I immediately burst into tears. And yet now that the time has come (after all, we're very close to the border, in a neutral zone), I can't quite take it all in. What I do know is that the journey itself has been an experience I'll never be able to describe in all its glory. And to think that last night, when we crossed guerrilla territory, the commission was scared to death.

The train is full of guards and has armoured cars in front and at the rear, with big searchlights. If you were to read that in a book, it would give you the creeps. We travelled through a region of bare rocks and caves and it's true that the train could have come under attack from anywhere. Still, we weren't scared at all. It seems we've been through too much. Not that I enjoyed it, I was certainly a bit anxious, but not as much as you might think. And the journey was incredibly beautiful. Large flocks of sheep with shepherds, simply biblical. We saw a trail criss-crossing the mountains and riding down it on a mule was a man in a black cape and a tall hat, holding a stick in front of him. Quite a picture!

And in the meantime, the people are getting all worked up about the food again. True, the restaurant car serves ridiculously small portions. Barely enough for a bird. But we don't let it worry us

107 Germany and its allies.

now that we know that we'll soon be fed properly again. At the same time, this transition is very good for us. A Turkish *Speisewagen* was attached to our train this morning, and it serves a fantastic breakfast. And now people are jostling each other to eat there. As if you can't wait that little bit longer. But eventually my turn came and I've just eaten at the Turks. Fried egg!! Need I say more! We celebrated our freedom, and we did so in amazing style. In the Turkish restaurant car, with a wonderful supper and lovely people. Friendly waiters. With the compliments of the Turkish government! Unforgettable.

Just crossed a yellow river. The Maritsa.[108] Buffaloes, mosques, storks, clay huts. This time last week we knew nothing yet.

6 July

We're living a fairy tale. At the moment we're on a boat, sailing on the Bosporus. Beautiful houses, too exquisite for words, and the water a shade of blue I never thought I would see. This is one big adventure. A newspaper. Parcels containing: Chocolate! Hazelnuts! Cheese! Egg! Fruit! Cigarettes! But there are downsides as well. We are *Schnorrers,* beggars. We're put on a boat, isolated from everybody else, and have to live off charity. And we've acquired the mentality of *Schnorrers,* i.e., we've learnt to beg and get everything for nothing. Perhaps we'll break this habit soon. And to think that we used to be the people who gave, rather than received, charity. Still, it's a fairy tale.

7 July

The Golden Horn. Mosques, the Sultan's palace, donkeys laden with baskets, beautiful round-bodied pitchers with narrow necks.

---

108   A river running through Bulgaria, Turkey and Greece.

Lovely boats and sailing ships, but most impressive of all: the blue, blue water. We'll be on our way again tonight. And we're coming closer and closer to you. We now have a magnificent train, incredibly stylish and beautiful. Father and Mother have a sleeping compartment, quite extraordinary. And yesterday evening we dined with the lights on! The mountains with thousands of illuminated windows, the full moon. All equally beautiful and divine. Veiled women. Graveyards with rough stones. Rocks, wadis. Everything we see here is biblical. Travelling along the edge of the desert. Primitive villages, camels.

8 July

In Adana now. At the station a plaque of Roosevelt and Churchill, who met here. We're riding through boiling hot tunnels.

9 July

Aleppo. Breakfast, washing and showering in a tent camp erected by the British soldiers who have escorted us from Turkey. People are sleeping on the roofs.

10 July

Hama, Homs, Tripoli. Desert wind, tent villages, humid heat, snow-capped mountains. Beirut, Mediterranean. Ras el-Nakura (Rosh Hanikra).

PALESTINE!!!

Mirjam and Leo on their wedding day, September 1944

Author's collection

Index

H

Haarlem 52, 78, 117
[The] Hague 38fn., 67, 78, 80, 87, 125,
131, 138, 178, 183, 200
Hama (city in west-central Syria) 278
Hamburger, Mr 125
Hanover 202, 209fn., 268
Hartog family
Gien (Karel's wife) 200
Karel 140, 142, 200
Karel and Gien Hartog's children
246, 271
Ro (Karel's sister) 171
Heertje, Mr 170, 180
Heilbut, Mr 154
Hendrix, Mr 143, 155
Herz, Mr 154
Herzberg, Abel 11, 238, 260
Heynemann, Mr 159
Hijmans, Dorus 142
Hildesheim 271
Hilversum 160
Himmler, Heinrich 194
Hitler, Adolf 14, 30, 93, 116, 206, 215, 273
Holland, the Netherlands 16, 25,
29fn., 35fn., 36fn., 38fn., 52fn., 62,
69–70, 77, 97, 114, 116, 126, 167fn.,
174, 178fn., 203, 207, 209, 214, 239,
242, 249fn.
see also Jewish Community in the
Netherlands
Homs (city in western Syria) 279
Hooghalen 163–164
Houthakker, Mr 210
Hungary 252, 273–274
Huysman family 58

I

Ichenhäuser, Elie 171
Imbach, Mr 159, 178
Israel (*Eretz Yisrael*; Land of Israel;
Mandatory Palestine) 7, 9–13,
18–19, 27fn., 32fn., 68fn., 71fn.,
76fn., 81, 94fn., 114fn., 120, 129fn.,
131fn., 154–155, 168fn., 172fn., 173,
254, 267
Palestine List; Palestine

certificates; immigration
certificates 23, 117, 128–129, 161,
168, 170, 173–174, 183, 190, 194,
196, 201–202, 239, 258
Palestine people 196, 216, 229, 236
see also Eretz Yisrael Office; Jews
exchanged for German citizens

J

Jacobs, Mr 155
Jacobson, Mr 155
Jewish Agency 128, 174
Jewish communities outside the
Netherlands
African Jews see Bergen-Belsen
American Jews 245
German Jews 15, 38–39, 63, 65, 70,
73–75, 106, 130, 180, 186
Association of Jews in Germany
(*Reichsvereinigung der Juden
in Deutschland*) 93
Spanish and Portuguese Jews 72fn.
Jewish Holidays and Remembrance
Days
Hanukkah 206–207
Holocaust Remembrance Day 7
Pesach (Passover) 7, 114, 119,
126–127, 129, 134, 251–252, 254,
256
Seder 7–8, 114, 119, 122, 237,
252–257
Purim 7, 94, 243–244
Rosh Hashanah 18, 119
Sukkot 54–55
Tisha B'Av (the Ninth of Av) 77
Jews exchanged for German citizens
9–10, 115, 129fn., 147fn., 201–203,
209, 211, 228, 264, 273
exchange camp (*Austauschlager*)
9, 211
Joint (American Jewish Joint
Distribution Committee) 70
Jorissen, Dina (household help;
appears as "Dina") 25, 45

K

Kan, Marinus 173, 228, 244, 259